The Seattle School
2510 Elliott Ave.
Seattle, WA 98121
theseattleschool.edu

Narrative Therapy in Practice

Narrative Therapy in Practice

The Archaeology of Hope

Gerald Monk,

John Winslade,

Kathie Crocket,

David Epston,

Editors

 JOSSEY-BASS
A Wiley Company
San Francisco

Published by

 JOSSEY-BASS
A Wiley Company
350 Sansome St.
San Francisco, CA 94104-1342

www.josseybass.com

Jossey-Bass books and products are available through most bookstores. To contact
Jossey-Bass directly, call (888) 378-2537, fax to (800) 605-2665, or visit our website at
www.josseybass.com.

Substantial discounts on bulk quantities of Jossey-Bass books are available to
corporations, professional associations, and other organizations. For details and
discount information, contact the special sales department at Jossey-Bass.

We at Jossey-Bass strive to use the most environmentally sensitive paper stocks available to
us. Our publications are printed on acid-free recycled stock whenever possible, and our
paper always meets or exceeds minimum GPO and EPA requirements.

Library of Congress Cataloging-in-Publication Data

Narrative therapy in practice / Gerald Monk...[et al.]., editors.
     p. cm. — (Jossey-Bass psychology series)
    Includes bibliographical references and index.
    ISBN 0-7879-0313-2
    1. Storytelling—Therapeutic use. 2. Personal construct therapy.
  3. Metaphor—Therapeutic use. 4. Psychotherapy. 5. Counseling.
I. Monk, Gerald, date. II. Series.
RC489.S74N37 1996
616.89'14—dc20   96–16258

HB Printing   10 9 8 7 6 5   FIRST EDITION

Contents

Preface

Although I appreciate being asked to introduce the writers of this book, I wanted them to be known to you in a more comprehensive manner than the usual protocols allow. I met both Gerald Monk and Wally McKenzie in the early 1980s, and although they did not know each other at the time, they both shared an irrepressible enthusiasm and took to narrative work like ducks to water. As fate would have it, their paths crossed in Hamilton in 1991, and they decided to co-teach in the Master of Counseling program at the University of Waikato. They joined and were joined by others who were like-minded. I have always felt connected to developments both at the Hamilton Therapy Centre and the Department of Education Studies at the University of Waikato in Hamilton. I had a strong suspicion that, as their "community" started to include their students and others at the therapy center and in the Department of Education Studies, something out of the ordinary might very well develop. I believe this book substantiates my convictions.

Since I feared that if I went further I would end up panegyrizing my friends and colleagues, I decided that the best introduction to this book would be a collective one. With that in mind, I took advantage of a "manuscript party" and sought permission to interview the community of authors and collaborators on this project so that they could speak for themselves, directly to you. My hope in doing so was that you might come to know them to some extent in the way that I know them, and that this would help you respond to the book in the spirit in which it was conceived. Good reading!

David Epston: I've often mentioned Waikato when I've spoken in North America, and I thought I was pronouncing the word pretty clearly until I recently got a letter back from an interested party referring to "Wild Kettle." So I guess I cannot assume that many readers of this book outside of New Zealand will know where that is, and what it is. I'd like some of you to tell them.

Bill Anderson: The Waikato region is the Tainui tribal area, named after a Maori canoe which brought our ancestors from Hawaiiki [the ancient land where the great migration began] to this country Aotearoa [New Zealand]. The Waikato river flows through this region, beginning at the mountains of Tuwharetoa, at Lake Taupo. The Maori people acknowledged the river as the source of sustenance for the people. The stories that have been written about it tell of many people living on the banks of this river right from its early beginnings. This was a time of wealth and prosperity for our people. And in Maori terms, we have a saying: "Waikato taniwharau. He piko he taniwha, He piko he taniwha." This translates [figuratively] as "The Waikato basin with a hundred chiefs. With every bend of the river there is a powerhouse both human and material." Subsequently, our land was illegally confiscated and the Tainui tribe betrayed and left landless and alienated.

Tuti Barrett-Aranui: Ko Kemureti toku oko horoi, Ko Arekahanara toku haona kaha Ko Ngaruawahia toku Turangawaewae. [Cambridge is the "wash basin" of my people. Alexandria is my fortress, while Ngaruawahia is my footstool where I will stand and be proud. (These are small towns in the Waikato region.)]

One of our early leaders in the 1860s, Tawhiao, prophesied that Waikato would be the basin for things to happen in years to come. It would be the seat of learning. The

University of Waikato is now moving into a
situation where they are creating the School
for Maori and Pacific Development, which
stands alone in its own right. To me, that has
answered the prophecy that was made by this
old gentleman who had so much to give.

Gerald Monk: In speaking about the specialness of this
area, I would like to make the comment that
the Tainui people of the Waikato have
agreed to a financial and land settlement
with the New Zealand government, making a
step toward addressing some of the injustices
imposed on the local people by the process
of colonization. It strikes me that this settlement is a step toward finding a way forward
for Pakeha institutions to attend to this
treachery of the past. I think it is rather profound that this settlement, this first one, has
happened in this area in the way that it has.

John Winslade: The land that the University of Waikato is
built on has been part of that settlement.
The ownership has been transferred. This is
quite fitting in relation to the ways of working we have been writing about, which have
been about an honoring of the indigenous
stories that all too often get colonized. And
narrative therapy can be likened to a process
of restoring rightful ownership of what has
been stolen away by dominant stories.

Wendy Drewery: The Maniapoto *iwi* [tribe] have made important contributions to the learnings of the
staff and students in our counseling program. These learnings are contained in the
pages of this book. The University of Waikato
has nurtured us and given us space to do the
things that we are doing. It is not an old, old
university; it is a new university, under thirty
years old. And it has made a deliberate policy
of working with interdisciplinarity.

David: Speaking of working with interdisciplinarity, I understand this book was a joint project of the Hamilton Therapy Centre [founded by Wally McKenzie] and the staff and graduate students of the Master of Counseling program. How did your organizations get together?

Wally McKenzie: I talked to Wendy Drewery about eight years ago and suggested that some changes to the counseling program needed to take place. That [the changes] happened when Gerald and Wendy got together and started setting up a quite different program in 1991. I had made contact with Gerald the year before and shortly after that began teaching in the counseling program.

David: I think it would be fair to say that your program at Waikato is the only university program I know that has developed narrative therapy to the extent it has.

Wally: Yes, it could well be.

David: The virtual process of writing this book is a story in itself, because really, you know, when editors here have multiauthored books like this, they usually don't agree to publish them, or even commit themselves to publication, because they don't get done. What interests me is that not only did this get done but everyone seems to thrive on the experience and revel in it, and it produced a true community of authors. How did you go about writing this book in such a communitarian way?

Wally: Well, David, you had been urging me for some time to get writing about what we were doing in the Waikato. Almost exactly a year ago, Gerald and I were sitting up late one night, and we got talking about writing a book and decided that it seemed a horrendous task for

us to sit down and do. So we thought, why
don't we enlist the experience of a whole lot
of people? We quickly brainstormed a whole
string of people and their areas of interest,
and thought, "Let's do it!" So I think that's
where the community of interest really
started.

Glen Simblett: I guess it is an amazing thing. I remember
coming along to the first meeting and just
reflecting, Wow! it's so big, this is so many
people!

David: Can I ask you, just for the record, how many
people were there?

Glen: There must have been nearly ten of us there
at those early meetings. And I remember, for
me, it was just an amazing experience. . . .
Within my own field [psychiatry], I'd struggled to find two or three people who were
interested in these ideas. To suddenly discover ten people was an amazing thing. I
remember all too well thinking, "Ah, it will
never work."

David: What were your reservations?

Glen: Ten or eleven people coordinating pieces of
work just seemed like an enormous task,
never mind getting over the fact that many of
us had never written before on this subject.
And all of us, I think, at times, were overwhelmed by the task or by the notion that we
didn't have a "right" to voice our ideas.

John: There is something about the myth of writing, where a spirit of competition can
descend when writing a book. You can somehow assume that you have to be special, or
distinct, or ahead of the pack in order to
write, or something like that. And yet, Kathie,
you said to us early on something that just
contradicted these myths. You said, "What
we're doing here is in a sense writing about

our ordinary work, about our ordinary thoughts, making our ordinary contributions, and taking them seriously enough that they actually become special, and they become important because we take enough care with them." And I think that process has been what has been distinctive for me about how we've gone about this. That's what's been really neat.

David: How did you gather the commitment to see this whole process through to a conclusion?

Bev McKenzie: Realizing that what I was doing in the community was actually at the cutting edge, and that I had to stay with it. Because I owed it to the community of people I work with. I've been part of a community of Maori women at the cutting edge of change in their communities. And seeing their commitment and what they put out, and what they've got to deal with, I began to see that narrative ideas help meet the aspirations of Maori people; and so I know there's something important in there, and I got carried along with that and the energy of the group—and the encouragement always of Wally to try and untangle whatever it was that was sticking.

John: I want to add that the way we've gone about this has been no accident. It does relate very much to several years of working together in our teaching. Like, all of our courses we've been involved with have been taught in the way that we've ended up writing. We have spent hours of time in our planning, talking in the ways we've actually now embodied in the writing. And we've had a commitment to not work in isolation. We've avoided each teaching our own course separate from each other. Instead, we've worked together and taught in dialogue with each other, and

sought to include the students in those dia-
logues; and they've become excited by that
process, which has just encouraged us to do
it more, and eventually to share it in a wider
way. I think that process of dialogue has
almost taken us over in the way that we've
been teaching and in the way that we've been
writing. And we've had a commitment to collaborative writing for some time.

David: Can I ask everyone, what would you consider
your most important ingredients for the
recipe for constituting this community of
authors? If people want to duplicate this
experiment in collaboration, what would
they need to do? What would be required?

Bev: I think being prepared to be vulnerable. It's
a vulnerable activity to display your writing.
To have someone else point out all of the
encouraging parts of it was just wonderful
and really validating. I think sharing the
work at a really early stage with one or two
who would encourage you in saying these
things. I think one of the other ingredients
for me was [that] there was a great deal of
joy in this process. But I think it's good to
credit suffering, too—not in the sense that
one must suffer for one's art, but I think
there was a suffering with a purpose going on
here. Initially, I had a lot of trepidation about
my writing. It was a painful experience
because the chapter I was writing was about a
passion for social change. To be able to separate myself from my writing was quite difficult. I spent the first few meetings crying part
of the time.

Wally: I think the thing for me that contributed
most to the success was that it was a large
group. We each agreed to produce written
work for each group meeting. We met every

two weeks. Then we would break into groups of three. One person would present to the other two what [he or she] had written, and the two would read it quickly and then have a discussion between them about it; so that the person who had written it didn't have to defend it in any way—[he or she] just had to listen to what was said. The writer made notes on the discussion. Everybody would end up commenting on everybody else's work, which was really leveling and encouraging and empowering. And I think it helped each of us . . . it helped me find some voice that I didn't think I had. Through this, we have formed a tight-knit group.

David: Anything else?

Glen Silvester: For me, the recipe is to do with collaboration. The bit that I'd like to underline is how with collaboration you bring your own unique skills, and that brings out the respect, I think. Realizing that whatever you bring needs some other parts to enhance it. That's probably the thing I saw happening in the group.

David: Bernadette, what do you think there was about this group that allowed everyone to shine? Every chapter, in my opinion, is exemplary.

Bernadette Simblett: I think it was amazing that there wasn't really one person taking any particular lead. At different times, different people were. When some people weren't feeling . . . things were going right, or they were sticking or whatever, somehow someone within the group came up with what was needed and ideas about how to proceed further. I'd say it's probably one of the more unique experiences I've ever had, having been the observer throughout the process. In a way, they were all leaders. At some point, everybody could come up with a question or something that pushed the group forward and kept the focus going. I think once people realized that nobody was going to say, "Well, that's not right," there was never a feeling that anybody was less than anybody else.

David: I think it would be fair to say that many of the graduate students have contributed the most innovative and exciting work that is storied in this book.

The graduate students David refers to are experienced practitioners in their own right, some of whom have spent a number of years teaching and counseling. However, it is also true that these graduate students have been exposed to narrative ideas relatively recently.

David: I think the readers of this book will be interested to have some feel for the nature of your training experience [referring to those authors who are completing their graduate studies] at the University of Waikato, because I consider it unusual that a book should be coproduced by students and staff, and I think American readers will certainly think that is the case. If you were speaking to some would-be students at Waikato, what would you tell them about what they should expect in this program? What should they prepare themselves for?

Aileen Cheshire: I think the biggest thing is being prepared to have most of your assumptions challenged and being prepared to put aside the divisions between work and your own ideas about yourself in your own life. What you learn about the work has such an impact on everything else that the divisions just get thrown away. This was sort of life-changing, really.

Lorraine Smith: It enabled me to make sense of how people's lives are constructed by dominant norms of the society that people grow up in, and it is when people feel out of step with the dominant culture that they blame themselves, and this is what often brings them to counseling. I've learned it is how people get positioned by these cultural values that is the problem rather than that there is something innately wrong with people. So this program gave me the language and the framework to practice from as a counselor. It gave me a framework to articulate my own experience and to make sense of the world in a way that suited me more, but also it gave me some ways to practice, to make a difference in this world.

David: Does anyone want to speak about anything else that just might feel pertinent?

Alison Cotter: One of the things I have enjoyed has been the relationships among the staff of the counseling program. They have a real respect for each other in the sense of excitement about exchanging ideas.

Lorraine: Not only do they share information, but [they] also share the ownership of the information.

David: What's your next book going to be about? Got a guess about what it might be?

Gerald: Some of us are involved in extending narrative ideas into the mediation field, and so some of us here will, I'm sure, be involved in this second book.

John: There are also about four or five other chapters that are in this book that could be elaborated into other books.

David: I'm very proud of the fact that there is now a New Zealand version of narrative therapy which is going to make itself known to a wider public. I want to acknowledge your faithfulness in your practice of teaching, and your ability to act as a collective, which in my opinion has exhibited the greatest integrity. How is it that you have chapters so striking and so innovative and so modest produced by people in the role of graduate students? How could that happen? But why shouldn't it? And the question people might ask you is, Why is it happening here? So that's what I've most appreciated about your program and this book. You have been faithful, right down to this very last moment as I finish my comments. That's what I've most enjoyed.

You've asked the hardest questions about how to make this talk walk. It seems to me it's walked all over your program, and into it, and outside of it. And if anyone asked me how I know this, the answer would be "Read the book."

Auckland, New Zealand   David Epston
August 1996

To those who have gone before us and have been the forebears of our thoughts, our practices, and our knowledges. You have left us a rich vein of stories to mine in our search for the meanings that sustain hope. We dedicate this book to you.

Acknowledgments

We wish to acknowledge all of the writers who have contributed to this book. Thank you for readily accepting invitations to contribute chapters and then working so hard as we encouraged and supported each other and provided commentary and critique of each other's work. We set about working as a community of authors, and we owe thanks to you, Wendy Drewery, Wally McKenzie, Glen J. Simblett, Lorraine Smith, Tim Harker, Aileen Cheshire, Glen Silvester, Alison Cotter, and Bev McKenzie, for making this possible. Our thanks go to Bernadette Simblett for her participation in our meetings as an encouraging and astute audience and to Jeffrey Kottler, whose knowledge and generosity started us on the track.

We acknowledge Bill Anderson and Tuti Aranui. You have brought a richness and diversity of voice to this project, and we thank you for the wisdom and generosity you have shared with us as the project has unfolded.

We are grateful to Alan Rinzler, our Jossey-Bass editor. Thank you, Alan, for your enthusiasm and encouragement, and for the support you gave to our approach in writing this book. Your experience and gentle guidance along the path were valued by us all.

We appreciate all those alongside whom we have learned so much of what we know in this field. We thank the students with whom we have worked at the University of Waikato, particularly those in the graduate program; the clients who have taught us numerous lessons that are not taught at university; our counseling colleagues for sharing your ideas and skills with us; and those with whom we have worked in supervision relationships.

We are grateful to the team at the Family Centre, Lower Hutt, particularly Kiwi Tamasese, Warihi Campbell, Flora Tuhaka, and Charles Waldegrave. We cannot consider our acknowledgments complete without expressing our sincere thanks for your leadership in family therapy and counseling in New Zealand. We thank you for your courage, which has both inspired and challenged us. We thank you, too, for your willingness to share your knowledge.

We thank Michael White. The chapter notes in this book are evidence of our indebtedness to you, Michael. We have learned from you directly in workshops and conversations and indirectly through your books, articles, and videos. We have also learned by putting into practice what you have taught us. For us, your work has been, as we are sure you would wish, a source of great generativity. We thank you for that.

We acknowledge David Epston. Thank you, David, for your pioneering work in this field and your willingness over the years to share your ideas, your genius, your ways of working. Thank you, too, for generously encouraging us to take on this task, and for your great enthusiasm for this project as it proceeded.

We thank Wendy Drewery. We would like to express our heartfelt love and gratitude for the leadership and mentorship you have provided for the counseling team over the last five years. We value your scholarship, wisdom, and perceptivity, which along with your willingness to challenge have made an enormous contribution to the developments we are all enjoying now.

Last of all, we acknowledge Wally McKenzie. We would like to thank you, our dear friend and fellow traveler, person of generous spirit, for your commitment, creativity, and constancy in this work. We want to acknowledge that it has been you who has advanced the practices and development of narrative therapy in the Waikato. Your enlivening stories have added a warmth, a richness, and a playfulness that have brought heart and soul to this way of working.

University of Waikato   Gerald Monk
Hamilton, New Zealand   John Winslade
August 1996   Kathie Crocket

Introduction

Gerald Monk

The authors of the chapters in this book are a diverse group. Some of us are experienced counselors, therapists, and community and mental health workers. Others are counselor educators, and four of us, though experienced counselors, have been completing graduate studies. We have been drawn together because of our attraction to a profoundly different way of theorizing the nature of counseling and practicing it.

Our work has been a collaborative process emerging from the therapeutic partnerships we have formed with our clients. The practice of forming alliances with clients in order to access, encourage, and promote their abilities was carried into our relationships as coauthors of this book. In fact, the process mirrored what we would consider to be the exemplary application of narrative thinking.

Some of us changed our views of ourselves and of what we do as a result of writing about our work in the precise and disciplined manner required by this book. Our focus was sharpened, and our understanding of how narrative ideas can be applied was deepened.

What Is This Book About?

The narrative approach to therapy has been one of the most exciting developments within the helping professions over the last decade. Numerous examples of the benefits emerging from this form of counseling can be found in the literature and on video. This book adds to those examples.

The major focus of the book is the work done by counselors using a narrative framework in a variety of settings. The clients may be individuals, couples, families, groups, or communities.

Narrative approaches to counseling are now used with a broad range of human difficulties, including relational and family distress, eating disorders, depression, various psychiatric illnesses, and problem issues in childhood and adolescence. Narrative ideas are applied in schools, psychotherapy groups, mediation, and in drug and alcohol counseling. They have contributed to new and innovative ways of conducting supervision and community health work.

The book has two parts. Part One covers some of the key features of narrative counseling, including its theoretical and philosophical underpinnings. Part Two discusses the applications of narrative therapy in particular professional and cultural settings.

Chapter One begins with an example of what narrative counseling looks like in practice. Some of the key concepts are brought to life through the exploration of a series of interviews with a client, Peter, who developed a fear of seeing. The chapter concludes by describing narrative counseling as an attitude and a way of thinking about problems rather than merely a box of tricks or clever techniques.

We felt it was important to present the significant theoretical ideas that inform the practice of narrative therapy. In Chapter Two, Wendy Drewery and John Winslade write about some of the major conceptual components that are a part of the construction of the narrative metaphor. These theoretical ideas were informed by the work of a variety of philosophers, sociologists, anthropologists, and literary theorists. Wendy and John write about the significance of social constructionism for counseling practice, and in doing so, address the interactive relationship between theory and practice.

There has been a general absence of discussion in the narrative therapy literature about the therapeutic relationship, an aspect of counseling that has been recognized as crucial in other modalities. Chapter Three focuses on the complexities of developing a collaborative relationship. John Winslade, Kathie Crocket, and I seek to move beyond the rhetoric that characterizes many discussions about partnership and relationships of empowerment with clients. We discuss how the construction of the counselor's identity is embodied in his or her language use and interactional style, and we look at the effects this has on the therapeutic relationship. We note the part counselors play in allowing the client to experience power and influence over the counseling conversation. Considerable attention is given to the audience role that both therapist and client fill as client stories are brought from the private to the public realm. We explore the possibility of a social constructionist view of transference replacing the one that has been traditional in psychotherapy.

In Chapter Four, Wally McKenzie and I elaborate on the phases of the narrative interview that are introduced in Chapter One. For the benefit of those who teach narrative ideas to therapists, we have included exercises that we have found useful.

Part Two of the book opens with a rare self-reflective discussion of the influences of narrative ideas on mainstream psychiatry. Glen J. Simblett's Chapter Five addresses some tough issues in modernist psychiatric practices. He explores the challenge of incorporating narrative practice, an orientation that accepts the subjective nature of knowledge, into a discipline that is based on the practices of objective science. Though venturing to critique modernist practices that serve to control, regulate, and order human experience, Glen identifies the strengths of conventional psychiatric practice and finds ways of combining these with narrative approaches to psychiatry. The result is a compelling practical resource that both advances narrative approaches to therapy and develops an innovative way of conducting psychiatric interviews.

The next two chapters are assembled around clients' presenting problems. John Winslade and Lorraine Smith, in Chapter Six, show how narrative therapy can be used in the field of drug and alcohol counseling. In this presentation, which we believe is the first of its kind, the authors offer a provocative argument for reviewing the dominant modes of drug and alcohol "treatment." We were tempted to soften the tone of the chapter and take a more tentative stance, but we decided that the strength of the argument would serve our goal of stimulating and encouraging discussion of this vitally important work.

Chapter Seven, which is based on Tim Harker's graduate research on the relationship between dominant masculine belief systems and male sexual abuse, shows how the narrative metaphor can be used to help clients escape from the totalizing effects of this childhood trauma. Tim offers numerous examples to illustrate how narrative questioning can be used with such clients. In addition, he demonstrates the therapeutic relevance of social constructionist theory to this area of counseling.

The last five chapters describe a variety of helping modalities that apply narrative ideas. Chapter Eight, by John Winslade and Aileen Cheshire, discusses how narrative methods can be incorporated into the work of a high school counselor. The authors describe narrative work with several clients and illustrate, by way of practical example, how narrative questions can be used with adolescent clients even when the constraining influences of high school culture are present. John and Aileen also show how this counseling method is grounded in a philosophical and linguistic practice.

Chapter Nine introduces a narrative perspective on psychoeducational group work. Glen Silvester relates in a practical and down-to-earth fashion her journey from a humanistic to a social constructionist perspective. With the help of many examples, she illustrates the subtleties of narrative questioning while also throwing light on the dynamics of group process.

John Winslade and Alison Cotter, in Chapter Ten, introduce an excitingly different way of conceptualizing the practice of mediation. They build on the innovative work of our small community of narrative mediators to show the potency of this way of working with disputing parties. Care is taken to explain the differences between mainstream practices of mediation and a social constructionist approach to this work. The chapter provides examples of questions suitable for a wide variety of mediation scenarios.

Chapter Eleven opens up a much wider frame of reference, as it moves away from the personal concerns of individuals to issues of health within an extended community. Drawing on her broad experience in community health development, Bev McKenzie demonstrates how narrative ideas can form the basis of a developmental approach to community health. This chapter outlines the damaging effects of colonizing practices associated with dominant medical discourse; these effects inadvertently undermine the contributions that can be made by Western knowledge. Bev demonstrates how collaborative interactions that combine both indigenous and Western knowledge open up possibilities of change in the quality of health and welfare among a formerly alienated group.

The book closes with Wendy Drewery's brief description of the unique group process that brought this volume into being. The writing of the book has moved our own ideas along, and we hope that your reading of it will contribute, in turn, to your work. We intend to continue to expand on our ideas, and Wendy invites you to share your thoughts and learnings with us.

We have attempted to present a rich array of practical resources for professional helpers seeking to introduce narrative ideas into their therapeutic work. You, the reader, may be a practitioner with many years' experience who wants to incorporate narrative ways of thinking, theorizing, and working into a practice with which you are already satisfied. Alternatively, you may be starting out in a career of professional counseling and may be hungry for new avenues to explore. These are but two possibilities. Whatever description fits your present circumstance, engagement with these ideas may well produce a conceptual leap in your approach to your work.

In our writing our aim has been to present our ideas in a relevant, accessible, and practical manner. Many of the ideas we discuss are at once simple and complex. We have sought to write about them in a straightforward way, yet to avoid an overly simplistic, technique-based account of narrative therapy. Furthermore, to ensure that we were not merely offering you a range of clever therapeutic strategies, we wanted to ground our work within a body of ideas that would help locate the nature of our practice. You will, of course, evaluate the degree of our success in achieving that goal. We invite you to read on.

Notes

P. xxiii, *and on video:* Sykes Wylie, M. (1994, November–December). Panning for gold. *Family Therapy Networker,* 40–48.

P. xxiv, *childhood and adolescence:* Epston, D. (1989). Nightwatching: An approach to night fears. In *Collected papers.* Adelaide, Australia: Dulwich Centre Publications; White, M. (1989). Ritual of inclusion: An approach to extreme uncontrolled behaviour in children and young adolescents. In *Selected papers.* Adelaide, Australia: Dulwich Centre

Publications; White, M. (1989). Fear busting and monster taming: An approach to the fears of young children. In *Selected papers*. Adelaide, Australia: Dulwich Centre Publications; White, M., & Epston, D. (1991). *Narrative means to therapeutic ends*. New York: Norton.

P. xxiv, *literature about the therapeutic relationship:* Johnella Bird is one of the few authors who examine relationship issues in narrative therapy. Bird, J. (1993). Coming out of the closet: Illuminating the therapeutic relationship. *Journal of feminist family therapy, 5*(2), 47–64.

Narrative Therapy in Practice

Part One

Theory

Chapter One

How Narrative Therapy Works

Gerald Monk

With meticulous care and precision, the archaeologist brushes ever so gently over the landscape with an instrument as small as a pastry brush. With these careful movements, she exposes a remnant, and with further exploration, others soon appear. Disconnected fragments are identified and pieced together as the search continues. With a careful eye for the partially visible, the archaeologist begins to reassemble the pieces. An account of events in the life of the remains is constructed, and meaning emerges from what was otherwise a mere undulation in the landscape.

The practitioner using narrative therapy needs all the observational powers, persistence, care, deliberation, and delicacy of the archaeologist. From a few small pieces of information, the beginning of a story located in a particular culture is constructed.

Unlike the archaeologist, the practitioner using a narrative approach is working with a bustling, dynamic, living, breathing culture, represented in the counseling setting by individuals, couples, or groups.

Narrative approaches to counseling invite clients to begin a journey of coexploration in search of talents and abilities that are hidden or veiled by a life problem. Unlike the passive soil that is excavated by the archaeologist's tools, the client is engaged as an active collaborator in the reconstruction of something of substance and value. The narrative therapist draws on her own patient and thoughtful persistence to help the client rediscover the remnants of favored experiences in his life. In some instances, these experiences will open up avenues by which clients can bypass the problems that have stalled them on their journey. In other instances, they may be the cornerstones with which persons seeking respite from their pain reconstruct their lives.

Narrative therapy requires an optimistic orientation. The main character in the plot is frequently positioned in the therapeutic conversation as the courageous victor rather than the pathologized victim, as a colorful individual who has vivid stories to recount rather than a hopeless individual leading a pathetic life. The stories will not only change the teller in the telling but will also change the counselor as a privileged audience of the tale.

This book is organized around a series of client stories that illustrate how narrative therapy can be used as a crucible from which stories of hope, success, and vindication emerge. The following account of a series of counseling sessions with a young man and his parents will serve as a brief introduction to narrative therapy.

Peter's Story

Twelve-year-old Peter had been virtually blind since birth, with only a sliver of vision that gave him a murky view up to a distance of ten feet. Nevertheless, according to his parents, he had been a well-adjusted boy, both at home and at school. In the year prior to counseling, he had undergone a series of operations that had resulted in his gaining completely normal vision, and this radical change had given rise to major problems.

The world was much uglier than Peter had imagined. Now he could see the background of life as well as the foreground. His greatest challenge was going to school each day and seeing all those people gossiping, laughing, fighting, grimacing. There was so much to take in all at once. The classroom appeared ugly to him, and the audience he saw looking at him when he spoke was overwhelming. Whereas previously he had had a dull view of perhaps one or two people who were close by, now he could see everyone focusing on him at once. He withdrew from some of his old friends; they looked different from the way he had pictured them in his mind. Some of them looked silly and did stupid things.

Peter stopped going to school. His parents, Joanne and Bruce, were devastated by this development. They had hoped that normal sight would mean a "normal life," but they were witnessing the opposite. Peter hated being able to see well and wanted to return to his more familiar world. Now, as the family came for counseling, the parents were at their wits' end.

"How has 'being able to see' changed things?" I asked Peter, focusing on him intently.

"Well, it's just that everything is different. . . . I hate school and I don't want to go back." Peter looked downcast.

"Has sight got in the way of your friendships?"

Peter said he didn't want to see his friends at the moment. In fact, he didn't want to leave the house if he could help it.

I asked, "Is sight keeping you a prisoner in your home, because before it sounded like you were free to come and go pretty much as you wanted?"

He replied that he was happy at home. He said he spent time on his dad's computer.

"What has the effect of 'being able to see' been on your mum and dad?"

There was a long pause. "I think Mom is really upset because she and Dad went through a lot with all of the eye operations, and now things are worse than before!"

Joanne stepped in. "We just can't believe what has happened. The family has been under so much pressure over the last two years. We didn't know how the operations were going to work out. There was a 60 percent chance that Peter would be able to have normal vision. There was also a risk that he could have lost the vision that he already had. We knew there would be huge adjustment problems, but we wouldn't have guessed that this would have happened."

Bruce, Peter's father, added with exasperation: "Peter has been such an outgoing kid. Even though he has had such major restrictions on his vision, he was always out with his friends . . . you know, into everything. This [problem of not going to school] has been going on for three months. Peter has missed an awful lot of school. We thought, we'll give him a few weeks to settle into life after his last operation. We're all feeling really disheartened."

The Uniqueness of Narrative Therapy

These interactions convey something of the flavor of a narrative therapy conversation. In many ways, this discussion may not be so different from many other ways of beginning a counseling session. However, one can already see some deliberate attempts to enter into the world of Peter and his parents in a way that will disrupt the common tendency to blame either oneself or others for one's troubles. In this counseling session, it would have been easy for Peter and his parents to engage in such blame. Peter felt he had let his parents and himself down. He was also a little angry at his parents for initiating the operations, as he figured he was doing pretty well before his eye surgery. Joanne and Bruce blamed themselves for instigating the operations in the first place, as they were both now aware that there were going to be unforeseen consequences. They were disturbed, frustrated, and hurt by Peter's behavior following the surgery.

One of the distinctive characteristics of narrative counseling is the use of externalizing conversations, as developed by Michael White. These conversations attempt to move the focus away from self-attack, recrimination, blame, and judgment—attitudes that work against productive and positive outcomes in counseling. Questions such as "What effect has being able to see had on you?" and "How is sight keeping you a prisoner at home?" clearly focus attention on the problem caused by sight rather than on Peter's personal inadequacies in choosing not to go to school or Bruce and Joanne's failure to ensure Peter's attendance. Through this linguistic shift, a small beginning is made in a process of marshaling the family's efforts to work together on the problems created by the return of Peter's sight.

Prior to surgery, Joanne, Bruce, and Peter had created a story about Peter having normal vision. The construction of this story had filled them with excitement, hope, and promise and had guided their decision to have the operations. However, Peter's lived experience of having the faculty of sight resulted in a story of frustration, chagrin, and regret.

Using the story metaphor for counseling, a narrative approach might focus on building a fuller picture of the plot development that followed Peter's cure. Each client will have his own version of events. By interviewing several members of a family concurrently, a fuller and richer version of the problem-saturated story can be woven together.

Influences on the Development of Narrative Therapy

The narrative metaphor as a therapeutic tool has emerged principally from the work of Michael White and David Epston. These therapists and authors have cast their nets wide for the philosophical underpinnings of their practices. Space does not permit a detailed exploration of these underpinnings; however, a few figures who have contributed a great deal to the development of narrative therapy deserve a brief mention.

The work of Gregory Bateson, anthropologist and psychologist, was an early inspiration to White and Epston. They were attracted to Bateson's concepts dealing with the subjective nature of reality and the nature of learning. Bateson's most profound contribution to the understanding of how learning occurs emerged from his discussion of the "news of difference." He suggested that in order to be able to detect and acquire new information, human beings must engage in a process of comparison, in which they distinguish between one set of events in time and another. White noted that many clients adapted to their problems and did not notice the extent to which those problems affected their lives. Often, clients were also unaware of their own resourcefulness in diminishing the extent of the problem. Building on Bateson's idea of "news of difference," White discovered that by drawing clients' attention to subtle changes accompanying the escalation and reduction of their problems, he could foster new insights into their abilities and thus help them develop a clearer perspective on how to address their concerns.

Further refinements in this work came out of dialogue between David Epston, Michael White, and Cheryl White, who shared with each other their understandings of the story metaphor. Edward Bruner, an ethnographer, had shown how people develop stories as a way of understanding and making sense of their experiences. The story largely determines which experiences will be selected for expression and performance in the world. As the story metaphor has been developed in counseling, it has proved to be a potent resource for working with a wide range of clients.

Perhaps the most outstanding figure to have intimately affected the shape of narrative therapy is Michel Foucault, a French historian and philosopher. Michael White has turned the intellectually obscure and esoteric writings of Foucault into a powerful but workable resource. It is not possible here to detail the wide-ranging implications of Foucault's writings for our understanding of the therapeutic process. However, one major theme throughout Foucault's work is the subjugation processes that become established in professional practice. He discusses how a society constructs "true" standards of behavior, with which individuals feel obliged to comply. The establishment of correct or "objective" standards leads the therapeutic professions (among others) to move, deliberately or inadvertently, into the role of classifying, judging, and determining what is a desirable, appropriate, or acceptable way of life. Foucault goes on to identify the harm that arises from this practice.

Foucault's thesis has led Michael White to develop a variety of therapeutic approaches that address the damaging effects of normalizing practices that confine, constrain, and undermine people's efforts to lead a life of their own design. Relevant aspects of Foucault's theory are discussed in Chapter Two, and White's development and interpretation of these ideas within the therapeutic context are described throughout the book.

Other relevant knowledges drawn from the social sciences and the humanities—in areas such as literary theory, hermeneutics, and feminist and critical theory—have been transposed by Michael White and David Epston to the territory of therapeutic conversation, opening up outstanding new possibilities in counseling.

Taking Apart or Deconstructing the Problem

A counselor using a narrative approach wants to deconstruct the problem that is presented. He or she asks questions that give the client an opportunity to explore various dimensions of the situation. This helps to reveal the unstated cultural assumptions that contributed to the original construction of the problem. The counselor wants to find out, for example, how the problem first arose, and how it affected people's views of themselves.

Peter's ability to see had exacted a price from everyone. What made Peter's story so ironic was how markedly it stood outside of the dominant norms of a society that places considerable value on sight and produces sophisticated technology to heal, repair, and restore the body. Unlike Peter, most of us are fearful of the possibility that our sight might be impaired. We take for granted that normal vision is a desirable and necessary faculty. Bruce and Joanne's original hopes had (not surprisingly) conformed to the norms of their community, where the inability to see was labeled a deficit or disability.

I told Joanne and Bruce about a group of young people I had known who were proud of their membership in a culture where entry could be gained only by being completely deaf. These young people could communicate in a very sophisticated way by nonverbal means and considered their abilities to be superior to those used in a talking and listening culture. I asked Peter's parents how they thought these deaf individuals could have arrived at this conclusion. Joanne and Bruce were thus encouraged to reflect on the issues of competency and deficit in a different way, and they began to understand the losses that Peter had suffered in leaving a world in which he had felt comfortable.

Peter had come to know that he had deficits only from the reports of others. Having never had "normal" vision, he had not known what he was missing and had been reasonably content with the direction his life was taking. Yet, as Peter grew older he had become increasingly aware of his difficulties in adapting to the environments in which he was expected to function. In school, his ability to cope was being strained more and more by the sophisticated tasks assigned to students. Difficulty in keeping up with his peers on the soccer field had also frustrated him at times.

Mapping Influences and Externalizing Conversations

As my conversation with Peter's parents continued, I became interested in what the problem had done to them, was currently doing to them, and might yet do, as matters were clearly getting worse.

This was no morbid fascination to satisfy my own needs as a therapist. Often, counselors will avoid engaging the family in the fullness of the problem story, fearing that either the client(s) or the therapist will be swamped or overwhelmed by the despair and frustration that the story might evoke. To minimize the likelihood of this occurring, I initiated an "externalizing" conversation about the problem—that is, one that separated the problem from Peter and other family members rather than giving attention to the internalizing processes of self-blame and recrimination to which I have already referred.

In this early phase of the interview, I was employing two tactics. First, I was mapping the influence of the problem on each member of the family. I wanted to know what normal vision had done to this family. For example, what effect had Peter's reaction to sight had on Bruce? Bringing these effects to light would give the family a clearer sense of the oppression that each and every one of them had sustained as a result of Peter's world being turned upside down. They would be much more aware of the costs to them as people. By asking these questions of each member of the family, I was giving them an opportunity to learn how problems can reverberate through relationships and affect each person.

Second, I did not talk about "Peter's problem" or "see" the problem as belonging to Peter. I was not interested in getting Peter to own the problem, nor did I want to talk in a way that would encourage the family to view Peter's difficulties as his fault. Instead, I used externalizing language to identify the problem as separate from Peter and his parents.

This problem had been generated in a culture that, like most other cultures in history, had placed considerable value on sight. The externalizing conversation served to locate the problem within the cultural meanings that were impacting the person rather than in some internalized pathological condition.

I asked Peter, Joanne, and Bruce when they had first become aware of the difficulties that were emerging for Peter as a result of developing normal vision.

"I think Peter was starting to struggle at school after the second eye operation," Joanne explained. "This operation had increased his sight from about 20 percent of normal vision to about 60 percent. He had been off school for about three weeks, and we really had to cajole him to go to school. That was the beginning of last year. Then he had a nasty run-in with a couple of boys in his science class. Well, . . . actually, that happened just before he stopped going to school, which has now been since late February [about three-and-a-half-months]!" Joanne glared in Peter's direction, and he looked very uncomfortable.

One of the hallmarks of narrative therapy is persistence. I continued to ask questions and to respond to the family's stories, seeking to provide an opportunity for a full account of their experience of the problem, its history, and its influence on their lives.

I asked each of them how their lives would go forward if the problem of normal vision were to continue to imprison Peter in his own home. Would his confinement become solitary? What would be the effect of such isolation on him and his parents? Could Joanne and Bruce foresee a time when they themselves would lose touch with Peter?

Such questions allowed us to speak of the future their story might predict. This was an issue they had not dared talk about, but privately, each of them had thought about it frequently. Because stories can sweep people along in their wake as they gather momentum, I was interested to determine how this one might unfold if it continued in its present direction. For the first time, the futures they were privately predicting could be speculated on in a "community of concern."

"I dunno," said Peter glumly, looking away from us and down at the frayed carpet. Joanne's and Bruce's gaze followed his.

"Well, let's think about what you are up against a little more," I suggested. "If normal vision continues to create difficulties for all of you, how will you be in a month from now?"

Peter and his father continued to stare at the floor.

Joanne broke the silence. "I just can't stand the idea that things will keep going on like this. I guess we may have to think about correspondence school, although now that Peter doesn't have any form of disability, I doubt whether he will be eligible. I can only see things getting worse." Her tone was despondent.

Bruce said, "I just feel sick thinking about everything that we [referring to Joanne and himself] and Peter have gone through. I sometimes think we would have been better to have not even started the whole damn process. Peter certainly is not any happier.

I just worry that we are not going to find a way out of this." Bruce's voice was quavering as he struggled to control his emotions.

In mapping the influence of the problem on each person, I was preparing the way for the family to line up together against normal vision. Family problems can be enormously divisive and, as I have suggested, can push family members into a search for who is to blame. Externalizing conversations, by contrast, invite them to work together against their problem.

I had begun by calling the problem "normal vision," but I now encouraged the family to come up with a new name. Joanne and Bruce responded by saying they thought "normal vision" was a good name. Peter suggested "trouble." We referred to the problem by a number of names, including "normal vision," "reacting to sight," and "trouble."

In the remainder of this first session, we made some headway in storying the development of the problem and were able to map the influence of the problem on all family members, including others who were not present. As this map was being drawn, a shift took place in the way Peter and his family thought about their difficulties. They began to see that their own lives and the life of the problem were distinct.

Prior to the end of the session, I asked each of them, "How much do you think normal vision and trouble have taken over your lives?" They sat in quiet contemplation for some time. Then both Bruce and Joanne talked at length about the troubles they had all faced.

I asked Peter: "Does this trouble follow you around all the time . . . like every waking and maybe sleeping moment? Is it kind of with you all of the time, talking you out of being able to have a life for yourself with your friends?"

Peter looked thoughtful.

I put the question again. "How much are trouble and normal vision the boss of you? Is it 100 percent in charge, or do you sometimes shake it off, even for a moment, and feel like you want to go out and see a friend?"

Peter again thought for a while.

"No, it's mostly around about," he said, looking a little confused.

"So it is not completely in charge of you all the time. Sometimes do you catch yourself thinking that you want to spend time with Ronald [one of Peter's old friends whom he hadn't seen for a couple of months]?"

I suspected that, given Peter's long-standing friendship with Ronald, he may have privately entertained the prospect of meeting up with him. I was engaging in an archaeological investigation.

A therapy of questions can easily make the client feel like the subject of an interrogation. To avoid the power imbalance that might follow from this kind of conversation, I sought permission from Peter to ask him some more questions, saying that if I asked too many questions, he could either not answer them or tell me he was "questioned out." But Peter was still thinking about my previous question and had come up with an answer that seemed important for him to state, as he now lifted his gaze from the carpet and met my eyes.

"The other day, I did think about going over to Ronald's, because we used to play computer games together."

I saw this response from Peter as representing a slight loosening of the hold of the old story about being imprisoned by normal vision. Michael White refers to such a shift in response to the problem as a *unique outcome,* but I prefer his alternative phrase, a *sparkling moment.* Peter's thought about leaving home was a fragment, a beginning point, for the construction of an alternative story.

This fragment was part of the raw material that could be used for the construction of an alternative description of Peter's present circumstances. This process is like the archaeologist's work of reconstruction. But unlike the archaeologist, I have the advantage of living experts who possess all of the necessary cultural knowledge, and I can collaborate with them in the construction of a valued account. They will be the senior collaborators in this therapeutic endeavor.

Michael White has suggested, in relation to the story metaphor, that the narratives we construct about our lives do not encompass the full richness of our lived experience. However, they do have real effects in shaping our lives. A problem narrative emphasizes certain experiences at the expense of others so that the coherence of the story line can be maintained. The ignored lived experiences go unstoried, the events unnoticed. They are never recounted or even understood. Aware of this tendency, the counselor stays alert to the mention of such events, which are often spoken of in little asides or hidden in throwaway lines. For Peter and his parents, although the dominant narrative had featured the theme of growing despondency, there were lived experiences that had occurred over the previous three months that told a different story.

These "pruned" lived experiences can be developed into a more favored story. In fact, we are keen to treat such prunings as cuttings that can be replanted, fertilized, nurtured, and grown into fullness.

Uniting Client and Counselor Against the Problem

In my work with Peter, there was value in finishing the first session by helping the family recognize the signs that progress was being made. To be sure that they were ready to speak against trouble on their own behalf, I asked them to evaluate the progress that Peter had already made in moving out into the world. I was not going to allow the problem to force me into taking up the challenge on my own.

"As we draw this session to a close," I said, "we have begun to identify experiences that Peter has had that have been related to his stepping out with normal vision rather than being imprisoned by it. Are you interested in our exploring further your abilities to find some more favored solutions to Peter managing normal vision, or should we stay with finding a way of accepting Peter living and being at home permanently?"

Peter, Joanne, and Bruce all favored the stepping-out option rather than the imprisonment option. When I asked why, Peter stated, "I don't want to live the rest of my life living at home all the time!"

Although it may seem obvious that people want to overcome problems rather than be overcome by them, we believe it is important that such questions be asked. They serve to align all family members and the counselor on the same side against the problem. They prevent the counselor from rushing on ahead of the family into an attack against the problem without the family's permission. When the family members choose to say no to the problem, the influence of the problem on their lives diminishes.

In the first session, Peter, Joanne, Bruce, and I had accomplished a number of things. We had begun to make the problem external to Peter, and we had all lined up against it. We had spent considerable time mapping the extent to which the problem had been ruling all of their lives, and we had explored more fully the implications for each of them, and for their relationships, of Peter continuing to be housebound. This form of exploration built on the concerns about Peter's motivation that brought the family to counseling in the first place.

Judging by their demeanor, it seemed to me that Peter and his parents had experienced considerable relief in being able to name out loud many of the difficulties they had been experiencing. They had given the problem story a name, and together we had begun to construct the beginnings of an alternative story. We all started to call it "stepping out"—*with* normal vision rather than *against* it.

After the session, I wanted them to focus on the ongoing effects of the problem-saturated story and invited them to consider any events occurring within the family that were free of those effects.

"Be on the lookout," I said, looking at Joanne and Bruce, "for how the effects of trouble might continue to tighten their stranglehold during this next week, and be watchful for hints that there might be some more activity in your household for the staging of a breakout."

In Search of an Alternative Story

At our next meeting, I wanted to explore with the family an understanding of events that had already transpired, both in the interval between sessions and prior to the start of counseling.

"Have there been any changes since I saw you a week ago?" I asked, looking at Peter.

There was a long pause. "No, I don't think so," Peter said, appearing somewhat miffed by the very question.

"Has being able to see made things a bit worse or a bit better for you since we last talked about this?"

Peter reiterated that there had been no changes since our meeting a week earlier.

This form of questioning is used to identify any subtle shifts taking place in the client's relationship to the problem. Minimal or contemplated changes are explored as examples of the strength of the dominant story or as an indication of the emergence of a new story. This focus is based on the assumption that human beings are never still. Even microscopical shifts in thinking or behavior are seen by the narrative counselor as a source of material to be worked with. Clients with long-standing problems like the one that Peter was experiencing typically report that nothing has changed in the early phases of counseling.

Although I was seeking something more than a nonchalant reply from Peter, I was aware that I would probably have to work hard to help the family identify any subtle changes taking place in their view of the problem.

"He's still not interested in going to school," reported Bruce, in a quiet and despairing tone. "Things are pretty much how they've been for the last few months. We really need help, because it just can't keep going like this."

"He did go to visit with his cousin on Wednesday," offered Joanne inconsequentially.

To a counselor using narrative ideas, such a startling development is a wonderful gift with which to continue building the alternative story. But neither Peter nor his parents had put any value on the event, as it seemed irrelevant to getting the problem fixed and having Peter return to regular school attendance.

I had to avoid showing too much excitement—a tendency of mine when I hear such an excellent indication of a new plot. Rather than jumping right in and pointing out to the family that this was exactly what we were looking for, I maintained a steady and inquiring stance.

I asked, "Were there any other occasions when Peter left the house within the last week?"

"Well, Peter did want to come to the supermarket, as he likes to make sure I buy at least some of his favorite food items," reported Joanne, again inconsequentially but somewhat less so.

Peter interrupted to remind his mother and father that he had taken the dog for a walk the day before.

Constructing a History of the Preferred Story

Such pearls of activity can now be strung together to develop the alternative account of Peter and his abilities. These sparkling moments, or new developments in relation to the problem-saturated story, need to be historicized so that they do not hang lifeless and disconnected. I like to describe this stage of the narrative interview as similar to the task of building a fire. To keep the first flickering flame alive, you place tiny twigs very carefully and strategically over the flame. If the twig is too large, the flame could be suffocated. If there is only one twig, it will quickly be spent and the flame will be extinguished. The fire needs to be gently nurtured by the placing of twigs in such a way that oxygen can feed the flames. Larger sticks are then placed on the fire, and soon the fire has a life of its own.

The twigs and sticks referred to here are the person's positive lived moments. It is my task as counselor to identify these favored moments and bring them to the awareness of the client. The art in this approach lies in both knowing where to look and recognizing the unstoried moment when you see it. The observational skills of the archaeologist are most critical at this juncture. The approach is simple in principle but it presents a difficult challenge: to be sufficiently persistent and observant to feed the fire with new possibilities.

In this second session I asked Peter: "How did you beat the fear of being able to see and end up breaking out of the house to go see your cousin? How did you do this?"

"I dunno! I've gone out a bit over the last few weeks," he said evenly.

"Yeah, but how did you get yourself out of the house? How did you get yourself to see me last week and again today?" (I was overloading him with questions—a bad habit I'm trying to contain.)

"I had to come here. Mom and Dad made me come," Peter replied.

"Okay. Did they have to force you much?" I asked, looking for a way to induce a recognition in Peter that his own will was at work in here somewhere.

"Nope, not really. They forced me last week," he said with a grin, while looking at Bruce. "They didn't have to force me today. I wanted to come." He smiled as he said this, looked again at his father, then at his mother. Bruce and Joanne were looking only slightly relieved.

I returned to my original line. "How did you manage to not let the fear of seeing at least stop you at your gate. How did you get yourself along to your cousin's and not bail out or run back home? This is a mystery to me. I would love to know how you did this. Will you let me in just a little on your secret about getting yourself back into the world?"

When narrative counseling is used, a stance of persistence and curiosity is essential for the development of the alternative story. This is sometimes like a very rapid birth. At other times, it can be a much longer labor. Counselors work best when they are enthusiastic about, and committed to, the search for sparkling moments and the history of how these moments came to be.

By focusing on how Peter and his family were overcoming their problem and by encouraging them to view the old story as redundant, I was attempting to build the foundation for a new story line. Peter must have drawn on past abilities to tackle his present problem. At this point, I was feeling confident that we were more than halfway there.

"Well, I like to go to my cousin's," said Peter. "He is building a battle cruiser, and I help him put it together."

"Is sight a friend to you sometimes?" I asked. "Like being able to see does have something going for it, too. Am I right?"

"Yeah, I guess so. But it's okay at my cousin's. He doesn't bug me like some of the kids did at school."

"What is the toughest thing you are getting yourself to do at the moment that stops you being cornered at home?" I asked. Peter paused, and Joanne and Bruce looked thoughtful. Joanne finally made a suggestion. "I wonder if it's going to the supermarket and when he comes into town with me. He often sees some of his school friends, and they natter [chat] for a while." Joanne turned to Peter. "Is this the hardest time in going out, because I know you don't find it easy to come out, and you hide in the car sometimes?"

"It's not really that hard," Peter replied. "I just hate some of the kids at school seeing me around town with you."

"What things do you privately think in your mind to prepare yourself to leave the house?" I asked, continuing with the same line of questioning.

It became clear that Peter would say things to himself that would encourage him to step out of the house.

"I tell myself that I can easily go home if it gets too much," he said quietly. He told himself that he wouldn't really come to any harm, and if he didn't like what he saw, he could still come home. But school was another thing altogether. He hated the idea of entering the grounds with all those kids coming at him asking, "Where have you been?" "Have you been bunking school?"

At this stage, we were continuing to assemble an alternative story. Peter was progressively becoming aware that he already had potency to take some action against the fears produced by his world being turned upside down. I was attempting to establish a trend toward Peter quietly opening up to the possibility of stepping back into the world. It was becoming clear that Peter was spending more time away from home, and he was enjoying going to his cousin's. Joanne reported that the other day Peter had asked if he could spend the weekend with his cousins.

Here are some other examples of questions that invited Peter to reflect on his abilities and competencies:

"How were you able to start getting back into life and going out when the world had really been tipped over on you?"

"Have you always seen yourself as someone with courage when you get to a really hard place in life? Is regaining your sight one such hard place?"

Peter's parents could recall his courage in facing the four eye operations that he had gone through over the previous year.

"Where did this courage come from?" I asked Peter, and looked to Joanne and Bruce for support. Numerous examples were gathered from Peter and his parents about his courageous acts in the recent past.

"When you were really little, were there any other moments when you were called on to have some courage like you have been showing lately?" I asked, wanting to place his courage within a historical context.

In these kinds of interactions, I am taking an active role in building the fire under the new story. I asked Peter to think about himself as a character in his own story who has strength that can be called on in the tough circumstances of life. It is also possible to widen the context of the story by moving back from such character descriptions to yet other events that exemplify these qualities. Peter's ability to manage the eye operations was seen as exemplary of his courage when the going got tough.

The Beginning of Self-Redefinition

A counselor using narrative ideas is interested in restorying a client's early life to demonstrate that the abilities currently being used to deal with the problem at hand are built on capability accumulated from when the client was very young.

For example, Peter and his parents all remembered an encounter with a German shepherd dog when Peter was five. Peter had stood courageously still, and the dog had lost interest in pursuing him, an event that provided an example of Peter's earlier abilities and talents.

I asked him: "Does the idea of being a courageous person suit you? Does that fit with the kind of person you tell yourself you are?"

"Oh, yes, I think so. When I was in the hospital, the doctors said that I was one of the toughest people there." He flashed a confident grin.

I asked Peter a variety of other questions to support the construction of the story of himself as a courageous person:

"Did the problem try to talk you into thinking you were a fearful kind of person?"

"Do you prefer yourself as a courageous person or a fearful person? Why is courage your preference? What has it got going for it, to your way of thinking?"

This form of interaction is a reauthoring process that promotes a person's redescription of himself. In this case, Peter is becoming reacquainted with his ability to stand up to a challenge. The stories of his courage and strength clearly do not fit with the story of being overwhelmed by the problems that have come with normal vision. Recounting them brings them alive in Peter's consciousness in ways that might be expected to influence his response to the problem issue if enough links can be drawn.

Creating an Audience

The preferred story—as chosen by the family—was still a fragile account of events that stood in direct opposition to the story of defeat by fear. But stories about ourselves are not just personal inventions. We learn them in conversation with significant people in our lives. We perform them in our actions, and the reactions of our audiences then become built into our stories about ourselves. In order for the client to make a successful departure from the identity offered by the problem account, an audience needs to be recruited to bear witness to the emergence of the client's new description of himself. The audience could include people significant to the client, such as the therapist, other family members, neighbors, friends, or anyone who is deemed of importance to the person.

Because our psychological relationships with the people we love do not end when they die, therapists using narrative ideas can often encourage clients to contemplate the imagined reactions of a loved one who, though dead, is very much alive in the client's heart or mind. Such relationships can be explored and may become important sources of support and encouragement as the client develops new or more positive self-descriptions. Because human beings are capable of reflecting on their own experiences, counselors can encourage a person to be an audience to his or her own desirable thoughts and actions.

I asked Peter who of the people he admired—including people who had died—would be least surprised to hear about the courage he had demonstrated in the face of the eye operations and his ability to get himself into a world that had fundamentally changed for him.

Remembering his relationship with his grandmother, who had died when he was nine, he stated, "My grandma wouldn't have been surprised to hear about my strength because she always used to say I'd never cry if I fell over and hurt myself."

As the conversation continued, we found other individuals whom Peter cared about who might authenticate his courageous character. The more people we brought into this affirming audience, the more Peter valued his new self-description.

Preparing the Future Through Possibility Questions

At this stage of a session an alternative story has begun to emerge. It is now appropriate to move into the realm of possibility questions and to anticipate the future history of the alternative story.

"Given your track record with courage," I asked Peter, "what is your current plan on how much courage you will be drawing on for your future? Are you going to call on courage all at once or let it slip in gradually?"

Peter thought that he would be drawing on courage gradually. I continued to follow his lead. Peter and his parents were genuine coauthors in this storying process. I found it easy to regard Peter as a young man who had some expertise and knew what he wanted for himself in his life.

I asked him what his current plans were for returning to school.

"I do want to go back to school. Maybe at the end of the month" (three weeks away), he said with some uncertainty.

I asked about his strategy for returning to school. Was he considering waking up one day and just going to school, or was he thinking he would approach school in small increments? Would he, for example, plan to go to school for an hour to begin with and then gradually extend the time, or was he favoring a full immersion?

"I want to go to school for a little while to start with," he replied. Joanne and Bruce looked a little more relieved.

In the next session, a week later, it was reported that Peter had quite deliberately made contact with Ronald, whom he hadn't seen for some time. He wasn't going to school, but he was preparing himself for a step toward entry into school.

As narrative therapy sessions continue, there is value in responding to the subtle and not so subtle changes that the client is making. Peter was moving toward a full reentry into the world. His parents and I negotiated with him a first step in returning to school: he would attend for one afternoon at the beginning of the following week, for just one class.

To make overt Peter's alignment against the problem, I asked him, "Are you sure you and your courage are ready to dip into life at school?"

"Yes, I want to have a go," he responded.

As a consequence of this third session, Peter wanted to prove himself and his courage. Rather than rush ahead of him in the process, I encouraged him to not overdo things.

When we next met, Peter stated that he had gone to school as planned for the one class and, after some initial adjustments, was attending school regularly by the end of that week. After two follow-up meetings at one month and three months, Peter was beginning to appreciate some of the advantages of being able to see, even if the world he saw was very different from the one he had lived in for the first twelve years of his life. During these meetings I had opportunities to hear about the progress Peter was making, and I continued to search with him and his parents for brief moments or larger events that were examples of the enactment and elaboration of the preferred alternative story, which we named "courage to see" or "seeing is believing."

As in most developmental processes, there were setbacks. On one occasion, Peter stopped going to school for a couple of days. He had had a humiliating experience in his science class. Joanne rang up most distressed, believing that things were going to "go back to square one." I invited Peter in for a booster session.

At this meeting, I invited him to consider being a consultant in our practice. I also asked him and his parents if they were interested in making a video of the story of his struggle. I asked Peter whether, if he did make the video, it would be possible for me to show it to some young people who had lost touch with their courage. He could at least tell them how he found his, I said.

Peter thought this was a good idea, and his parents agreed. He enjoyed being videotaped as he described his challenges and the way he beat the fear of living in a world that had completely changed.

This phase of narrative work is as vital as any other. The status of consultant is a fitting acknowledgment of Peter as the senior coauthor in the therapeutic conversation. Peter articulates for himself and for others who will follow him a knowledge that he has been privileged to learn and discover from his own life experiences. Not only does this demonstrate to similarly troubled persons that somebody of their age has knowledge and ability to unravel difficult human problems, but it also suggests to his peers that they, too, are likely to possess talents, abilities, or knowledges that may be both respected by and of use to others. Furthermore, Peter's consultant role provides him with an important audience for his alternative account of himself and his resources, and the influence of that account is thereby expanded. In completing this process, Peter gains the status of "expert," which replaces that of a helpless, dependent person who needs to be fixed. The distinction was not lost on his parents as they saw him shine and bubble with confidence in his new role as an authority on his life.

Finally, if Peter were for any reason to have a temporary problem with fear, he would now have an excellent resource to consult: himself, in living color!

A Way of Being—Not a Formula

The story of the counseling work with Peter has provided a vehicle to introduce you to some of the features of the narrative conversation. Of course, the approach will vary with each client. Narrative counseling is not a formula, although it may be tempting to teach people about it as if it were. In fact, if it is seen as a formula or used as a recipe, clients will have the experience of having things done *to* them and feel left out of the conversation.

The co-creative practices of narrative therapy require a particular ability on the part of the therapist to see the client as a partner with local expertise whose knowledge may, at the beginning of the counseling relationship, be as hidden as the artifacts of a civilization buried in the soil of centuries. However, with tenacity, persistence, enthusiasm, and skill, the counselor, with the aid of the client, will begin the uncovering process. This therapeutic process is a deliberate yet respectful and reciprocal activity. It is reciprocal in the sense that the counselor typically gains knowledge and understandings for herself as a result of the client's disclosures. And because the narrative conversation is a process of unearthing dormant competencies, talents, abilities, and resources, it tends to produce numerous moments of excitement and vivacity.

Stances for Narrative Counselors

When I ponder the differences between narrative therapy and other ways of working with clients, I am drawn to a comparison of what I call the modernist and postmodernist ways of understanding the therapeutic process.

The "knowing" position in therapy (a stance promoted by modernist therapies) has been for me the least satisfying approach to working with clients. Taking the expert position, I found fewer and fewer surprises in my work as the years went by. The normative position invites the professional person to look for commonalities among people; to predict, interpret, classify, and deploy ideas that are considered tried and true. In fact, this position encourages us to be confident about the direction our work will take. Our main stimulation comes from the introduction of new ideas that we have gleaned from a course or workshop and want to try out in our work. From the conventional normative standpoint, energy and excitement for our work is dependent on what we as practitioners introduce by way of new expertise and new knowledge, as little value is placed on the local knowledge of our clients.

This stance requires us to work especially hard to generate the solutions or answers for the clients who seek out our knowledge. It is a path that can lead easily to boredom and tediousness, because we become locked into drawing only from our own expertise.

In contrast to the normative, knowing stance, a narrative way of working invites the counselor to take up the investigative, exploratory, archaeological position. She demonstrates to the client that being a counselor does not imply any privileged access to the truth. The counselor is consistently in the role of seeking understanding of the client's experience. When clients ask a direct question to elicit some expert guidance from the counselor, the latter may indeed offer to provide it but will first want to seek further understanding from the client. The aim is to progressively discover the client's experience of therapy so that the therapist can learn what is helpful and what is not. Counselors are invited to express interest and curiosity in the preferences of clients by seeking an awareness of their moment-to-moment experiences. During a counseling session, many opportunities occur for the identification of knowledge and competency. The narrative counselor learns how to listen for these opportunities to promote the emergence of a counterplot to the dominating problem story and to give the client's hinted-at competencies the acknowledgment they deserve.

Using this orientation, the counselor is mindful of taking a tentative position—one based on what the well-known family therapist Lynn Hoffman called *deliberate ignorance*. Prediction, certainty, and expert interpretation do not fit with a narrative style of working. Developing too much certainty about how to proceed runs the risk of producing a rigid and inflexible practice. The unchecked power or certainty of the counselor's expertise may easily silence knowledges and abilities that might otherwise have come forth from the client.

This way of working requires therapists to squarely face the moral and ethical implications of what it is they create in their interactions with their clients. They can no longer hide behind a "truth-based theory" in accounting for their ethical behavior.

The Importance of Curiosity

Curiosity can be seen as one safeguard against the use of counselor expertise to steer the client in the direction that the counselor deems appropriate. Curiosity about the client's experience brings forth numerous private thoughts about the client's perspectives, realizations, and orientation to the issues at hand. Genuine curiosity opens space for the client and the counselor to observe what is taking place in greater breadth and depth. It is a specific kind of curiosity giving rise to questions that highlight new possibilities or directions for the client to consider. This kind of curiosity, says Michael White, "falls outside of the totalizing stories that persons have about their lives."

When the counselor uses an inquiring stance, the client is given the opportunity to discover the strengths that are present within himself. The counselor can view problematic behavior as a potential resource and look for the special indigenous knowledge of the client.

An attitude of curiosity allows the counselor to live with confusion and ambiguity and to avoid moving too quickly to a therapeutic fix.

The Person Is Not the Problem, the Problem Is the Problem

I have already discussed the use of externalizing conversations in my work with Peter, but there is more to say on this subject. Such conversations are a feature of narrative work that produces the greatest excitement among counselors. The immediate value of externalizing conversations is that the subtle change in the counselor's language promotes a separation between the person and the problem. As a result, clients' tendencies to inflict blame on themselves or others begin to be undermined.

The idea that people are not to blame for their problems may at first sight seem simplistic. It flies in the face of the humanistic tenet that only when therapists help clients to take full responsibility for their inadequacies and behavior can the clients make significant changes in their lives. Many counselors have assisted clients in powerful ways when they have adhered to this formula, and you may well ask, "Why change? Won't seeing the problem as external to the person diminish the client's volition and responsibility to make changes?"

Far from being simplistic, narrative counseling is based on the understanding that problems are manufactured in a social, cultural, and political context. The newly born child is instantly bathed in a cultural "soup." From a narrative perspective, problems may be seen as floating in this soup. The problems we encounter are multisourced, they are developed over a long period of time, and they come together through the medium of human language to construct and produce our experience. To illustrate how cultural context contributes to the production of problems, I refer to the story of Harold.

Harold speaks of the strong influence in his early life of the values of hard work, material accumulation, provision for the family, and individual freedom as the measures of success. It was not just his parents who taught him these things, or his grandparents, his great-grandparents, his schoolteachers, or even the movies he watched as a child. It was all of those influences and more that constructed what he sees, values, and strives for. Harold is not the only person to have been influenced in this way. I would suggest that the values he names characterize the dominant cultural habits of many Western, white, middle-class men. They are values that have been promoted from a variety of sources within white, middle-class culture. If Harold continued to remain "true" to these values but was unable to fulfill them in his life—perhaps because of a job loss, or the birth of a severely handicapped child, or the need to nurse a sick parent—he might adopt a problem story about himself. His sense of success as a person might be significantly undermined, and he could fall into depression. In this case, the fault could be seen as lying with the values imparted to Harold rather than with the dysfunctional nature of his psyche.

From such a perspective, clients are viewed as being positioned by social and cultural factors that shape their desires, ambitions, and purposes. The counselor does not see the person as embodying the problem. Externalizing conversations help to locate the problem within the beliefs of the culture from which the problem emerged. An externalized description can serve as shorthand for a set of values or for cultural *discourse* (discussed by Wendy Drewery and John Winslade in Chapter Two.) These cultural factors can be identified by questioning the client about their effects on his life and their role in creating problems. For example, using narrative approaches, Harold might come to see how distress and depression associated with rearing a child with high dependency needs are influenced by the discourse concerning "the right to complete individual freedom to pursue material wealth."

We have found that narrative ideas have opened up a new range of possibilities in therapeutic practice. If the counselor is genuinely able to incorporate the story metaphor, he is well on the way to becoming a successful practitioner in the narrative style. In this book, we consider examples of the wide range of applications of narrative therapy.

Notes

P. 4, *an optimistic orientation:* Dickerson, V., & Zimmerman, G. (1993). A narrative approach to families with adolescents. In S. Friedman (Ed.), *The new language of change: Constructive collaboration in psychotherapy.* New York: Guilford Press; Epston, D., White, M., & Murray, K. (1993). A proposal for re-authoring therapy: Rose's revisioning of her life and a commentary. In S. McNamee & K. Gergen (Eds.), *Therapy as social construction.* London: Sage; Griffith, J., & Griffith, M. (1993). Language solutions for mind-body problems. In S. Gilligan & R. Price (Eds.), *Therapeutic conversations.* New York: Norton; O'Hanlon, B. (1994, November–December). The third wave. *The Family Therapy Networker,* pp. 19–29.

P. 6, *by Michael White:* Madigan, S. (1992). The application of Michel Foucault's philosophy in the problem externalizing discourse of Michael White. *Journal of Family Therapy,* (14), 263–279; White., M. (1989). The externalizing of the problem. *Dulwich Centre Newsletter,* special edition, 3–21; Adelaide, Australia: Dulwich Centre Publications; White, M., & Epston, D. (1991). *Narrative means to therapeutic ends.* New York: Norton; White, M. (1992). Deconstruction and therapy. In D. Epston & M. White (Eds.), *Experience, contradiction, narrative and imagination.* Adelaide, Australia: Dulwich Centre Publications.

P. 7, *the nature of learning:* Bateson, G. (1972). *Steps to an ecology of mind.* New York: Ballentine Books; Bateson, G. (1980). *Mind and nature: A necessary unity.* New York: Bantam Books.

P. 7, *how to address their concerns:* White, M., & Epston, D. (1991). *Narrative means to therapeutic ends.* New York: Norton.

P. 7, *understandings of the story metaphor:* White, M. (1995). *Re-authoring lives: Interviews and essays.* Adelaide, Australia: Dulwich Centre Publications; Bruner, E. (1986). Ethnography as narrative. In V. Turner & E. Bruner (Eds.), *The anthropology of experience.* Chicago: University of Illinois Press.

P. 8, *historian and philosopher:* Foucault, M. (1980). *Power/knowledge: Selected interviews and other writings.* New York: Pantheon Books; Foucault, M. (1984). *The history of sexuality.* New York: Pantheon Books; Foucault, M. (1984). Space, knowledge and power. In P. Rabinow (Ed.), *The Foucault reader.* New York: Pantheon Books; White, M. (1992). Deconstruction and therapy. In D. Epston & M. White (Eds.), *Experience, contradiction, narrative and imagination.* Adelaide, Australia: Dulwich Centre Publications.

P. 8, *Michael White and David Epston:* Chafe, W. (1985). Linguistic differences produced by differences between speaking and writing. In D. R. Olson, N. Torraru, & A. Hildycrill (Eds.), *Literacy, language and learning.* Cambridge, England: Cambridge University Press; Chatwin, B. (1988). *The song lines.* London: Picador; Geertz, C. (1983). *Local knowledge: Further essays in interpretive anthropology.* New York: Basic Books; Geertz, C. (1986). Making experiences, authoring selves. In V. Turner & E. Bruner (Eds.), *The anthropology of experience.* Chicago: University of Illinois Press; Fay, B. (1977). How people change themselves: The relationship between critical theory and its audience. In T. Ball (Ed.), *Political theory and praxis.* Minneapolis, Minn.: University of Minneapolis Press; Goffman, E. (1974). *Frame analysis.* New York: HarperCollins; Harré, R. (1985). Situational rhetoric and self presentation. In J. P. Forgas (Ed.), *Language and social situations.* New York: Springer-Verlag; Hare-Mustin, R. (1990). Sex, lies and headaches: The problem is power. In T. Goodrich (Ed.), *Women and power: Perspectives for therapy.* New York: Norton; Mishler, E. (1986). *Research interviewing: Context and narrative.* Cambridge, Mass.: Harvard University Press; Myerhoff, B. (1982). Life history among the elderly: Performance, visibility and remembering. In J. Ruby (Ed.), *A crack in the mirror: Reflexive perspectives in anthropology.* Philadelphia: University of Pennsylvania Press; Spender, D. (1983). *Women of ideas: And what men have done to them.* London: Ark; Stubbs, M. (1980). *Language and literacy: The sociolinguistics of reading and writing.* London: Routledge; Turner, V. (1986). Dewey, Dilthey, and drama: An essay in the anthropology of experience. In V. Turner & E. Bruner (Eds.), *The anthropology of experience.* Chicago: University of Illinois Press; van Gennep, A. (1960). *The rites of passage.* Chicago: University of Chicago Press; White, M., & Epston, D. (1991). *Narrative means to therapeutic ends.* New York: Norton.

P. 8, *new possibilities in counseling:* Epston, D. (1992). Temper tantrum parties: Saving face, losing face, or going off your face! In D. Epston & M. White (Eds.), *Experience, contradiction, narrative and imagination.* Adelaide, Australia: Dulwich Centre Publications; Kamsler, A. (1992). Her-story in the making: Therapy with women who were sexually abused in childhood. In M. Durrant & C. White (Eds.), *Ideas for therapy with sexual abuse.* Adelaide, Australia: Dulwich Centre Publications; Seymour, F. W., & Epston, D. (1992). An approach to childhood stealing with evaluation of 45 cases. In D. Epston & M. White (Eds.), *Experience, contradiction, narrative and imagination.* Adelaide, Australia: Dulwich Centre Publications; Adams-Westcott, J. (1993). Escaping victim life stories and co-constructing personal agency. In S. Gilligan & R. Price (Eds.), *Therapeutic conversations.* New York: Norton; White, M. (1986). Anorexia nervosa: A cybernetic perspective, In J. Elka-Haraway (Ed.), *Eating disorders and family therapy.* New York: Aspen; White, M. (1986). Family escape from trouble. *Family Therapy Case Studies, 1*(1); White, M. (1989). Family therapy and schizophrenia: Addressing the in-the-corner lifestyle. In *Selected papers.* Adelaide, Australia: Dulwich Centre Publications; White, M. (1989). The conjoint therapy of men who are violent and the women with whom they live. In *Selected papers.* Adelaide, Australia: Dulwich Centre Publications; White, M., & Epston, D. (1991). *Narrative means to therapeutic ends.* New York: Norton.

P. 10, *each member of the family:* White, M. (1986). Negative explanation, restraint, and double description: A template for family therapy. In *Selected papers.* Adelaide, Australia: Dulwich Centre Publications; White, M. (1989). The externalizing of the problem and the reauthoring of lives and relationships. In *Selected papers.* Adelaide, Australia: Dulwich Centre Publications.

P. 11, *"community of concern":* Epston, D., & White, M. (1992). Consulting your consultants: The documentation of alternative knowledges. In D. Epston & M. White, *Experience, contradiction, narrative and imagination: Selected papers.* Adelaide, Australia: Dulwich Centre Publications.

P. 13, *sparkling moment:* White, M. (1992). Deconstruction and therapy. In D. Epston & M. White (Eds.), *Experience, contradiction, narrative and imagination.* Adelaide, Australia: Dulwich Centre Publications.

P. 13, *shaping our lives:* White, M. (1992). Deconstruction and therapy. In D. Epston & M. White (Eds.), *Experience, contradiction, narrative and imagination.* Adelaide, Australia: Dulwich Centre Publications.

P. 16, *and his abilities:* White, M. (1989). The externalizing of the problem and the reauthoring of lives and relationships. In *Selected papers.* Adelaide, Australia: Dulwich Centre Publications.

P. 20, *redescription of himself:* White, M.(1989). The externalizing of the problem and the reauthoring of lives and relationships. In *Selected papers.* Adelaide, Australia: Dulwich Centre Publications.

P. 21, *new description of himself:* Epston, D., & White, M. (1992). Consulting your consultants. In D. Epston & M. White (Eds.), *Experience, contradiction, narrative and imagination.* Adelaide, Australia: Dulwich Centre Publications.

P. 21, *the alternative story:* White, M. (1989). The process of questioning: A therapy of literary merit? In *Selected papers.* Adelaide, Australia: Dulwich Centre Publications.

P. 23, *in our practice:* Epston, D. (1992). Consulting your consultants: The documentation of alternative knowledges. In D. Epston & M. White, *Experience, contradiction, narrative and imagination.* Adelaide, Australia: Dulwich Centre Publications.

P. 23, *his own life experiences:* Foucault, M. (1980). *Power/knowledge: Selected interviews and other writings.* New York: Pantheon Books.

P. 25, *deliberate ignorance:* Hoffman, L. (1992). A reflexive stance for family therapy. In S. McNamee & K. Gergen (Eds.), *Therapy as social construction.* Thousand Oaks, Calif.: Sage.

P. 26, *about their lives:* White, M. (1992). Deconstruction and therapy. In D. Epston & M. White (Eds.), *Experience, contradiction, narrative and imagination* (quote, p. 146). Adelaide, Australia: Dulwich Centre Publications.

P. 26, *therapeutic fix:* Amunsden, J., Stewart, K., & Valentine, L. (1993). Temptations of power and certainty. *Journal of Marital and Family Therapy, 19*(2), 111–123.

Chapter Two

The Theoretical Story of Narrative Therapy

Wendy Drewery
John Winslade

This book is about ways of using language for therapeutic purposes in the context of a counseling approach often called "narrative." The various chapters offer examples of therapeutic possibilities based on this approach. The book itself arises out of our enthusiasm for these ideas and our desire to communicate their power in an accessible manner. We are not entirely happy with the term *narrative,* however, because although the approach certainly makes good use of the notion of storying, it is much more than that. *Narrative Therapy in Practice* is about doing therapy respectfully—that is, promoting the construction of a client's life without enfeebling her in the process.

For many of the contributors to this book, the project is about more than therapy: it is about learning to avoid ways of speaking and listening that unintentionally express disrespect for others. We want to focus on ways of producing our selves differently. It is a lifestyle and a political project as much as a therapy. The project is based on a belief that the success of Western psychology has become its limitation: in the mental health area in particular, we have learned to focus on personal deficits in ways that speak of failure rather than accomplishment, that produce social hierarchies (experts who often appear to know more about people's lives than they do themselves), and that erode our sense of communal interdependence and common purpose.

In this chapter, we outline some of the ideas that have contributed to our belief in the importance of narrative therapy. In certain respects, we are only just beginning to learn about the power of these ideas, even though they have been around for some time in one form or another. What we are doing is looking at how an apparently simple theoretical perspective can be intentionally turned to therapeutic use. One central discovery is that Western language habits are often productive of negativity and pathology. As Gergen argues, many of the labels used in the field of mental health focus on individual deficits, on what is "wrong" with us. Like Gergen, we believe that this way of speaking is not helpful—that it can maintain the very effects we as therapists are concerned to erase. In narrative therapy, therefore, much of the skill of the therapist lies in attending closely to the ways we use language: to the positionings we call people into by the words we use and the ways we organize our sentences. The approach requires intentionality on the part of the therapist (although client-centered, the approach is not "nondirective"), skill in language use, and systematic attention to the hidden assumptions in the ways people tell their stories.

These requirements sound simple but they are not. It is important to emphasize that there is no recipe, no set agenda, that the aspiring narrative therapist can follow to guarantee success. The best we can offer is our (developing) understanding of the process of "speaking ourselves" differently. Other chapters in this book demonstrate the application of this approach in a variety of contexts; this chapter will look at the underlying theory. We hope you will not be deterred by this pause to discuss theory, and that here also you will exercise your curiosity: for we believe very strongly that to know the underlying theory is to become empowered in a way that is not possible when applications are employed in a purely mechanical manner.

Language and Power

The simple idea from which the narrative approach developed is that people make meaning, meaning is not made for us. This simple statement contains a wealth of implications. For one thing, it puts people in the driving seat of their lives: *we* produce the meanings of our lives. Certainly, the ways we speak and the things we speak about are part of our cultural heritage; they are handed down to us, and they are our tools for making sense. The argument of this book is that these ways of making sense are susceptible to change. We can change the ways we speak. In doing so, we can also change much about the way we organize and understand our worlds. Language is not simply a representation of our thoughts, feelings, and lives. It is part of a multilayered interaction: the words we use influence the ways we think and feel about the world. In turn, the ways we think and feel influence what we speak about. How we speak is an important determinant of how we can be in the world.

So *what we say, and how we say it, matter.* As will be explained below, we can apply this idea not only to objects in the world but also to our selves and to our relationships. This grounding idea about the relation of words to reality has far-reaching consequences that are now being harnessed for therapeutic ends.

Producing Lives That Make Sense

Narrative therapy is underpinned by a philosophy of language that suggests that meaning arises in particular contexts, rather than being given and then applied in those contexts. Meaning is constructed socially. It is not possible for any one of us to decide to use words in particular ways without regard to whom we wish to speak with. To have community, we need some common conventions that we all follow. But commonly accepted meanings can vary, too. The same words can be used with different meanings in different contexts, and different people make meaning differently, sometimes using similar words. (This idea is the basis for mediation in the narrative mode.)

Thus, we make sense of our lives in the context of our social history, shaping stories about the groups we belong to and about how we came to be who, how, and where we are. Such stories constitute something of our identity; they are the background context that gives the possibility of coherence to our lives. Our daily practices and ways of organizing are meaningful because of such contexts. It follows that to make sense of how other people are understanding their lives, we need to understand their background—the contexts, stories, histories they habitually relate. And this is at least a two-way process: the stories can become constitutive of our lives, to the extent that we may sometimes feel that our lives are being storied for us by external forces. It is often at this point, when people feel that their lives are out of their control, that they come to counseling.

The perspective taken in narrative therapy is that it is more useful for people to think of themselves as drawing on the stories or discourses that are available to them for making sense of the world than to think of themselves as in direct contact with reality. This kind of philosophy raises lots of questions about the nature of reality. We do not argue that reality does not exist—only that we cannot know it directly. Further, we certainly accept that different people describe reality differently, and that sometimes their descriptions are at odds with those of their therapists and others in their social world. There may also be divergent descriptions issuing from a single person: an individual's world view is never completely consistent. This is an important springboard for therapy.

It is important to distinguish this constructionist perspective from others that describe the same phenomenon—multiple realities—but that nevertheless differ in their underlying theoretical orientation. Here we are focusing on the idea that in spite of operating within different realities people still need to make meaning together; therefore, no single person has total control over the meanings in his or her life.

Discourse and Power Relations

The notion of discourse is useful because it helps to draw attention to the idea that what counts as coherent or meaningful depends very much on power relations. A discourse is a set of more or less coherent stories or statements about the way the world should be. When we acknowledge that there are many valid ways of seeing the world, what is interesting is which accounts dominate and which are less often heard. Within human communities, what can be said, and who may speak, are issues of power. Discourses organize and regulate even interpersonal relationships as power relations. Discourses are social practices; they are organized ways of behaving. They are the frameworks we use to make sense of the world, and they structure our relations with one another. Seen in this context, power is not the "possession" of particular persons, nor is it a finite quantity so that the more power is possessed by certain persons, the less there is for others to exert. Rather, power operates at the lowest levels of society; it is at work in everyday interactions in homes, playgrounds, workplaces—wherever there are attempts to make sense of living. Power in this sense is something that can be positive and productive rather than repressive and negative.

This understanding of the operation of power is quite different from the humanistic interpretation that is familiar to most counselors. In humanist discourse, the (ideal) person is positioned as a kind of "prime mover," a metaphorical source of primary power. The well-functioning person in the humanistic mode is one who is "in control of her life," a person who "has choices" and makes them consciously. Our theory suggests that healthy personal positioning is quite different from this, but we would not want to say that persons have less power. Indeed, making meaning is a serious and ethical business in which what each of us does counts, and we have no option but to take notice of one another. Appreciating this difference in the way the workings of power are viewed is of primary importance in understanding and using narrative therapy. It repositions the counselor and has important implications for all interpersonal relationships.

Positioning

Our analysis suggests that no one has complete power over himself or his environment, and that we live in social contexts where many different, often potentially conflicting, discourses operate. Discourses, the more or less consistent sets of ideas we draw on to tell about ourselves, offer us positions in patterns of relationship with other people. Discourses often come to have a prescriptive function. For example, the family discourse in New Zealand has positions for wife, husband, mother, father. There are dominant stories about how a wife is expected to be positioned in relation to the husband and about how a father is expected to be positioned in relation to the mother. If a person wants to take up a position different from that identified in the dominant story, she may have to engage in some quite significant, and ongoing, negotiations. People can give new meaning to the term *husband* or *wife,* but it may be difficult to do so. The measure of difficulty is related to the power relations that are signified within the family discourse.

A familiar example may be of use here. Meeting someone for the first time, it is common to ask what they do (meaning, of course, in the paid workforce). If I, Wendy, meet a couple, I try to ask both the man and the woman this question. Both women who hold responsible positions and those who do not are familiar with the situation of having their occupation presumed to be of little interest. In some circles, it takes a particular effort not to talk with men as if they are more interesting (and more important) than the women who may be present. That many people now make this effort amounts to a cultural change. But the example demonstrates the way discourses operate and the embeddedness of the power positionings we have been talking about. It also points to some of the ways in which positionings can be challenged. Such social and cultural changes are happening all the time, as different discourses collide and new meanings and new positions are negotiated.

Some of the ways positions can be given to us by the discursive conditions within which we try to produce our lives can be very subtle. Discursive conditions are often implicated in the problems people bring with them to counseling. A child in a "reconstituted" family told Wendy that his father's new partner "bullied" him. Although the conflict was, of course, more complicated than space allows us to describe, it hinged on the fact that the partner had decided on the choice and arrangement of some furniture in the boy's bedroom, against his wishes. Ever since he was young, this boy had been encouraged to make his own decisions about his life. In his view, parents were people whom he consulted about his financial needs and little else. His new "parent," on the other hand, felt that parenting meant more than that. Thus what seemed like interference to one was responsible behavior to the other.

Noticing the effects of this kind of difference in naming is not new in counseling, but what narrative therapy draws attention to is the process of meaning-making: both the child and the new partner brought into the situation their own assumptions about the proper authority of adults in relation to children in their care. In narrative mode, neither view is seen as "right." The parties could be seen as engaged in creating new meaning—a complex process of negotiation. In such situations, neither person "wins": the narrative therapist presumes the sovereignty of each person over his or her own life, and works within this framework. Thus the child can emerge feeling as respected as the adult, even if the furniture stays where it is. From the point of view of the therapist, neither has final authority over the meaning of their relationship. "Parent" and "child" are discourses that can be drawn on but that will not, finally, decide the form of the developing relationship (which could, of course, be viewed as a negotiation about power positionings). The determination of how this relationship plays itself out will be an ongoing, creative process.

Utilizing the changeable nature of meanings and their relation to the complex webbing of power in social interactions is fundamental to narrative therapy. We shall return to this point briefly when we come to speak about deconstruction.

Shaping Ourselves Through Discourse

Let us now draw your attention to another aspect of this idea that the way we speak positions us: the notion of multiple positionings. The example of the family discourse demonstrates that it is possible to hold more than one position within the same discourse—for example, wife and mother, husband and father. Each of these positions brings with it a variety of expectations about how the person relates to certain other people in socially organized (in this case, family) interactions. However, it is also possible to hold positions in several discourses at the same time. Thus, for example, a wife may also be mayor of the local council. At the same time, she may be a self-professed feminist. Each of these descriptions produces a set of expectations that positions her differently in other discourses. In each of these discourses (family, local politics, feminism) the power relations into which she is called are likely to be very different: each of these *subjectivities* reflects a particular kind of positioning in relation to others—to her husband and family, in the one case; to the people of the city, in another; and to quite different relationships in feminist discourse, with their own (equally contested) sets of expectations. Each *subject position* is a position in a possible conversation, and each signals something about the individual's power relationships too.

Thus, we tell a distinctive story about identity. We do not assume that people's identities are primarily stable and singular, which is the basis of many descriptions of identity formation in personality theory and counseling practice. For us, who people are is a matter of constant contradiction, change, and ongoing struggle. Because this concept is very different from the one that most counselors are familiar with, we prefer to speak about subjectivities rather than identities. It is not unusual, of course, for different positionings to conflict with one another; often, such conflicts bring people to counseling. This account of subject position differs from that of simple role conflict because of the power dimension that determines whether a person may speak, what he can say, whether and how he is likely to be heard, whom he may speak with, and so on. Thus our positioning in discourse is important in relation to our ability to contribute socially. The subjectivities that we live are not necessarily of our own making but are the products of social interactions that are themselves practices of power relations. When we speak to or about others, we are giving them parts in a story, whether we do this explicitly or implicitly. Thus a speaker makes available a subject position that the other speaker, in the normal course of events, will take up. In this way, we influence one another's subjectivity, often without a conscious intention to do so.

Position Calls

Discourses offer subject positions in many socially defined ways. The discourses around counseling, professional relationships, learning and teaching, and ethics are examples. We show that we "know how to go on," in Wittgenstein's phrase, when we respond appropriately to these position calls. An accomplished speaker not only is aware of the meaning of the words used and their grammatical positioning in sentences but also knows the "rules of the game" and understands what behavior is expected of her in the situation. Ready-made meanings are brought to any interaction, together with expectations about how that interaction will be played out. The parties may then negotiate. Conversation is a very good metaphor for the social process of meaning-making, as it has just the right pattern of to-ing and fro-ing. It focuses our attention on the interactions between people rather than on the intrapersonal dynamics of the individual. Narrative therapy seeks to harness such ideas about the power of language and how the self is formed and reformed. This is an ongoing process, and one that is never finished. Even after death, others will continue to restory our lives.

Realities/Reality and Knowledge

The way we speak about "things" determines a lot not only about how we understand them but about what those things are. This theory about the production of what we treat as reality suggests that the reality we work with is not "out there" but something we produce—and something that can change as well. The theory is an extremely important aspect of the narrative approach to therapy, not just because it points to the constancy of change, but mainly because it challenges the idea that true and certain knowledge is possible. However, the implication is not that the material world does not exist, only that what we say about it (including how we name it and what we count as objects) is influenced by the meaningfulness of the contexts and histories in which we find ourselves. At the same time, however, we influence our worlds; the interaction is at least two-way. But we can create the world only in the terms we have available to us. This is what it means to say that we are "always-already social": we are born into a context that we have no option but to react to. Far from being in control of the world, we seem to be at the mercy of myriad influences, and these are not always obvious; indeed, many are hidden or unknown. Further, because the social context is itself constantly changing, there can be no one true story—no single, correct account of what is. Different stories are possible, even about the same events. How we talk about what happens to us depends on our starting point, and how we explain what happens to us depends on the questions we ask. This kind of understanding of the workings of language can be used intentionally for therapeutic ends.

Rather than taking knowledge as given, somewhere "out there" to be discovered, we prefer to speak about *different knowledges* and *preferred knowledges*. Different knowledges have different claims to validity, depending on the contexts within which they arise and on their relationship to different purposes and histories. This is an enormously complex point that positions our theory within a particular context in the history of ideas—that of *constructionism*. Not all forms of constructionism are the same, and the reader should be aware that we are defining our own usage of the term. This form of epistemology, or theory of knowledge, is located in a very different philosophical tradition from the one that produced most of Western science and technology.

Relativism and Ethical Practice

Our theoretical story involves, it seems, a loss of some deeply held Western values, such as truth and the immutability of selfhood. Rather than the individual being seen as the focus or source of motivating power, the emphasis falls on the outcomes of social interaction. It is a sharp move away from individualism, and certainly challenges some strongly held Western ideas about personal responsibility. The constructionist account suggests that the social rather than the individual realm is the primary ground from which the human being may be understood. But this does not mean that we can shrug off moral responsibility for the way the world is. Far from it. In fact, we are participants in producing other people's worlds as well as our own. The adoption of this viewpoint would bring Western culture into line with many other cultures in the world, particularly some indigenous cultures where there is a closeness to the land and collectivity is valued highly. It is also possible to argue that constructionism brings relationships into the foreground: we are "in it together," in a manner of speaking.

Putting the Ideas to Work

One of the social practices where this kind of responsible coproduction of social relations can be seen at work is counseling itself. The counselor is involved in influencing the production of meanings in the client's life. But unlike some other therapists, the narrative counselor is not concerned with diagnosing "the problem" or with offering "treatment." The objective is not to find a "solution." Narrative therapists are resigned to the possibility that they may never "get it right" in any final sense.

What we do say is that problems are the products of discursive conditions, or ways of speaking, which have placed the person in problematic positions in the story he is telling about his life. Different subjectivities can be presented together in ways that create conflict and unhappiness. The counselor can help the client to understand how these different claims on his subjectivity are producing discomfort. Often the counselor needs to do little more than this. Part of our philosophy is that people work all the time to make sense of their own lives and that it is not up to the counselor to do this work for them. One of our students remarked with some relief that this stance allowed her to be less stressed in the counseling process. The counselor is not expected to be an "expert" but rather to be a curious, interested, and very partial participant (rather than claiming an objective neutrality in regard to the forces that shape the problem) in the production of the meanings of the client's life. This stance reflects the deep commitment that is required of the narrative counselor, at the same time as it displays the productive yet nontechnological nature of the therapy.

Stories and Alternative Stories

Narrative theory suggests that we do not have complete control over the possibilities for our lives: we can only ever speak ourselves into existence within the terms or stories available to us. But if we grow up thinking that things are so and so, how can we "know" any other way? For example, if we have taken in the belief that the earth is flat and that if we go too far in any direction we will fall off, then that becomes a "fact." From our perspective, there is no other possibility. The stories we tell come to be the "natural" state of the world—the way the world is. Often, this kind of sense-making becomes a credo—the standard by which all other stories about the same phenomena are told and the basis of judgments about what is right and what is not. Our stories can blind us to other possibilities. The narrative counselor listens for alternatives to the "problem" story that the client is telling. Although we believe people struggle to give coherent accounts of their lives, no account is so consistent that we cannot find elements that contradict the problematic story. Every life is fraught with contradiction, and it is possible to make use of this fact in therapy.

Agency, or Speaking in One's Own Voice

Often, it seems to us, problems are such because we feel unable to move them—we have lost agency in our life. What is happening is that the stories we are telling ourselves about what is happening are disabling. These are stories in which the client is position*ed*, or subject*ed*: he is not the actor but the passive recipient of the given positioning. The narrative counselor looks for alternative stories that are enabling—that allow the client to speak in his own voice and to work on the problem himself. This process can be described as repositioning, or reclaiming the voice of the client.

We often use the terms *speaking* and *voice* as metaphors for the agency of the client. We believe that stories that are spoken in the voice of the client are experienced as more enabling than stories that tell the client's story for him. The narrative therapist's objective, then, is to reposition the client as the speaker or teller of his own story. Throughout the present volume, we give examples of how this can happen in therapy. The objective is to enable clients to speak from subject*ive* positions rather than as subject*ed* persons. Some readers may see this theoretical explanation as an account of empowerment; others may see it as an account of consciousness-raising. Certainly, our understanding of the processes of coming to speak one's own life owes a great debt to feminist theorizing, radical pedagogy, and community activism. We acknowledge these links, as we also acknowledge that this aspect of our theorizing is still in process of formation. We hope that you will join us in exploring, in theory as well as in practice, what we believe is a therapeutically potent theory, as we also hope that you will exercise your patience with the gaps in this exposition.

Listening and Deconstruction

One of the interesting practical aspects of narrative therapy is what it suggests about listening. Unlike the Rogerian therapist, whose active listening is intended to reflect back the client's story like a mirror without distortion, the narrative therapist looks for hidden meanings, spaces or gaps, and evidence of conflicting stories. We call this process of listening for what is not said *deconstruction*.

The narrative therapist is actively involved from the outset in delving into the meanings of the client's life. The notion of looking for hidden meaning has an interesting history, deriving from the work of French philosophers such as Jacques Derrida and Michel Foucault. Derrida pointed out that in order for words to have meaning, we must be able to distinguish that meaning from what it is not. He was pointing to the role of the opposite meaning in enabling a word to make sense. He claimed that the opposite is always present in any positive meaning, and that meaning-making depends on the possibility of perceiving a difference. This is a very powerful idea. Some of the stories clients tell can seem to make no sense at all until we ask ourselves, What are the backgrounding assumptions that enable this story to make sense? We can listen for what is not being said, or we can ask, *In distinction from what* is this story being told? or What unnamed background assumptions make this story work? Listening this way often renders rational the apparently irrational; it can enable us to understand some forms of "madness," for example. The complexity of deconstruction in this sense and its potential for use in therapy deserves an entire book of theory on its own. Certainly, the area is ripe for renewed commitments to research in the counseling field.

We draw another useful sense of the term *deconstruction* from the way Foucault wrote many of his books: he was largely concerned to uncover the hidden workings of power relations in claims to knowledge. Although he was originally concerned with large bodies of knowledge (or social practices) such as medicine, education, and the law, toward the end of his life he became more preoccupied with what all this meant for producing an ethical life. This could easily be a description of the purpose of therapy. Like Foucault, we argue that power relations characterize all of our social interactions, and that these power relations are played out (among other ways) in the language we use to describe our lives. It behooves us, then, to pay attention to how the language we use speaks us, to examine the sources of authority for the claims we make about ourselves. The counselor "unearths" the ways in which clients have had their power to tell their story reduced by their acceptance of less preferred ways of speaking—less preferred because they reflect authorities other than the client. Once having "gotten" this way of listening, we find it is possible to uncover and to challenge a lot of taken-for-granted assumptions about the way the world should be, and thereby to open up possibilities and offer spaces that were previously hidden. "Old" ways of thinking can thus be revealed to have been hampering us in ways we had not noticed. When this happens, we may feel that scales have fallen from our eyes. Taken together with the notion that because the world is constantly changing, there is no single "right" way, these ideas about language can be experienced as enormously liberating. Throughout the body of this book, we offer examples of these processes at work in different contexts, so that you can make your own assessment of their potential.

Externalizing

People within a culture share a dominant set of discourses, or ways of making sense. But each one of us puts our own individual story together in our own particular way, often changing the story depending on whom we are talking to, when, and why. Because each story is particular, there are no formulas that will definitively teach you how to use deconstruction in counseling. For this reason, some people find it very difficult to learn the narrative approach. As will be evident from Chapter Four, we are still in the process of developing our own understanding of how narrative counseling "works" and how to teach it. For our present purposes, we will offer some principles by which the process can be made more understandable and we will indicate areas for further reading.

Some people speak about deconstruction as a process of "externalizing the problem," without necessarily discriminating the nuances of the term. The process, which was called deconstruction by Michael White, focuses on the problem rather on than the person and then mobilizes the client's resources against the problem. *Externalizing* was proposed as a mode of working by White and David Epston, the original exponents of narrative therapy. Several of the authors in this book talk about this process of externalizing.

More recent formulations of this approach have adopted the notion of ongoing *externalizing conversations*—a more fluid idea than that of "externalizing the problem." Externalizing is a rhetorical device that opens up a slightly different way of speaking about one's life. It seems to achieve several things.

First, if the dominant discourses of twentieth-century Western culture have promoted a view of individuals as prime movers in their own lives (as argued above), then externalizing conversations create space for a different understanding in which discourses are accorded more influence in the shaping of experience.

Second, the device of externalization helps to reverse the trend in psychology toward seeking more and more deficits in individual character and encouraging clients to relate to themselves as deficient human beings. Separating the person from the problem often comes as a pleasant surprise to people who come to counseling with the expectation that they will have to walk across hot coals in penance for the inner deficiencies that "must" be causing their pain. Instead, they are immediately given the status of agents in their own and others' lives and regarded as resourceful, intelligent persons engaged in common human struggles.

Third, externalizing has an ironical effect. In a world intent on maximizing the disciplinary power of internalizing logic, the process of externalization parodies the dominant ways of thinking in our culture. The discourses in which problems have previously been located are thus travestied. For example, in the well-known narrative story of "Sneaky Poo," the professional knowledge of encopresis is travestied by the externalized description of the problem Michael White adopts in a way that enables the family that has consulted him to take back from the professional grasp their own agency to deal with the problem. Thus, the previous discourse can almost be laughed at from the new perspective; certainly, it has been gently undermined. This ironical effect is, we suspect, far more potent than any kind of direct confrontation.

Fourth, the process of speaking in an externalizing way provides counselors with a discipline to maintain—a discipline that alerts them to the possibilities for agency in the lives of the people who seek their help. This discipline trains them to listen for discourses at work in the production of problems and breaks the unconscious habit of imputing to clients a sense of deficit. It moves them into a more respectful way of speaking to those who consult them.

Thus do externalizing conversations serve the purposes of deconstruction. In this section, we have attempted to sketch the origins of the notion of deconstruction, locating it—as does White himself—in a much wider philosophical context. However, in the narrative literature, the notions of externalizing and deconstruction are sometimes used interchangeably. Our discussion is intended to augment understanding of, and to some extent to challenge, this limited usage.

"Problems" Revisited

One of the most powerful examples of how deconstruction can be used is Foucault's own method of working. He "unearthed" the workings of power through discourses, as indicated by the title of one of his most famous works, *The Archaeology of Knowledge*. Foucault was also able to show how some of our most institutionalized ways of speaking are produced rather than given. The idea that meanings of words are constantly changing contradicts another "commonsense" notion: that words stand for things. This is especially relevant to the language of mental health. Words such as *happiness, sadness,* and *anger,* even *personality* and *self-esteem,* are often used as if they refer to some inner state of a person. The constructionist perspective challenges this view, suggesting that such words simply provide convenient ways of speaking about patterns of behavior. The immediate experience of a person is never captured for certain by the words used to describe it. The constructionist framework makes it easier to rename one's experience—to make sense of it differently.

But this idea can be taken much further, to challenge the grip of diagnostic labeling. In particular, narrative therapists have been concerned to work actively against what we perceive as the damaging effects of many "scientific" psychological labels. This theoretical area has been well explored by feminist writers in relation to the naming and invisibility of women's experiences through centuries of changing fashions in diagnostic labeling. We want to point to the strong cultural pressures (calls to an authoritative positioning of the therapist) in the language of therapy. We invite engagement with the type of language that *produces* the deficit positioning of clients and encourage resistance to it. Chapter Five, in particular, discusses this issue, highlighting some of the difficulties such a positioning raises for the therapist in the dominant scientific paradigm.

Identity, Again

We are suggesting that if words stand for things, this is only a temporary state, and that we can always name things differently. Of course, this is also true of people. Our theory is that who we are is a constantly changing reality—a dynamic process of being rather than something essential or hidden somewhere inside us. Our potential is infinite, our developmental paths are not set. What we do in our lives makes a difference to where we will end up, but this process is also subject to constant change, to known and unknown influences. As we have said before, what we do matters, but we do not have full control over our circumstances. We have a major part to play in our own becoming, but we cannot simply decide who we will be. This perspective foregrounds the contexts of our lives as influences in producing who we can be while at the same time leaving some agency with the person. It is important to note that this account of personal identity is very different from the model of the single, unitary self most generally assumed by counselors; the differences are subtle but central to the working of our theory, as the unitary self is central to many other forms of counseling. Although many of the words appear to be the same, the totality of the world view we are promoting is very different from that which would have the self "developing to its full potential," for example. It seems to us that what most people do is muddle along, making sense as best they can, making decisions and acting on them in the face of the uncertainty, complexity, and novelty of the situations that are constantly arising and demanding a response. As complexity increases, we recognize ourselves with more difficulty. But we also must learn to forgive ourselves.

Positioning Ourselves

The story we have told in this chapter is part of an epic that involves the evolution of scientific knowledge and our growing awareness of the possibility of many different ways of making sense of the world. Major elements in this story are language, power, knowledge, and the self. It is a theoretical story with a very practical application. This is a story with no end and no beginning, though for our purposes (and at the risk of inviting debate on an unsubstantiated claim), we will suggest that it began with the conjunction of the phenomenological approach pioneered in counseling by Carl Rogers and movements in the philosophy of science, humanism, and the Christian heritage. All this history is bound up with who we, the group who wrote this book, are—with our "identity" as a group. Of course, we are all deeply involved in counseling in one way or another; we are also writing from New Zealand. Both of these positionings are important in our thinking about counseling as we do.

It is no surprise that counselors may be central to the unfolding of this epic story. Carl Rogers's theory of counseling depended deeply on his perception of the therapeutic importance of understanding the person's own experience. Counselors in the Rogerian mold often quote the Native American proverb about not judging the behavior of another until you have "walked a mile in their moccasins." What this proverb points out is that what can seem incomprehensible, even bizarre, from one person's point of view can be seen as entirely sensible from another's. The idea that sense is something we make—rather than something that is given, separate and apart from us—underpins the perspective on the production of healthy lives suggested in this book. It is a kind of philosophy of science, representing a particular perspective on what knowledge is, on how we come to say that we "know." It asserts that there are many truths, and that what one person holds as sensible and true may not be so for another. Truth is made, not given. Although on the face of it this may seem an attractive idea, it may run counter to many of our most dearly held beliefs about nature and the universe. We are working with the possibility that nature is not given, to be discovered, but is itself produced.

In this case, "we" are people who live and speak from within a highly industrial and technological culture that has been achieved through a very developed form of rational thought—for many people, the highest possible form of striving known to human kind. But it is now quite well accepted that Western scientific knowledge is only one form of knowledge. Women's knowledges and indigenous people's knowledges are examples of domains where the issue is vigorously debated.

From our perspective, it is important to see how an entire value system (a "cultural soup," as Gerald Monk called it in Chapter One) has grown up alongside the Western "scientific" ideas about how knowledge is created. How facts are known and how change is brought about in the world are intimately bound up with our ideas about how we make our lives or have them made for us.

"We" who make our selves within the Western cultural perspective are used to thinking about our selves as individuals or single units, and about our relations with the world as resembling those of billiard balls, bumping against one another when their paths cross. We strive for control over our world and hold ourselves responsible for failures to perform according to standards that are often set for us. It is possible to argue that the entire project of developmental psychology (perhaps even the basis of the Western education system) depends on the idea that we can achieve a particular kind of rational control over ourselves and the world in which we live. Through the ways our lives are constructed, we tend to have a big investment in these ideas about progress and what is good. In supporting the narrative approach to therapy, we are very deliberately opposing these ways of thinking, because we believe that they exclude other perspectives that, although we may not always share them, we recognize as also worthy of respect. The persistent struggle of the first people of Aotearoa/New Zealand, the Maori, against the swallowing up of their own perspectives by the powerful discourses of Western colonizers has taught us much about the propensity of Western ideas to dominate and to presume their own rectitude. When you read Chapter Eleven, we hope you will get a flavor of how the engagement with Maori has touched many of us, teaching us to question our perspective very deeply. We are sure other First Nation people are having similar effects on colleagues elsewhere.

These matters are closely bound up with who we know ourselves to be—with our common professional project and with our location as participants in an ongoing therapeutic conversation of which this book is a part. We have deliberately talked about "us" as working within a particular "cultural soup," or discursive context, to draw attention to the idea that all people, including us, come to understand and evaluate themselves within such frames of reference. We want especially to underline the idea that who we are— the common threads of subjectivity that constitute our group's "identity" or "voice"—is produced in relation to this discursive background, and that it is easy to overlook how deeply a philosophy of knowledge can affect the production of our sense of ourselves as powerful people. This is particularly important if what we take for granted is at the same time that which oppresses others. Development of the necessary capacity for reflexivity is a project that is not easily achieved and, we believe, demands lifelong application. It seems to us extremely important that we, who as counselors deal daily with the effects of colonizing power, continue to search out and uncover the building blocks of this ancient edifice that is "our" civilization. The benefits of doing so might be that we more easily engage with others whose constructions of civility differ from ours. Above all, and at a profoundly professional level, we are engaged in learning about respect.

Notes

P. 32, *enfeebling her in the process:* Gergen, K. J. (1994). *Realities and relationships: Soundings in social constructionism.* Cambridge, Mass.: Harvard University Press.

P. 33, *what is "wrong" with us:* Gergen, K. J. (1994). *Realities and relationships: Soundings in social constructionism.* Cambridge, Mass.: Harvard University Press.

P. 35, *we cannot know it directly:* Harré, R. (1986). *Varieties of realism: A rationale for the natural sciences.* Oxford, England: Blackwell.

P. 35, *depends very much on power relations:* Gordon, C. (Ed.). (1980). *Power/knowledge: Selected interviews and other writings by Michel Foucault.* New York: Pantheon Books.

P. 35, *interpersonal relationships as power relations:* Davies, B., & Harré, R. (1990). Positioning: The discursive production of selves. *Journal for the Theory of Social Behaviour, 20*(1), 43–63.

P. 35, *Discourses are social practices:* Fairclough, N. (1992). *Discourse and social change.* Cambridge, England: Polity Press.

P. 35, *a finite quantity:* Gore, J. (1992). What we can do for you! What *can* "we" do for "you"? In C. Luke & J. Gore (Eds.), *Feminisms and critical pedagogy.* New York: Routledge.

P. 36, *positive and productive:* Fraser, N. (1989). *Unruly practices: Power, discourse and gender in contemporary social theory.* Cambridge, England: Polity Press.

P. 38, *multiple positionings:* Weedon, C. (1987). *Feminist practice and poststructuralist theory.* Oxford, England: Blackwell.

P. 38, *change, and ongoing struggle:* Weedon, C. (1987). *Feminist practice and poststructuralist theory.* Oxford, England: Blackwell.

P. 39, *a subject position:* Davies, B., & Harré, R. (1990). Positioning: The discursive production of selves. *Journal for the Theory of Social Behaviour, 20*(1), 43–63.

P. 39, *"know how to go on":* Wittgenstein, L. (1958). *Philosophical investigations.* Oxford, England: Blackwell.

P. 40, *"always-already social":* Walkerdine, V., & Lucey, H. (1989). *Democracy in the kitchen.* London: Virago.

P. 40, *that of "constructionism":* Monk, G., & Drewery, W. (1994). The impact of social constructionist thinking on eclecticism in counsellor education: Some personal thoughts. *New Zealand Journal of Counselling, 16*(1), 5–14.

P. 41, *moral responsibility:* Shotter, J. (1989). Social accountability and the social construction of "you." In J. Shotter & K. J. Gergen (Eds.), *Texts of identity.* London: Sage.

P. 42, *expected to be an "expert":* Anderson, H., & Goolishian, H. (1992). The client is the expert: A not-knowing approach to therapy. In S. McNamee & K. J. Gergen (Eds.), *Therapy as social construction.* London: Sage.

P. 42, *terms or stories available to us:* Davies, B. (1991). The concept of agency: A feminist poststructuralist analysis. *Postmodern Critical Theorising, 30,* 42–53.

P. 42, *contradict the problematic story:* White, M. (1995). *Re-authoring lives: Interviews and essays.* Adelaide, Australia: Dulwich Centre Publications.

P. 43, *what it is not:* Derrida, J. (1978). *Writing and difference.* Chicago: University of Chicago Press.

P. 44, *claims to knowledge:* Foucault, M. (1979). *The archaeology of knowledge.* London: Penguin.

P. 44, *an ethical life:* Foucault, M. (1989). *Foucault live.* New York: Semiotext(e).

P. 45, *called deconstruction by Michael White:* White, M. (1991). Deconstruction and therapy. *Dulwich Centre Newsletter,* (3), 21–67.

P. 45, *White and David Epston:* White, M., & Epston, D. (1990). *Narrative means to therapeutic ends.* New York: W. W. Norton.

P. 45, *externalizing conversations:* Roth, S., & Epston, D. (1996). Consulting the problem about the problematic relationship: An exercise for experiencing a relationship with an externalized problem. In M. Hoyt (Ed.), *Constructive therapies II.* New York: Guilford Press.

P. 46, *well-known narrative story of "Sneaky Poo":* White, M. (1989). "The externalization of the problem and the reauthoring of lives and relationships." In M. White, *Selected papers.* Adelaide, Australia: Dulwich Centre Publications and White, M. (1989). "Pseudo-encopresis: From avalanche to victory, from vicious to virtuous cycles." In M. White, *Selected papers.* Adelaide, Australia: Dulwich Centre Publications.

P. 46, *produced rather than given:* Foucault, M. (1973). *The birth of the clinic.* London: Tavistock.

P. 47, *fashions in diagnostic labeling:* See, for example, Chesler, P. (1972). *Women and madness.* New York: Doubleday; Ehrenreich, B., & English, D. (1979). *For her own good: 150 years of the experts' advice to women.* London: Pluto.

P. 47, *the unitary self:* Henriques, J., Holloway, W., Urwin, C., Venn, C., & Walkerdine, V. (1984). *Changing the subject: Psychology, social regulation and subjectivity.* London: Methuen.

P. 48, *an unsubstantiated claim:* For more on this, see Drewery, W., & Monk, G. (1994). Some reflections on the therapeutic power of poststructuralism. *International Journal for the Advancement of Counseling, 17,* 303–313.

P. 49, *but is itself produced:* Olssen, M. (1991). Producing the truth about people. In J. Morss & T. Linzey (Eds.), *Growing up: The politics of human learning.* Auckland, New Zealand: Longman Paul.

P. 49, *is vigorously debated:* See, for example, Kramarae, C., & Spender, D. (Eds.). (1992). *The knowledge explosion.* New York: Teacher's College Press; Gunew, S., & Yeatman, A. (Eds.). (1993). *Feminism and the politics of difference.* Sydney, Australia: Allen & Unwin.

Chapter Three

The Therapeutic Relationship

John Winslade
Kathie Crocket
Gerald Monk

"You're not really counseling me, are you?" said Lisa. "It's more like I'm bouncing my ideas off you, and checking in and telling you about the changes I'm making."

This comment was made by an astute client during a counseling interview. At first glance, it may seem that she is drawing a disconcerting distinction between "proper" counseling, in which she might expect the counselor to impress her with some form of expert knowledge, and this approach that leaves her less conscious of the counselor as an authority.

However, from a narrative perspective, the comment indicates that her counselor is doing her job. It is a statement about the politics of counseling relationships. In order to make such a statement, Lisa must be experiencing *senior partnership*. Counseling is not just something that she is the recipient of, or something that is being done to her; she is noticing herself as a significant agent in the production of the counseling process from which she is benefiting. Not coincidentally, she is also increasingly noticing this same sense of agency in her life.

Lisa's comment seems to us an outcome of the type of counseling relationship we seek to establish with our clients, and this in turn depends greatly on certain ways of speaking. This chapter will focus in more detail on the ways in which we speak *about* relationship, and also on our ways of speaking and being *in* counseling relationships. We begin by describing the overall stance we take in relating to the people who seek our help—with attention given also to the politics of this stance. We then outline some of the practices and emphases that are used as we develop the relationship.

Before We Enter the Room

It is customary for a textbook discussion of therapeutic relationship to focus immediately on the exchanges that take place between the participants and on how these might be intentionally developed. We prefer to start earlier in the process and to consider some of the influences that are present before such exchanges even begin. The social constructionist thinking outlined in Chapter Two teaches us that much of what happens in the relationship between counselor and client is shaped by discourse. We therefore want to begin with an examination of such discourses.

In our view, professional roles require the establishment of a relational stance that is ethical and that takes cognizance of the shaping effects that operate in the cultural world around the meeting. If the client is going to experience herself—as Lisa did—as the senior partner in the discussion of her own life, then certain moves are likely to be necessary. Some of these are attitudinal shifts on the part of the counselor. Specifically, if the relationship is to become truly collaborative, the counselor needs to be sensitive to how power manifests itself in social and professional practices, and he must develop a facility for reflexive thinking about his own practice. He also needs to find ways to communicate the results of such thinking to the client, through his moment-by-moment responses.

Coauthoring or Sharing Authority

To us, the term *coauthoring* describes a relational stance that we want to express in our actions and words with clients. It implies a shared responsibility for the shaping of the counseling conversation. The idea of coauthoring challenges the portrayal of counselors as followers, who must be very cautious about treading on the toes of clients lest some emergent buds of those clients' true inner nature be prevented from flowering. It also challenges the

view of the counselor as wise, all-knowing expert, sharing the bless-
ings of his years of training with clients who sit in awe at his feet.
Rather, we prefer to speak of identity and personhood as emerging from conversations in social contexts, including the context of
the counseling relationship. To be an author is to have the authority to speak—especially to speak in one's own terms and on one's
own behalf. To coauthor a conversation, counselor and client will
achieve shared meanings and coordinate their relationship according to their mutual meaning-making.

Professional Practices

Shared responsibility for shaping the conversation also has implications for the use of our authority in working with clients. There
is much rhetoric in the field of counseling in general about establishing collaborative relationships and giving the people who consult us plenty of opportunities for exercising their will over the
content and direction of the conversation. However, there are also
a number of ways of speaking about the counseling relationship
that work against this spirit of collaboration. These ways of speaking are products of professional discourses that, when embodied
in practices, create distance between professionals and those who
seek their help.

When we speak about collaborative relationship, we are seeking to foster alertness to those aspects of professional discourse
that set up a relation in which authority lies principally with the
professional person and very little with the client. The following are some areas of therapeutic practice that are often assumed
to come under the authority of the professional rather than the
client:

- Diagnosis of client concerns according to external definition
  criteria
- The asking of questions in order to interpret the answers
- Knowledge of what the client needs to do to overcome the
  problem she is concerned about and the development of a
  treatment plan
- The writing of reports in which the professional is the first-
  person author and the central character in the story is rele-
  gated to third-person object status

- The conveying of information about the client to other people or agencies in referral situations
- Discussions with other professionals about the client and her life
- Note-taking at the counseling meeting, decisions on what is appropriate to include in the notes, and the maintenance of such notes for professional purposes—all without reference to the person about whom the notes are written

The narrative perspective gives us cause for concern about the effects of these practices. We frame this concern within a set of ideas about how discourses offer people positions in relation to each other and how these positions are often inadvertently taken up, with consequences for the way relationships are experienced. Counselors engaging in the practices described may offer positions to their clients without either person noticing the fact. If counselors assume these kinds of authority without sharing the authorship of the professional relationship, they may be usurping clients' authority over matters that are important to them. They are acting against the interests of the clients' evolving subjectivity. They are taking up the position of the one with the right to act while giving the client the position of being acted on, of being the "object" of professional practice.

If we want people to know that we support them in taking up opportunities for agency in their own lives, we need to offer them genuine agency in the relationship they have with us. This stance leads us to want to share the authority to do all of the tasks mentioned earlier and to take great care with the way we speak about our work in order to avoid objectifying modes of thinking and behaving. For example, we might avoid the use of words like *diagnosis* and *assessment,* which grant precedence to professional "regimes of truth" over clients' knowledge about their own lives. We would hesitate before describing our practice as "treatment" or "intervention" lest we ascribe to ourselves the major role of taking initiatives in someone else's life or usurp the position of actor in bringing about change.

When therapy becomes difficult, we resist the temptation to locate the difficulty in the person of the client and to attempt to convince him of his failure to fit into our professional mold. So we do not subscribe to the use (even in private conversations between professionals) of internalizing concepts like "resistance" or "denial," which suggest that we know clients better than they know themselves. Locating "resistance" in the person of the client is a blaming response that lays at the feet of one person what has happened in a relationship. It serves to shore up the power of the professional person vis-à-vis the client. Instead, we might examine the restraints that are operating in the conversation between us or in the cultural world around us, and we might invite our clients to take part in this examination.

We want to honor the subjectivity in all our clients by consistently speaking to them and about them as people rather than as "cases" or "two o'clock appointments" and by avoiding the use of diagnostic categories ("the alcoholic," "a borderline," "that dysfunctional family") when referring to them. Such words shape relationships, even if they are not uttered in the therapy room. In everyday practice, we have worked with our receptionists on generating alternatives to statements such as, "Your two o'clock is here." In staff meetings with colleagues or in discussion with students, we seek to speak in ways that we feel our clients would be comfortable with if they were present.

The use of terms such as *case study* is not neutral or trivial, and we don't believe we are being pedantic to think carefully about it. For if we hold that relations are constructed in the language patterns we employ, then it follows that the language we habitually use to speak of our clients and of our work will exert an effect on our thinking. This in turn determines the background assumptions with which we walk into the room on first meeting a new person.

Before We Open Our Mouths

Counselors need to understand how attitudes and beliefs about counseling influence an initial meeting even before any words are uttered. The context of the meeting (referral process, venue, appointment delay, historical context) will also have an influence on what takes place. As the client and the counselor present themselves to each other, they present as well the cultural backgrounds that have shaped their physical appearance, posture, dress, and sexuality. They must draw from cultural traditions when they participate in rituals of greeting and acknowledgment. The financial contract of the meeting (however that is determined) will constrain the relationship in particular directions. In the first words spoken, both people will tell much about their cultural history through their vernacular patterns, voice inflection, accent, vocabulary, and register. In each act that takes place in the encounter, whether through speech or through nonverbal activity—even at micro levels—people embody their cultural location in ways that offer a limited range of positions for the other.

We conceive of this as an exchange in which two people offer each other *positions* (see Chapter Two). That is, each takes up a discursive position in relation to the other and offers the other a corresponding position. From this basis, a relationship is negotiated. Sonya, a counselor with whom we have worked, writes about her awareness of these issues.

> At the very outset, on first meeting with the client, I am positioned by discourses about being a woman, white, middle-aged, educated, of comfortable means, a "professional"—a person privileged by power . . . relative to my client's positioning within these and other discourses. In the face to face meeting, assumptions may be made by the client that locate me as subject within the dominant discourses about being a woman, white, etc. It will only be as the counseling relationship develops, as I am subjectively present, and become visible to the client, that my positioning vis à vis the client will change. . . . Where the client is a woman, there is straight away a basis for commonality around gender issues and our positioning within the discourse of being a woman. . . . This positions me as a person with a rich stock of "woman's experience" as a resource. . . . On the other hand, when the client is a man, there is straight away a factor of difference by virtue of our positioning within our respective gender discourses. There is a whole dimension of male experience that I do not know about from my own lived experience. And the discourses of female submission and male dominance are likely to colour and be overtly present in our relations.

Many of these position calls are initially nonverbal in character, but they develop in words when people start to speak to each other. Moreover, there are often critical moments when such negotiation takes place. One such moment occurred when Jeanette, a client I (Gerald) had worked with over several sessions, said, "I would like you to tell me the current thinking on how homosexuality occurs."

This question was pertinent to her, as she had previously reported that she thought her son was homosexual. In this moment, I was clearly called into the position of an expert who had important knowledge to impart about the etiology of homosexuality. Her request was made in a spirit that implied a privileged status to my knowledge as compared with hers. Indeed, anything she knew about homosexuality was not likely to feature further in the conversation. But this would have depended on how I responded to her position call. Perhaps the obvious response would have been to answer her as an expert and report my views on homosexuality. As the counselor, though, I knew that I had choices in how I might reply. And my choices would in turn offer her a position from which to respond to me.

If I took up the expert position she offered me and gave her the information she had asked for, the relationship between us would then be constructed as that of expert-to-client. Alternatively, I could have declined to take up her offer of the expert position and risk her forming a lowered opinion of what I might have to give in the relationship. Another possibility would have been to ask her about her views on homosexuality and the sources of influence on her thinking. In this way, I would have called her into a more active position in the relationship and into an exchange of knowledge. Yet another option would have been to point out her acknowledgment, in her use of the expression "current thinking," that opinions on these issues change, that there are no "correct" answers. The possibility of some shared discussion about current ideas would then have opened up. This might have been supplemented by some readings that could also have formed the basis of a shared discussion. Despite the variety of positions I could have taken, I launched, surprisingly early, into the position of expert-authority. I happily spoke at length about a variety of theories pertaining to sexual orientation. To my chagrin, I believe that Jeanette received the second-best solution to her inquiry.

Position calls and the responses to them form the basis of the counseling relationship. It is inevitable that this will be, in some sense, a power relation. The role of counselor itself gives a person an advantage in the decisions about what is to be the legitimate focus of any conversation. We therefore believe that counselors should adopt a deliberate ethical stance in this relation that yields significant authority to the client without giving away potency.

Creating Connection

As the counselor and client begin to speak, the question that arises is what to begin to speak about. The traditions of therapy have, by this late stage of the twentieth century, established some patterns of expectation about what might happen in the genre of conversation that we call counseling or therapy. There might, for example, be an expectation of an early naming of a problem issue by the client. There might be an accepted pattern of not wasting appointment time with small talk and a pressure to get down to business.

The family therapy literature has traditionally emphasized a *joining* stage of the interview, in which counselors seek to make connection with the persons who are consulting them. As Pakeha (white) New Zealanders, we have been influenced by the Maori perspective on this joining process. Maori processes of welcome stress certain traditions that are expressed in their fullest ritual form on ceremonial occasions on a *marae* (a tribal meeting ground). But the same elements of ritual may be found in microcosm in many different meetings. These rituals direct attention to establishing relation through the concept of *whanaungatanga,* which traditionally refers to family connection through shared ancestry. Often, this has been presented to us as a way of speaking that makes easier the building of rapport with Maori clients. But we have found that this knowledge teaches us not just about culture-specific ways of speaking but about how we might take more serious account of the process of building connection with all our clients, both Maori and non-Maori.

This was underlined at a recent meeting where we were showing a video of a family therapy interview featuring Michael White. In the group watching the video were two Maori colleagues. In this interview, which was videotaped before a large audience at a conference, White takes some time (about ten minutes of the fifty available for the whole interview) making "small talk" with each of the family members, inquiring about where they live, what jobs the adults do, what class the children are in at school, and how they traveled to the meeting. After these inquiries, which have established conversational exchanges with each of the family members, White attempts to ask about the problem issues that the rest of the meeting might focus on.

But he is interrupted by Michael, an eighteen-year-old man who has been living away from the family for some years as a result of a fire-setting episode. Michael asks a question that seems to come from nowhere, at least to my ears, about whether White has been on television. He recalls having seen White on a television program about the 1989 San Francisco earthquake. White answers the question respectfully and takes seriously this seeming distraction from the purpose of the meeting—which then continues purposefully.

What my Maori colleagues pointed out to me as we discussed the videotape was that this question could be understood not as an irrelevant distraction but as a part of the process of establishing *whanaungatanga* (traditionally understood as kinship-based connection in Maori culture but more recently widened so as to be interpreted as connection on a wider basis). The young man is reversing the process of the conversation, in which thus far the therapist has been the one asking the questions and establishing the connections. He is trying in the only way he can think of (one assumes) to find some point of connection with this stranger who has come into his life for a brief time. Television is the possibility he appears to hit on to make a link between himself and the therapist.

What this Maori perspective had to teach me was the importance of the connecting process. This young man with his "unconventional" approach was not so much asking an eccentric question as contributing significantly, in his own way, to the development of a relationship in which he could invest his trust. Such moments of connection are developed through rituals that are culturally inscribed in consciousness. The proper honoring of these rituals augurs well for the work that will follow.

Of course, not all clients come wanting to engage in this kind of connection process. As Foucault has suggested, the modern world has taken on many of the aspects of a "confessional society," and counseling is one of the arenas in which people seek to exercise their desire to "confess" their private experiences. Hence many people come along to a counselor ready to launch into their stories with little preliminary. Some of these stories are of the "once upon a time" variety: they start at the beginning and work through a chronological development, the connection between counselor and client being established along the way. Other stories start from a position of crisis, like "slice of life" short stories, and are characterized by the urgency of establishing purposeful connection.

In this phase of the interview, it is quite common when using a traditional counseling approach to establish some form of contract between counselor and client so that there is an acknowledgment that what the client is seeking is something the counselor can provide. Developing some agreement about how to proceed is an important part of the counseling process, particularly when the client is paying for the service and wants to ensure that she is getting value for money. When this negotiation about the purpose and direction of counseling is not properly conducted, the client may leave the counseling session, or the series of sessions, feeling disappointed or even distressed by the process. At that point, some form of litigation or complaint may be initiated.

When we use a narrative approach, these issues are dealt with slightly differently. First, we are less likely to make claims of expert knowledge in the particular problem areas being presented. This is not to say that we lack competence and specialized skill in addressing clients' concerns. But it does mean that the contract is less likely to be built on the assumption of a privileged position for the counselor's knowledge. Instead, we might present to the client our chosen method of working, making clear that we would want to explore clients' abilities and talents so that these became more available for use in addressing our concerns. We cannot make any promises about the final outcome but can talk simply and openly about our approach and emphasize our preference for a partnership relation in the counseling conversation.

Of course, some clients may be preoccupied with their difficulties and not particularly interested in hearing how the counselor works. Nevertheless, we find it useful to be prepared to talk about our role, because clients may be expecting us to provide specific solutions. We want to be open with clients so that they are prepared for what will take place. This declaration of approach does not necessarily have to be done verbally; it can be attended to by presenting clients, before the counseling commences, with a brochure about our preferred way of working.

Using Our Authority

The stance of coauthoring does not need to imply that we give up our authority as professionals. We do not withdraw completely from the authoring role in counseling relationships. But we do endeavor to use our authority in ways that put our weight behind the client's preferences for agency in his own life. We do this by deliberately choosing what we give attention to and how we align ourselves. The narrative alignment we seek is *against* problems, against isolating, deficit-inducing discourses, and *for* people. In a recent counseling meeting, I spoke with a client, almost in passing, against depression, one of the difficulties that were troubling her. She immediately looked up and articulated her desire to "move depression on." Her posture changed, her voice tone changed, her relationship with depression changed. It seemed that my taking a position against depression, using my authority, opened up a space for her to also take a stand in opposition to the problem.

Hearing the Story

What is it that enables us to hear our clients' stories? Like the archaeologist referred to in Chapter One, we are mindful of the need for patience and delicacy. Lisa, with whose comments we introduced this chapter, had something to say about this. What she appreciated about her counseling sessions with me (Kathie) was the sense that she could take her time in processing her own experience. She never felt hurried.

At times in counseling, we are careful followers, not knowing where the story will take us but convinced of our courage to be present to and for our clients. As Lisa put it, "It was always what I was experiencing that was important."

There is a sense of fairness about our need as counselors to show some courage in hearing the story. After all, the client has had to show courage in coming to see us. So we seek to offer the courage and patience, mixed in with respectful curiosity, that make possible the fullest expression of the story. Again, in Lisa's words, "No matter how sordid my story became, she never let me feel her fear, pain, or judgment."

Such hearing can have profound effects. In the session subsequent to the one in which Lisa remarked about her senior partnership, a particularly poignant story came to her mind. She was continuing to bounce ideas and reflect on her experiences. She told of a family Christmas when she was a young child.

On Christmas morning, Lisa had woken up and, with her younger brother, opened her presents under the tree. In their excitement, the two children had taken their presents into their parents' room. There, Lisa recalled meeting two parents hung over from drunkenness the previous evening. She also remembered her mother's rage at her for opening the presents. With much emotion, she told how she had taken the presents back to the tree and tried to wrap them in newspaper so that they would be as they were supposed to be for her mother.

As a counselor, I am a witness to the pain of this story. But I am not a neutral witness. I am moved personally by what I hear. Yet I also know that Lisa is giving an account of her life that is about freeing herself from this pain. The Christmas story is an experience that Lisa is now storying more fully, not in terms of details but in terms of being both teller and audience. As she reflects on the little girl rewrapping the presents in newspaper, she is telling herself and me, "I shouldn't have had to do that." I agree with her that she shouldn't. However, again I am conscious that Lisa is the senior partner, this time as the audience. Her own compassionate hearing of her story is more significant than my hearing. My contribution to the relationship has been built on my belief in my own trustworthiness. By being willing to hear her story on her terms, without imposing any knowing from a place of expertise, I have opened up room for her to be compassionate with herself.

From this point, she begins to story the pain of abandonment and tells of the injustice she has encountered. She traces the effects of abandonment and injustice in her life. We both acknowledge that she can survive this pain. She has already done so as a child, of course. But now, as an adult, she is bearing witness both to the struggles she went through and to her own strengths at this time in her childhood.

I have not been especially curious. I have not asked a lot of questions. I have offered no clever deconstruction of her language. I have only tried to remain respectful of her strength and to privilege nothing except Lisa's account of her experience and her statement, "I shouldn't have had to do that."

When courage prevails in the therapeutic conversation, the client will often discover the opportunity to escape the isolation and excruciating loneliness of her private negative evaluation of herself. Often, she feels relief at discovering that this evaluation is less compelling when brought into the arena of the narrative conversation. When we counselors have knowledge of our own trustworthiness, we can in turn help clients to experience their own resourcefulness in their struggle with the problem and to more fully appreciate the progress they have already made in managing their concerns.

In order to explore her concerns, the client needs to trust and believe that the counselor will not be consumed by her troubles, and she will want the counselor to provide boundaries so that her concerns can be fully expressed in relative safety. Lisa wrote about her counseling relationship that she had trusted Kathie to be "strong enough, bold enough and intelligent enough to challenge me when required. It was really important to me that she was not intimidated by me. This way, I was able to start respecting her."

Counselors must be willing to explore their own painful stories and gain a greater understanding of themselves with the help of people they trust. By doing so, they can develop confidence in their ability to respond appropriately to their clients' most painful stories. When narrative therapists are confident of their own trustworthiness, they are better prepared to meet their clients in rich and uncensored interactions.

Counselor as Audience

We have been speaking about the emotional involvement of the counselor in her role as coauthor and her openness to being moved by the painful stories that clients recount. But our emotional responsiveness is not just to the pain of the dominant story. In narrative work, we tend not to ask clients to stay connected to and to amplify the feelings of pain they might be experiencing with a view to some kind of cathartic release. This preference has caused some therapists schooled in other ways of working to question whether narrative counselors consider people's feelings important. We protest this suggestion. Of course we care deeply about the pain people disclose to us and are very moved by what they say. We are not trying to direct them into some form of "cognitive processing" that might deny their feelings. It is just that we prefer not to give emotional catharsis the prominent place in the process of change that it receives in some other therapies.

Instead, narrative thinking directs us to pay attention to alternative stories of protest and resourcefulness. As we do so, we find ourselves wanting to communicate their impact on us as well. We are often genuinely humbled and awed in the face of people's courage and resourcefulness, which are just as moving as their expressions of pain and isolation.

Through the counseling conversation, what may have been a quite private experience for the client is brought into a more public world of discourse. However, this world is constrained (there may be only one other person serving as audience), and it has boundaries, like the professional ethic of confidentiality, that seek to establish some safety for the public telling. The relationship thus created between counselor and client might be thought of as representing a positive use of power that positions the client in the counseling session as a person with a voice—and a voice that is being offered some legitimacy by being heard. Through careful listening and attentive reflection, summarizing, and paraphrasing, the counselor invites the client to listen to himself in a new way, to be an audience to his own production of self, to hear himself speak in ways that will engender growth in courage, resourcefulness, and hope.

There are several kinds of audience activity that might be conceived of. The first might be just noticing and acknowledging the client's presentation of his story. The significance of telling a story and having another human being listen closely to it should not be underestimated. If the client has previously experienced exclusion and the denial of his voice, it is most important that the power of the counselor be concentrated toward legitimation of that voice.

Second, the counselor might offer audience response. She shares the impact that the client's story is having on her as someone who has been affected by discourses similar to those being described. She is able to say with genuineness, "Yes, I've noticed these same kinds of 'rules for women' influencing me in difficult situations having to do with whether or not I have the right to challenge." At other times, the appropriate audience response might be applause or laughter. In each case, there might be an implicit or explicit invitation to the client to join the counselor in the audience and listen to his own story. This process justifies the continuing use of traditional counseling skills such as reflection and accent.

Third, the counselor might take on the role of chorus with respect to the client's story and again invite the client to join in this role. One way of doing this is to share the task of naming the discursive positions that have been spoken of in the telling of the story. These positions are often experienced by the client in uncomfortable or painful ways but are not clearly articulated as power relations. An example that comes to mind is of a counseling session in which a young woman spoke of a "bad sexual experience" she had had on a recent date. It was only after she had spent half an hour telling the details of the story that together we arrived at the point of naming the experience as rape.

At times, the counselor as audience might become more discriminating—even to the point of acting like a reviewer. This is a role that develops more strongly as the counseling relationship proceeds, but it can begin in the early stages of the process. For example, the counselor may make clarifying statements that sharpen the client's awareness of the significance of what he is saying, particularly when power relations or processes of exclusion are thrown into sharp relief. Counseling also involves contributing to coherence through summarizing, a story-building activity in which the counselor reviews the salient aspects of the story.

Sonya, the counselor mentioned earlier, writes about the early stages of a counseling relationship with Jack:

> I know that the first thing Jack did on meeting me was to size me up to see/feel if I was the sort of person he could open his heart to. He said as much. . . . He came with a clear agenda of what he wanted to deal with. The first session was no exception. Jack was in a hurry to unload and my first role was in listening and helping Jack to weep and express his pain and grief for past hurts, loss

and abuse—for his remorse for harm done to others. In terms of my understanding of the . . . healing process, I had no doubt that this was an important step in the work that was to follow.

Sonya was the first person in Jack's life to engage with what had been up until then a private story. Once a story has been told, an opportunity opens up for the person to develop a relationship with himself and with his story. The situation is different, of course, for someone whose story has already been made part of public discourse within a family, an institutional context, or a public arena such as a courtroom. But even then, there are likely to be aspects of the story that remain very private to the people involved. The process of engagement needs to take into account the interplay between the public and private elements of the story.

Validating the New Story

What kind of relationship might validate a person's own voice so that she can speak about her life on her own behalf? This is an important concern for narrative therapists. We want to make several points in answer to this question and then tell a story that illustrates the spirit of conversation that we would wish to foster in a counseling relationship.

First, we would want to take into the therapy room the same sense of care with language that we mentioned earlier. When we are discussing with a client the things that she is finding problematic, we want to avoid ways of speaking that might have the effect of isolating her in her struggle with the problem. So we would deliberately avoid using words or expressions that might imply a personal deficit. We would not ask the client to take responsibility for the problem, as this might suggest that we believe she is currently irresponsible. Instead, we would be careful to ascribe responsibility for the problem's effects to the problem itself. Further, we would seek to identify and maximize the responsibility, resourcefulness, ethical respect for self and others, and courage that are already evident in the client's struggles with the problem.

One thing we would do is work with her on the question of what to call the problem. Treating people as experts in their own lives includes giving them certain naming rights. So after the problematic story has been aired, we might initiate a conversation about how to refer to the identified problem from then on. If we take the trouble to ask our clients how they would like us to use the chosen name, we are validating their role in the construction of discourse and therefore in the construction of their own consciousness. Externalizing conversations with a series of clients in which exactly the same description was used in every case that had similar features might lead us to expect that the narrative therapist was imposing language on clients. "Sneaky Poo," for example, has become a narrative cliché and has therefore lost some of its therapeutic freshness. One way of avoiding the imposition of clichés on our clients is to constantly seek to learn from them new ways to name problems. If we cannot think of an inventive name at a particular moment, we might say, for example, "I've talked with other people about 'couples culture.' Does that make any sense to you as a name for what we have been talking about, or do you think perhaps there is a more useful name for it?"

Michael White speaks about the value of *experience-near* descriptions rather than descriptions that show deference to professional knowledge. He offers the example of a conversation with a man who has been diagnosed as manic-depressive in the psychiatric system. At first, White uses the label that the man has learned to use to describe his experience: for example, he asks about the effects of the mania in the man's life. Later, though, after the problem has been more fully explored, he raises the naming issue again. He invites the man to consider whether this is the best name for the problem and to suggest some better names. The man comes up with the word *overenthusiasm* to describe the problem that has been oppressing him.

At a follow-up interview, White asks about the use of this term, and the man replies that it has been useful because it has helped him to feel much more in control of the problem, to see it as more manageable and less overwhelming. This is an example of how collaborative use of language can help a person redefine experience in ways that alter its trajectories. A by-product of using experience-near descriptions is the privilege they grant to localized, particular knowledge as opposed to generalized, expert knowledge drawn from grand narrative canons of truth.

Another area in which we exercise care in our use of language is the ascribing of agency to our clients. The language of externalizing conversation deliberately speaks of problems as being outside of the responsibility of the client and in the world of discourse. But it would be a mistake to speak all the time as if people were not moral agents in their own lives. We do not want to convey the idea that human beings are no more than tumbleweed blown about by the winds of discourse.

Therefore, as the alternative story begins to emerge, we seek to stay alert to the possibilities of writing agency into the story. Sometimes, this means stopping to ask how the person has achieved something that she is scarcely noticing to be an achievement at all. Sometimes, it means listening for and commenting on the throwaway lines, the plot developments whose significance is discounted, or changes that are not being incorporated in the story being told. Michael White speaks of looking for the "agentive self gap" between the changes people bring about in their own lives and the incorporation of such changes into their account of themselves. When we notice this gap, we seek to draw connections between significant developments in people's lives and the sense of their own resourcefulness or competence that might result if they were to take seriously these achievements.

Marion's Story

The following story illustrates the process of validation of the client's authority:

Marion had come for counseling following a series of contacts, over several years, with mental health professionals who had given her a number of diagnoses. She was now hoping that counseling would help her to establish which diagnosis was right—that is, which label she should defer to for its authority to define her identity.

I (Kathie) was interested to know what names *she* gave the problem, but this was confusing and somewhat frustrating for her. She was not used to being given naming rights, let alone the authority to define her own experience. However, she became intrigued by my respectfulness toward her, and we agreed to work together. At the start of our second session, Marion said she had been "blown away" by the letter I had written to her after our previous meeting. She was clearly moved by the fact that I had not only communicated to her an understanding of her confusions but had heard her story and recorded it in a way that confirmed her sanity. She had anticipated that I would label her crazy. It was clear that this experience of having her story heard accurately and represented in an affirming way was quite new to her.

As we spoke further, the problem acquired a name. What that name was is of no particular importance; it was simply a useful way of talking about the problem—and it helped Marion to increasingly separate the problem from herself. I was quite frank about my unwillingness to engage in diagnosis, saying that diagnoses gave too much importance to problems, which already claimed enough attention anyway. Marion was developing some enthusiasm for putting herself center stage in her own life and telling her own story—a story that had not had an audience before. Rather than a third-person story that had been dictated by someone else, this was a first-person narration. It was especially distinguishable from those expert narrations told from the "eye of God" position that had been inflicted on her many times before.

Not many sessions down the track, as we were exploring the relationship between Marion and the problem, she leaped up, grabbed the whiteboard marker, and began writing about what she was saying. I asked questions as she wrote, not in order to apply my expertise, but to understand what she was telling me. I was encouraging her to deconstruct her experience and reconstruct it in ways she preferred. I was asking her to be an authority and to inform me as a learner about what she already knew. Suddenly, she became self-conscious and stopped.

"Hey, this is weird! I'm standing here like an expert!" she exclaimed.

We then examined this experience in which she had taken the role of knower while I sat there as the person being taught. What was noticeable to Marion was the developing account of herself as having expertise with respect to the problem. Further, as a result of my questioning, Marion learned to build subtleties into the description of herself that she carried around with her. She could now think of herself as a person who could notice her own knowing and grant recognition to her own expertise. This noticing gave her added strength to deal with the problem, and the sharing of such noticing strengthened the alliance between her and me against the problem.

As she began to tell the alternative story of her competence in dealing with the problem, she commented on a piece of the problem that she said she had never told anyone before. I asked her what it was like to tell it, and she spoke about the value of being understood. I was, for her, a witness to her sanity.

The task of bearing witness to what has been a very private, very delicate, very much overlooked version of experience is an important one for the counselor to shoulder. The counseling relationship may be the first place where such a version is given voice and heard, and thereby validated and strengthened.

Bringing in Our Own Stories

One of the things we find curious in the literature about narrative therapy is the scant mention of the counselor's use of his own experience as a resource to share with his clients. Given that we live in communities shaped by similar discourses, we may expect to have had experiences of positioning not unlike those reported by clients. Feminist writing about therapy, for example, has laid considerable emphasis on how women can sit side by side and register with each other the effects of the gender relations inscribed in patriarchal discourse. Particularly when the effect of oppressive problems is to isolate individuals, we think it is valuable to offer clients the alternative experience of shared knowledge and shared stories. Breaking the sense of isolation with (or by) the problem can itself be deconstructive of the isolating discourse because it reveals not just how the mechanism of isolation works but also that it affects many other people.

Moreover, when people are engaged in a struggle to build ways of thinking, feeling, and acting that minimize the power of the problem in their lives, it is strengthening for them to know that other human beings, including counselors, have had to wage similar battles. If courage is needed to move forward, it can often be found in the realization that others have taken similar steps, with positive results. And if a person is faltering, he may be reassured to know that others have faltered too. Stories that lend encouragement or support can come, of course, from other clients or from books, films, or literature, but they can also come from the personal experience of the counselor.

However, there are certain cautions that must be added to these comments:

- If, as counselors, we engage in lengthy tales about our own experiences, we may thereby call our clients into a position of audience and witness to our own development, which is not what they came to counseling for.
- There is also a danger of mistakenly reading our own experiences into the client's story and overlooking the subtleties of difference between us. The result can be that we unwittingly subordinate the other person's experience to our own.
- If, as we rush to be encouraging, we run ahead of the client's discovery of his own unique outcomes and alternative self-descriptions, we can end up sounding prescriptive of what he should do or think.

Like all therapists, those of us working with narrative ideas have been motivated to join the helping professions for particular reasons. Many counselors were designated helpers within their families, among their friends, and in the community long before they became helping professionals. It is well known in the counseling profession that helpers are often attracted to the field because they like to be needed and appreciated by others. Although this might be one of the primary reasons for entering the profession, the compelling desire to be of help is one we take care to avoid in our work with clients, as it can produce harm in the therapeutic relationship. The danger is that it will focus the counselor on her own position of power and blind her to opportunities for helping the client to connect fully with his own competencies and talents. In the quest to be needed, the counselor can be seduced into seeing herself as the only competent and resourceful party in the therapeutic relationship, the client being regarded as fragile and weak.

However, there are things we can do to avoid falling into these kinds of traps while still finding appropriate moments to share our own stories with clients. Such sharing usually comes after we have allowed the client plenty of time to find his own voice and develop his own story. It is usually brief, and it is supportive of the client's developing resourcefulness rather than didactic in tone or instructive in intent. Our sharing of our stories needs to arise out of our response to the client's story rather than out of our own desire for an audience. It represents a meeting of our storied experiences and hence a meeting between us as people. We can avoid imposing our own stories onto another person's by listening carefully for the differences rather than just the similarities between the client's story and ours and then referring to these as we share our experience.

The narrative perspective requires in counselors a commitment to seeking out and acknowledging, and then amplifying and building meaning around, clients' resourcefulness. Because narrative ideas direct us away from deficit-oriented diagnosis, they themselves help us to avoid slipping into the kind of relationship that some analyses of countertransference caution counselors about. The role of a narrative counselor is not to provide the interpretations, diagnoses, reinforcements, or positive reframings that will bring about change—a role that can potentially intoxicate with its power. Instead, the counselor's role is to invite the client to do all these things for himself.

Transference

There is a long history in therapy of paying close attention to matters of transference. This has been a topic of some awkwardness within the therapies that have grown out of the family therapy tradition. Some have argued that the ideas of transference simply belong to a different paradigm and therefore do not have relevance to counselors working within a narrative framework. Although there is something attractive about such a cavalier stance, we cannot sustain it when we think about our practice. We have to acknowledge that there are times in the relations between counselors and clients when people respond to each other as if they were someone else, when stories about other relationships impose themselves on the counseling relationship. Therefore, we cannot abandon into silence the relational phenomenon that the metaphor of transference seeks to explain.

On the other hand, we are not happy with the available descriptions of this phenomenon. They tend to be narrow in their focus and to foster thinking about counseling that does not fit with narrative principles. The tendency to regard transference as an essential or universal phenomenon and as pivotal to every counseling relationship appears to us to be an exaggeration that carries with it dangers of subjugating people's experience beneath a secret professional knowledge. In fact, talking about transference as a phenomenon that, in the first instance, is only discernible to those with a vast amount of training tends to privilege the knowledge of the counselor over that of the client in potentially dangerous ways. Transference ideas can be used to validate the knowledge in one seat and disqualify the knowledge in the other seat.

We are seeking in this section not so much to summarize a narrative position on issues of transference as to open up for discussion an area that has seemed to us marked by silence. Therefore, we want to advance a few tentative thoughts in the hope that other practitioners will pick them up and respond.

First, we expect that a social constructionist version of what has been called transference would move away from the intrapsychic terms in which the phenomenon has usually been discussed. The frame of reference of the autonomous individual psyche and the assumption of the all-powerful determining influence of a person's family of origin—complete with rigid, gendered notions of mother and father—cannot be considered adequate within a social constructionist view of the world.

Simple mapping of the politics of the family of origin onto all subsequent relations is too rigid an approach. We expect a narrative rendering of transference to take account of how positions in relationships are subject to the influence of discourse. For example, the relationship between a counselor and a client might have some elements in common with the many other relations in which we engage with persons in authority, including parents. And such similarities might lead to responses patterned on what has been learned in previous relationships. But we would argue that such patterns are located in discourse rather than in any psychic damage or deficit in the individual.

The concept of position calls discussed earlier is also useful here. In any exchange, people offer each other positions that they might take up, and as responses are made to such offers, the positions are modified. In a series of moves in conversation, a cluster of positions might merge into a defined relational position. The selection of such moves might be expected to reflect patterns of relation that the parties have been exposed to historically. In this sense, they might transfer patterns from one relationship to another and might call others into positions that appear more relevant to another relationship or to another discourse. Clients caught by a limited range of discourses might "call" the counselor into the role of an ideal or perfect person or an all-knowing or all-powerful expert. In addition, dominant sociocultural traditions might lead a client to anticipate that a counselor will take up a position as a nurturing parent. In responding to the client's "call" or the influences of dominant discourses about the therapist's role, a counselor may inadvertently act in an overprotective manner and find herself seeing a client as fragile, infantile, or damaged. A relation built on such positioning can invite from the counselor a form of compulsive advice-giving or inappropriate breaches of client boundaries.

Relating to another person is a complex process always affected by multiple discursive influences. As we seek to manage the complexities of relationship, we often have to make rapid decisions about people we have just met. In our urgency, particularly in the first or early set of interactions, we construct our view of the other out of our knowledge of familiar discourses. Based on apparently superficial pieces of information, in a split second we decide what we will say and how we will be with the person. These decisions might be made on the basis of the links between discourse and dress, tone of voice, social position, occupation, skin color, gender, or any one of a number of other characteristics. It is within this territory that what has been called transference comes into play.

Other therapeutic orientations have suggested that transference contributes to the forming of an unreal relationship based on distorted or incomplete relationships within childhood. Distorted projections developed in childhood are seen to be triggered for clients by a therapist's behavior. However, from a social constructionist standpoint, we would not expect a relationship ever to be based on "reality" in some pure form. All relations could be said to be "distorted" by discourse, including those within counseling. Therefore, the hope of engendering a counseling relationship based on "reality" disappears like a mirage. Our reference points can only be provisional at best. We therefore see past associations as packaged within discourse that becomes activated by the characteristics we attend to in our current relationships.

Counselors can also transfer a strong need for approval or regular reinforcement onto their clients, exposing them to the development of sexual or romantic feelings or inappropriate social relationships. Counselors using a narrative approach are as vulnerable to unethical forms of connection as any other. Such inappropriate feelings or behaviors transferred into the therapeutic arena must be attended to. Viewing this from our social constructionist orientation, we would suggest that counselors need to learn to maintain an awareness of the discourses at work in the situation, to continually check on their purposes within the counseling relationship, and to give a reflexive account of their values, prejudices, assumptions, and ethical conduct. There should be no shame in acknowledging the potency of discourses that can lead counselors to transfer inappropriate feelings into the therapeutic arena. But we would suggest that it is professionally inexcusable for counselors not to do something to address inappropriate thoughts and feelings toward clients. Supervision may be the most fitting way to deal with feelings that threaten to produce an abusive relationship. But sometimes it may be necessary to terminate the relationship so as to avoid harm to the client. This would be the case, for example, if a counselor had strong negative feelings toward a client that originated in another relationship.

Transference Illustrated

We will risk extending these ideas further while admitting that they represent no more than early attempts to grapple with the phenomenon of transference from a social constructionist orientation. To prevent this discussion from becoming too esoteric and intellectualized, we need to ground our ideas with an example. I (Gerald) had an experience when participating in a therapy group a number of years ago that bears on these issues.

A woman who was a member of the group behaved in an unusually negative fashion to me during the early part of the workshop. I had not presented myself in a disrespectful way and was surprised by the strength of her negative reaction. Later, it transpired that I both looked and sounded like an uncle who had sexually abused her when she was a child. Her discovery of this connection produced a change in her behavior toward me and a recognition of the redundancy of her previous evaluations and judgments.

This event would fit within a classical description of transference because of both the rapidity with which it occurred and the "unconscious" nature in which it was applied. However, we are seeking to break away from the traditional explanation that locates the source of transference within the nuclear family system. We prefer to locate the phenomenon within a much wider social context. Instead of inviting clients to establish a direct correspondence with particular people or places to explain the transference, we leave open the possibility of multiple connections to a variety of experiences within discourse itself.

In the example given, the woman's response may have had some connection to the particular abuse by her uncle, but such abuse can take on meaning only within particular social contexts. These contexts would include the historical conditions of gender relations pertaining at the time of the abuse and those at the time of the group at which I met her. What is more, her response to me might have been affected by further discursive influences built up within the therapeutic context in which we were both positioned. We thus move very quickly to a much more complex perspective than one that stresses a simple correspondence between the trauma of the abuse and the woman's reaction to me in the group. What gets transferred may be said to have its origins in the sociocultural milieu as much as in the family.

What we are reaching for here is a social-interactional description of the phenomenon rather than an intrapsychic one. However, it is also important to say that we would not wish to establish transference phenomena as foundational concepts in therapy, or changes in transference patterns as the ultimate aim of therapy or as the key to real change in people's lives. We see change in the pattern of involvement with the discourses that shape our relations as a more important counseling goal than close interpretation of what has been transferred from other relations into the counseling relationship. Yet there is much value, we believe, in noticing how discourses position us in the counseling relationship itself. So as well as pursuing a social-interactional, less intrapsychic explanation of the process of transfer of information from one set of relations to another, we would argue (tentatively at this stage, for the reasons we have stated) for the re-situation of the concept of transference in the field of therapeutic logic. These few comments are a brief attempt to suggest how this might be accomplished, but we acknowledge that a more thorough study of the subject needs to be undertaken.

What takes place in the counseling relationship is, then, a particular genre of conversation. It is not a "natural" genre, but then nor are other types of conversation. All are products of culture and historical tradition. In other words, conversations are products of, and at the same time the sites for, the production of the social conditions of our lives. The traditions of counseling that we are drawing from as we consider how we might operate in such conversations are diverse. We are conscious of the influence of the family therapy tradition in our approach to narrative conversations in counseling, but we are also conscious of the gaps in that tradition, one of which has been a lack of attention to the relationship elements within the dialogue. We also acknowledge within our own backgrounds other traditions of individual counseling that have directed our attention to these relationship elements. To some extent, this chapter has been an attempt to draw from these various traditions for the purpose of contributing to the development of narrative therapy.

As counselor educators, we are very conscious of needing to offer our students—and to continue to develop in ourselves—practices that embody the kind of "relational and dialogical rigor" that James and Melissa Griffith concluded was a necessary part of training their psychiatry residents. To engage in a counseling conversation that is distinctively narrative in its character (a subgenre that is still in the process of development), we believe we need to attend to the disciplines of thought that this chapter has outlined. The work done by discourse is central to the particular version of counseling relationship for which we are arguing. It operates, as we have said, on the positioning of the client and the counselor before they enter the room, before they open their mouths, and then in the exchanges that take place as they evolve the counseling story together. What we are advocating is an approach to counseling that begins from these positions in discourse and works toward a relationship that can be respectful, ethical, and collaborative. A relationship will always be productive in some sense, but we are constantly seeking for it to be productive of a subject position for the client that enables her to speak in her own voice and act on her own behalf.

Notes

P. 53, *senior partnership:* David Epston and Michael White have used this term in regard to the ownership of therapeutic documents. Epston, D., & White, M. (1992). Consulting your consultants: The documentation of alternative knowledges. In Epston, D., & White, M. (Eds.), *Experience, contradiction, narrative and imagination.* Adelaide, Australia: Dulwich Centre Publications. Gerald Monk and Wendy Drewery have gone on to suggest that the counselor "see the client as the senior partner in guiding the process of the therapy." Monk, G., & Drewery, W. (1994). The impact of social constructionist thinking on eclecticism in counsellor education: Some personal thoughts. *New Zealand Journal of Counselling, 16*(1), 5–14.

P. 55, *mutual meaning-making:* Weingarten, K. The discourses of intimacy: Adding a social constructionist–feminist view. *Family Process, 30* 285–305.

P. 56, *"regimes of truth":* Tomm, K. (1990). A critique of the DSM. *Dulwich Centre Newsletter,* (3), 5–8; White, M. (1995). *Re-authoring lives: Interviews and essays.* Adelaide, Australia: Dulwich Centre Publications; Bird, J. (1994). Talking amongst ourselves. *Dulwich Centre Newsletter,* (1), 44–46.

P. 58, *awareness of these issues:* Extract from a University of Waikato course assignment by Sonya Roussina.

P. 60, *a "joining" stage of the interview:* The term *joining* has become familiar in the family therapy field since Salvador Minuchin focused therapeutic interest on this aspect of interviews. Minuchin, S. (1974). *Families and family therapy.* Cambridge, Mass.: Harvard University Press. Its use is continued in Michael White's discussion of the development of reflecting teams. White, M. (1995). *Re-authoring lives: Interviews and essays.* Adelaide, Australia: Dulwich Centre Publications.

P. 60, *featuring Michael White:* White, M. (1989). *Escape from bickering* (video). Washington, D.C.: American Association of Marriage and Family Therapists.

P. 61, *As Foucault has suggested:* Foucault, M. (1978). *History of sexuality,* vol. 1. New York: Pantheon Books.

P. 63, *our authority as professionals:* Carpenter, J. (1994). Finding people in family therapy. *Dulwich Centre Newsletter,* (1), 32–38.

P. 66, *protest and resourcefulness:* White, M., & Epston, D. (1990). *Narrative means to therapeutic ends.* New York: Norton.

P. 68, *the work that was to follow:* Extract from a University of Waikato course assignment by Sonya Roussina.

P. 69, *deference to professional knowledge:* White, M. (1989). *Selected papers.* Adelaide, Australia: Dulwich Centre Publications; White, M. (1992). *Learning edge* (video). Washington, D.C.: American Association of Marriage and Family Therapists.

P. 70, *"agentive self gap":* White, M. (1992). *Learning edge* (video). Washington, D.C.: American Association of Marriage and Family Therapists.

P. 74, *within a narrative framework:* For example, Furman, B., & Aloha, T. (1992). *Pickpockets on a nudist camp: The systemic revolution in psychotherapy.* Adelaide, Australia: Dulwich Centre Publications.

P. 79, *training their psychiatry residents:* Griffith, J., & Griffith, M. (1992). Owning one's epistemological stance in therapy. *Dulwich Centre Newsletter,* (1), 5–11.

Chapter Four

Learning and Teaching Narrative Ideas

Wally McKenzie
Gerald Monk

We have been collectively exploring and experimenting with the teaching of narrative therapy to people both new to the helping field and to those who are experienced in other orientations. The ideas that form the basis of this chapter are drawn from our experiences of teaching narrative ideas to counselors, therapists, teachers, psychologists, and other helping professionals. We are anticipating that most readers will be interested in learning how to apply narrative therapy in their work. The material that follows includes a number of teaching exercises that we have found useful in our workshops. We think there will be value for both learners and teachers in working through and reflecting on these exercises.

We have also identified some of the difficulties and challenges in using narrative therapy that have arisen for us and the participants in our workshops. We anticipate that some of these struggles might be similar to your own as you begin to incorporate this way of working into your practice.

Narrative therapy is based on some very simple and accessible ideas. However, in our experience, it takes two to three years to integrate it into one's own style of therapeutic work. Because narrative approaches to therapy are evolving and changing all the time, we are continuing to develop and expand our ideas in both our teaching and in our therapeutic practice.

Narrative Approaches Compared
with Other Orientations

After our first narrative intensive, we received feedback from some students saying that they had difficulty in bringing the work through into their day-to-day practice. Eileen made the following comments: "I struggled with the content, enormously. The biggest problem for me is that White and Epston's approach is different from your traditional eclectic approach to counseling. I had a problem integrating it and finding a place for it against the other work I was doing. Like I was in love with it intellectually, but I couldn't get it to work."

In response to these kinds of difficulties among trainees, we have been constantly revising our presentation of these ideas. Now, we often begin a training course by providing background to some of the common therapeutic metaphors so that these can be compared and contrasted with those used in narrative counseling. The following is a description of three different metaphors that we use to illustrate the philosophical and theoretical differences between narrative and other approaches.

Mechanistic Therapy: Repairing the Faulty Machine

We begin by talking about those therapies that utilize the faulty-machine metaphor. Such therapies encourage counselors to investigate what's broken so that it can be repaired. The metaphor promotes ways of speaking that require us to locate, identify, and label problems in people's lives. Many of us have been trained in a set of techniques designed to correct the deficits, inadequacies, and malfunctions within the client—for example, mental breakdown, social skills deficits, disinhibition problems with anger. Having established the nature of the problem, we then introduce a set of strategies that will help the client develop competencies and skills where they did not exist before. People are often spoken about as if they were machines. In earlier psychologies, the machine of choice was often a steam engine, whereas more recently the computer has become a reference point for our descriptions of human psychology.

This way of working often presumes that there is some kind of objective truth that can be known about a person or a problem, and once it is discovered, the counselor can be confident in proceeding with the intervention. This helping metaphor encourages the counselor to give the client new knowledge, techniques, and skills to correct her irrational thinking, cognitive distortions, faulty processing, or maladaptive functioning.

Clients are invited into the unknowing position at the beginning of the therapeutic enterprise, and the counselor is encouraged to take up the knowing position, with expert knowledge that can be transmitted to the person impaired by some form of disability or deficit. Success is measured by the degree to which the client accepts the counselor's expert knowledge. This is evidenced in the implementation of specific plans and objectives, the acquisition of and demonstration of new skills, the development of correct and rational thinking, and the application of problem-solving procedures.

Romantic Therapy: Peeling the Onion

We refer to other therapies as following the "peeling of the onion" metaphor. These therapies subscribe to the view that there is some deep inner core of a person that has been covered up by a series of protective layers like the layers of an onion. These layers or defenses have been put in place during the course of the person's growing-up to protect his "inner self" from harm and pain.

This way of thinking encourages us to think in terms of major surgery to peel away the layers. The lengthy process involves exposure, vulnerability, and pain. It represents a significant reconstruction of the psyche. The counselor is encouraged to interpret the presenting issues in therapy as superficial concerns generated from the protective layers of the defended self. The task of helping is to cut through and strip the outer layers and expose the inner concerns and inner workings of the person—the essential attributes. This inner core is seen as the essential self, the inner guide, the source of truth or divine knowledge.

This metaphor invites the counselor to work for the release of the true feelings of the person, who has become dissociated or disconnected from his life force or passions. The expression of feelings is encouraged in the therapeutic encounter and seen as a reliable guide to the progress being made; thinking can be seen as a distraction from the real work and regarded with suspicion. It may be associated with the defensive function of the outer layers of the onion.

Success is measured by the expression of authenticity and spontaneity, the degree to which the person can express his inner truth in the world. The successful therapy involves the direct and passionate expression of emotion unencumbered by intellectual barriers and defenses.

Postmodern Therapy: The Story

Narrative counseling belongs to a new group of therapies that align themselves with the philosophy of postmodernism. As we have already described in previous chapters, these approaches use the story metaphor.

Helpers are interested in knowing about the meanings people have constructed about themselves on the basis of their lived experiences in the world. Stories serve a meaning-making function. From this perspective, we both create stories about ourselves and become positioned in story lines that other people have created about us. People are seen as making sense of their lives by assembling significant events together into a series of dominant plots.

Narrative work is not seen as a process of discovering the truth about who people are but as an exploration of how people construct truths about themselves and their relationships. In their feelings and behaviors, people are viewed as performing the meanings developed in the storying process.

People experiencing problems are thought to be located in a problem story line. Positive outcomes are identified when the counselor is able to take up a coauthoring role with the client to develop a story line that the client prefers. The client's preferred story is based on lived moments that can be performed as a counterplot to the problem-saturated story.

The participants in our workshops tend to be familiar with the first two metaphors. For some, these metaphors are seen as serving what many believe therapy is designed to do. To a large extent, the mechanistic and romantic metaphors have become incorporated into our history and mythology. Many of us unquestioningly and implicitly accept these constructions *as the helping process*. We do not ask those working with us to abandon these metaphors, claiming that the story metaphor is the true and correct approach to training. However, we do consider the story metaphor to be powerful, and worthy to be offered alongside the more traditional modes of training employed in the West.

Major Concepts and Techniques of Narrative Therapy

In this next section, we cover some of the key principles of working effectively with narrative ideas. If counselors ignore some of these principles, they may never experience the pleasure of witnessing clients produce favored accounts of themselves that color their lives in the way that their difficulties had done previously. We begin by looking at the preferred descriptions that counselors would like to activate in their work.

Preferred Descriptions

We explore with the participants in our training the stories they bring with them as counselors. In our early training, we noted that little attention was paid to the new recruits' previous life experiences. Often, students new to training erase or render invalid many of the experiences that might have contributed to the ongoing development of their *preferred descriptions* of themselves as counselors. They disconnect their personal experiences from the professional training context, and the relationship between the two is lost.

Exercise: Preferred Self-Descriptions

To promote connections for workshop participants between their everyday experience and their professional development as counselors, we use the following exercise when there are periods of time between the workshop sessions. Many participants have identified this training exercise as the single most important activity in their development as counselors.

> You are invited to work in pairs for about thirty to forty minutes. Each of you will take turns in outlining your preferred description of yourself as a counselor. Each of you is asked to consider sharing with your partner your own

history and life experiences that will be useful to you in the development of your preferred description. To help you do this, we want you to consider the following questions to guide you in this exploration:

1. What experiences have you had in your life [or since you last met as a pair] that have assisted you in moving toward your preferred description of yourself as a counselor?

2. How have you been curious about your work with your clients and yourself, and what came from that?

3. How have people been responding to you differently as you move toward or embrace your preferred description?

4. How do you account for these changes?

5. Are these changes similar to any you have experienced on other occasions in your life, or are they absolutely new? Have a conversation about this.

These reflections might help you recall events in your own history that are helpful to you, and increase your appreciation of yourself.

Some of the connections that are made relate to previous sources of employment, religious upbringing and experiences, survival of family difficulties, and philosophies of life. Here are some examples:

"I relate back to my training as a teacher . . ."

"I think it's partly my religious beliefs that come through."

"Violence has been a problem in my family, and I've gained lots of insights into how to work with these issues."

"I've always had a suspicion of the individualistic nature of counseling. I've wanted to challenge individualism since my student radical days in the early seventies."

Reflection on such life experiences brings alive many of the participants' stories, which provide powerful resources for the ongoing construction of an identity as a professional counselor.

A Stance of Persistent and Genuine Curiosity

We have discovered through trial and error that our training works best if we spend time focusing on the development of curiosity, as this stance is crucial to working with narrative ideas. As has been mentioned in Chapter One, curiosity should be used by the counselor in a respectful manner, as it is oriented toward people's strengths and competencies rather than to their deficits or faults. Curious questioning is often associated with discourses of interrogation, and clients may feel defensive about it. An attitude of respect on the part of the counselor tends to allay such reactions.

In our experience, people who are new to this orientation often give up too quickly on their inquiry into clients' stories of competency. For example, if they ask, "Have there been any experiences recently that were examples of your eliminating or diminishing the damage that the problem was causing you?" clients who are in the midst of struggling with their difficulties may respond with a "No." Often, counselors new to narrative work take this response at face value.

Participants in our workshops can be easily satisfied with the client's initial response and feel somewhat constrained in further examining an area of life that the person may have seldom reflected on. Counselors trained in a client-centered modality are accustomed to accepting the client's offerings and may feel they are intruding on the client if they ask for additional information or ideas.

Here are some exercises we have used in our workshops to show people how to sustain their persistence and curiosity.

Exercise: Practice in the Use of Curious Questioning

We have found that people need practice in being curious. Some people find this approach natural to them, whereas others feel initially very uncomfortable. We give participants in our workshops plenty of practice in being respectfully curious and persistent. Curious questioning is a good early exercise.

> Work in pairs. One person is the interviewer, the other the storyteller or interviewee. Talk to one another for about fifteen minutes about a regular routine activity like fixing breakfast, getting out of bed in the morning, going to work. The interviewer is to ask questions of the talker, seeking more detail about the routines and their significance. The interviewer takes up a position of respectful and genuine curiosity and avoids an interrogating tone. The task is to help the interviewee to discover new information about himself or herself, or about the activity being discussed, by means of sound curious questioning.

This is a good warm-up activity and a safe way to practice respect-ful curiosity.

Exercise: Brainstorming "Smalling Questions"

Asking *smalling questions* is another useful way to be persistent and curious in exploring resources and talents that have been unavail-able to a client and hidden by the problem narrative. "Smalling" refers to a particular way of phrasing questions that invites the client to think about experiences in his life that have not been fully developed. These experiences may be fragments of memory or what clients may regard as insignificant moments that nevertheless hint at competence or ability.

> In this exercise, we brainstorm a series of questions to help counselors get access to fragments of experience, vague memories, or apparently insignificant moments or thoughts that hint at alternatives to the problem story. Some examples are
>
> Can you recall a brief moment when the problem was not influencing your thoughts?
>
> Have there been times during our conversation when the problem hasn't totally controlled or dominated our time together?
>
> Are there small areas of your life that the problem hasn't yet occupied?
>
> Have you had any dreams recently that have not been tainted by the problem?

This form of questioning opens up prospects for new possibil-ities of which the client is unaware. When the person becomes aware of more positive events operating in her present life, a plat-form of hope begins to be established.

People who are most successful in using this approach tend to have developed an unshakable belief that somewhere in their client's recent history, there are life experiences manifesting frag-ments of ability, competence, or talent that the client is not pres-ently able to notice or apply to her concerns.

If the counselor is confident in the client's resourcefulness, as narrative practitioners tend to be, he will persevere in helping the client to discover incomplete or half-assembled story lines. This approach will provide the material for the development of an alternative account of the client's problem and a more preferred self-understanding.

What follows is an example of an interaction in which the counselor is demonstrating the use of curiosity and persistence. Maria is a participant in a workshop and has agreed to be interviewed. The purpose of this interview is to assist Maria in developing an alternative story of her life that demonstrates from her early history that she is able to take a stand against injustice rather than passively participate in somebody else's story of who she is as a person.

Initially, Maria is unable to identify these events.

Counselor: Would you mind me asking a series of questions to better understand some of your earlier experiences that have helped you to deal with your present non-judgmental position and not think the worst of people?

Maria: No, that would be fine.

Counselor: What are some of your earlier experiences that have helped you develop your present abilities to be not so critical of people—say, when you were a little girl?

Maria: Well, I can't really think of any.

Counselor: When you were young, my guess is that you learned about not prejudging people and wanting to be fair. Am I right?

Maria: Well, probably.

Counselor: Can you think back to when you were a little girl, maybe four or five years old. Were there any events that you witnessed or were involved with where you were concerned with fairness or justice?

Maria: It was a long time ago, and I'm not sure about any specific thing.

Newcomers to narrative approaches might want to give up on this line of inquiry. The narrative counselor does not want to invade another's privacy. But permission had already been granted by Maria to explore her hidden talents. The counselor is prepared to persist in his curiosity because he sincerely believes that Maria has developed some earlier competencies that she has not yet accessed.

Counselor: Maybe when you were a little older, you could remember an incident that stands out that was an indication that you have been concerned with fairness for a good part of your life?

Maria: When I was eight, I think I remember something that might be relevant.

Counselor: Please tell me about it.

Maria: When I used to go to church when I was little, I was aware that the rich people sat on one side of the church and the poor sat on the other side, and I remember thinking that this was really wrong, even though everybody accepted that this was the way things should be.

Counselors just starting out with narrative approaches tend to be satisfied with some of the early or first responses of clients. But the counselor continues to be persistent, inquiring how Maria registered that there was something wrong in separating people based on material wealth. He is of the view that there are probably numerous early stories that, if Maria could access them, would explain why she registered the incongruity of the rich people being on one side of the church and the poor on the other. So he asks for more.

Counselor: Maria, my guess is that you learned about injustice and fairness even before your experience at church.

This is the fourth "question" that has been asked about this issue.

Maria: I'm not sure if there are any others.

Counselor: Would you be offended if I spent a little more time figuring out with you some other experiences, because I feel pretty confident that we could discover some more?

Maria: No, I don't mind.

Maria is still fully involved in the process at this stage, despite the fact that the interviewer has asked the same question in different ways. She is intrigued by the prospect that there might be other accounts in her early life that reflect on her competencies, and she is enjoying the attention that the interviewer is giving to her childhood.

Counselor: When you were very tiny, maybe even four years old, did anything happen at home that stays with you now that taught you that you care about injustice and inequality?

Maria: Now that you mention it, I do remember from as early as I can recall my upset toward my grandparents who treated my female cousins more unfairly compared to my male cousins. I would say to my grandparents that it wasn't fair how the boys got the best food and were more spoilt than us girls. I guess I have always felt strongly about injustice and unfairness.

Persistence is a virtue for a counselor using this approach. However, the challenge for the newcomer is to be persistently curious without the client feeling interrogated. People tend to appreciate the counselor's vigor in seeking out the lost remnants of their lived experience that may provide the beginning of a more favored description of themselves than the one developed from the problem.

It is often a good idea to seek permission from the client to ask a series of questions before forging ahead, making it clear that they do not have to answer any of the questions. This puts the client in control of the process. A positive relationship between counselor and client is crucial to curious and persistent questioning. We also find that this way of working respectfully maintains a collaborative stance while minimizing the risk of inadvertently pressuring the client to understand her concerns from the counselor's point of view. This is an ethical aspect of narrative practice.

In the next section, we present a variety of exercises that prepare people to recognize the ongoing significance of the wider sociocultural context and its relationship to the activity of counseling.

Discourses

Early on in the training, we introduce participants to the language of discourse, positioning, deconstruction, and reconstruction. These concepts become the tools with which narratives are assembled.

The term *discourse*, which refers to a cluster of ideas produced within the wider culture, is a useful backdrop to the understanding and application of narrative ideas. At first, discourse is a difficult concept to grasp. In presenting it to students, we work at making it accessible and enjoyable. There are lots of resources available to illustrate discourse. We use nursery rhymes, poems, cartoon strips, stories, television advertising, talk shows, and movies to demonstrate how discourse works. Discourses about love, sex, body shape, desires and how they are generated differently for men and women are excellent topics to introduce these concepts. Discourses underlie the operation of power in the counseling relationship. They place people in particular positions or relationships with others and themselves and prompt them to describe the world from particular vantage points. Discourses are the material from which narratives and metaphors are produced.

Exercise: Discourse in Practice—Headlines and Magazines

Collect some covers of well-known magazines and focus on the pictures and words. Draw on your collective cultural understandings to determine what has been taken-for-granted in the construction of these covers.

For a more specific focus on gender discourses, choose for comparison covers of some popular magazines that are aimed at women and others that are aimed at men.

As a group, talk about the discourses that promote these meanings and positions in relations. What kind of person does this discourse call into being? What kind of relationships?

The group can then design new magazine covers for women's and men's magazines promoting alternative discourses, meanings, and positions. They should work only on the cover/title/headlines/layout for the proposed stories inside.

Positioning

Discourses position us in particular relationships with others, and these can emerge from the conversations in the story line. Teaching positioning in relation to discourse is best done through examples. We have found that one of the most useful ways of illustrating positioning in discourse is to study both live and videotaped counseling sessions. In one recent example, we had participants in our workshop view a counselor working with a young family with two preschoolers. The parents were from different ethnic backgrounds: Mi'i was a Cook Island Maori, and Paea was raised in Tonga.

Mi'i took all the responsibility for child care and was feeling overwhelmed by the demands of two young children. She was also grieving the loss of her career. Paea worked for long hours in a menial occupation for little pay. Mi'i wanted to return to her well-paid work and wanted Paea to be the primary caregiver; if this was not possible, she would reluctantly place the children in child care. Paea was against this.

We asked the participants to identify the major discourses in this counseling session and the positioning of Mi'i and Paea. We found that the best way of teaching positioning is to name the discourses first. The participants identified the following:

A father should be the primary breadwinner.

The father should be the head of the household who is entitled to make executive decisions.

A mother belongs at home beside her children in their early years.

A mother is neglecting her responsibilities to her children if she relies on child care.

A husband who works long hours at his work is demonstrating his love for his family.

A man is failing in his abilities as a provider if he is "kept" by his wife.

A woman is designed to be the primary caregiver due to her biological makeup and therefore is naturally more able to be a more competent caregiver than the father.

The participants noted that Mi'i and Paea were placed in contradictory positions in relation to one another. Paea felt that if he became the primary caregiver of the children, he would not be behaving in an appropriate male way in a marriage. Mi'i felt that placing the children in day care was a betrayal of her caregiving responsibilities as a mother. Neither of these subject positions was assisting them to deal with the conflict in their relationship.

In like manner, counselors and clients are positioned in multiple discourses that will have real effects on the counseling relationship, the nature of the problem, and how it will be solved.

Deconstruction

The process we have described of identifying discourses in Mi'i and Paea's story is in fact an example of deconstruction. As we have already mentioned, deconstruction is the process of disassembling the taken-for-granted assumptions that are made about an event or circumstance. These taken-for-granted assumptions about a problem often close down opportunities for both client and counselor to explore new possibilities for change. Deconstruction is a process in which discourses are exposed and people's positions within them are revealed. We explore in training how our identities have been constructed within a sociocultural environment. We are mindful, for example, of how the discourses associated with ethnicity, gender, and sexual orientation influence what we do in our counseling work.

The following is an example of an exercise in which we deconstruct identity in relation to heterosexual or homosexual views.

Exercise: The Deconstruction of Identity

Participants are asked to signal the wants that go along with their identity as a woman or man, heterosexual or homosexual, in the context of selecting a partner for a long-term relationship or an ideal union. Participants can be invited to discuss the most desirable qualities sought in an intimate partner or companion. The task is to deconstruct the history of these wants and how they might have changed over time.

> Work in pairs. In turn, discuss some of your wants that relate to selecting a partner for an ideal union. If appropriate, make visible your own orientation and talk about the most desirable qualities that would be sought after.
>
> Explore these wants and where they came from.
>
> As the interviewer, search out the history, the influences, and the development of such desires and the ways they may have entered this other person's life. It will take respectful searching out to expose some of the discourses that have contributed to the construction of these wants.
>
> Here are some questions to assist you in this mutual search:
>
> What were the vehicles of influence for these wants?

Are these wants currently useful in the ongoing development of who you really prefer to be?

What ways have you found to be most successful in keeping these wants working for you rather than against you?

This exercise can also be adapted to explore the influence of your ethnic or class identity.

Exercise: Working with Strong Beliefs

This exercise is very useful for the deconstruction of the effects of strong beliefs or values. It provides a brief overview of many features of narrative work, including externalizing, historicizing, mapping the influences, relative influence questioning, discourse, positioning, and deconstructing. It quickly introduces key ideas, unaccompanied by jargon or a set of labels that might be off-putting to those seeking just a taste of narrative therapy.

In the next ninety minutes, we are going to work from two principles:

1. The person is not the problem, the problem is the problem.

2. Whatever gets talked about should not be presumed to be a problem.

Each of you think of a belief that is influential in your life and that you care about greatly. This can be any belief relating to anything. It might be about race, lineage, privilege, culture, social group/class, education, religion, sexuality.

Work in pairs and talk about the specific belief.

One person begins to talk about this belief and its influence in his or her life. The other listens with an attitude of interested curiosity. The listener encourages the teller to explore the effects of the belief on his or her life. Focus on family, work, spirituality, relationships, history, future, life position, and any other dimensions that come to mind. This should be an extensive conversation that goes beyond a superficial discussion.

Your task is to obtain an in-depth understanding of the effects of the belief.

As you explore the influence of the belief, explore its history and search out its origin and development through this person's life.

During this exploration, consider the intentions of such a belief and its usefulness in the person's life.

What are the person's thoughts about the possible historical and future implications of the belief, in terms of gender, race, age, class, and the like?

Because of the intimate nature of the exercise, it is useful to process the conversation. Here are some questions that may assist with this processing:

1. Do you have a sense of knowing or being known by your partner more fully than before?

2. How has this conversation affected your liking of or closeness to your partner?

3. Was this person born with these beliefs, or do they have some other source? Have the beliefs helped to create this person's identity?

4. What effect has this conversation had on you and on your understandings of your own beliefs in your life and relationships?

We have found this approach to be a helpful way of deconstructing some of the dominant beliefs that have an impact on the participants in our courses.

Exercise: Deconstructive Questioning

Typically, we move from the students' deconstruction of their own beliefs and values to the application of the narrative approach to working with clients. We begin this transition with a series of role plays. Groups of students construct a make-believe family based on their knowledge of families and helping experiences. At other times, students become one of their clients and act out a narrative session. One of the exercises that we have had a lot of fun with and that gives the participants plenty of practice with narrative questioning is introduced as follows:

Get into groups of three. The tutor, acting as a client, introduces a problem and prepares the small groups to produce deconstructing questions.

Each group of three is given a period of time (up to thirty minutes) to generate questions collectively. When ready, they can take turns at trying them out on the tutor, who continues in the role of the client.

The other groups listen and observe the process. After each group has had an opportunity to try out its questions, the small groups meet again to refine and develop new questions.

The process is then repeated.

This exercise takes approximately two hours for a group of fif-teen to twenty participants. We have found that it provides numer-ous opportunities for generating questions and benefiting from the ideas produced in the small groups. In addition, participants gain an opportunity to observe other groups in action.

Agency

As teachers, we believe it is important for participants in training to act on their own initiative, without a particular focus on satisfy-ing the story line of the teacher or tutor. Participants are encour-aged to produce their own accounts of their professional growth by being reflexive in their work. This process is facilitated by ask-ing participants to make audiotapes of their counseling conversa-tions, with clients' consent, and to study and reflect on segments of those conversations. Participants then discuss these segments with peers, tutors, and supervisors. During this process, they iden-tify aspects of their work on which they wish to focus for further development, and they name aspects of their narrative counseling in which they experience a growing sense of competence. This naming is part of the adoption of a new position in the discourse of counseling.

Navigating Around the Stumbling Blocks

In the remaining section of the chapter, we identify some of the difficulties that arise for participants in training who are actively applying these ideas in their work. Then we explore options for circumventing these difficulties. We also discuss additional features of narrative work to flesh out some of the therapeutic possibilities in narrative conversations.

One of our concerns has been that people new to this method might feel that they could master narrative work using a paint-by-numbers approach to learning. From time to time, we have seen counselors try to use narrative ideas in a mechanistic fashion. We are convinced that this approach does not work.

One of the risks in producing some kind of map of a narrative orientation is that the beginner will follow the map rather than attend to the person he is working with. Instead of responding to the unique events that arise in the conversation, the counselor will be inadvertently seeking to have the client conform to the next theoretical stage in the process. If the issues that arise in the counseling session do not fit the delineated stages of the narrative interview, it is very easy for the counselor to move from a collaborative relationship to a rigid and controlling one, where he is orchestrating every element of the session. This obviously undermines the quality of the therapeutic relationship. As a result, some people conclude that narrative approaches do not deal with the emotions of the person and are too cognitively focused. Take, for example, this statement made by a participant: "Narrative therapy creates some difficulties for me because there seems to be little space for working with people's feelings. I couldn't find a way of respecting people's feelings." We would suggest that it is the attention to a narrative formula that undermines the newcomer's quality of engagement with the client.

Our other concern is that the further we move toward categorizing this form of therapy, which began as an orientation or a metaphor for a therapeutic conversation, the more easily it can be turned into a set of procedures that establishes a right and a wrong way of using narrative ideas. It is then very easy to set up some truth-based philosophy or orthodoxy. Rigid hierarchies can readily form around this way of constructing knowledge.

What follows is an identification of some of the problems that arise, in part because of such rigid adherence to a set of stages in the interview.

The Use of Externalizing Conversations

The counselor using narrative therapy moves from the internalizing language of the client—for example, "I've been very weak and ineffectual"—to an externalized question—such as "What does weakness or ineffectiveness have you do?" The purpose, as has already been explained, is to open up new possibilities for interacting with the problem without being paralyzed by the effects of self-blame and self-judgment.

Typically, newcomers to the narrative metaphor actively externalize the earliest statements made by the client. Although this may not necessarily be detrimental, the beginner may want to stay with the first externalizing description that she has identified. Unfortunately, when a counselor clings to an early externalized description, it tends to rapidly become redundant. The client has moved on in the account of the problem story and has started to identify themes that are far more central to his concerns. When a counselor keeps reworking the early externalized description, the client can become quickly disillusioned. He may not feel listened to and may also be confused by the rigid repetition of an early statement that has little or no bearing on major worries.

In our experience, counselors new to this approach latch on to the idea of externalizing conversations and want to give any form of difficulty an externalized name. It is sometimes preferable for the counselor to use the words *it* or *this problem* before assigning a specific label in the early part of the interview. It may take as long as one or two sessions before the counselor and client have become sufficiently clear as to the major concerns that are troubling the client.

Despite these caveats, there is value in being able to produce a name that is fitting for the client as early as the client supplies the necessary information. However, it is important, in our experience, to stay with the client and follow the unfolding of the story. It may be that the externalization needs to change. In some circumstances, it may be appropriate to use more than one externalization early on, to capture the complexity of what the client is describing. For example, in Chapter One, the problems that challenged Peter, Joanne, and Bruce after Peter gained his sight changed from "this problem" to "normal vision," "trouble," and "fear," depending on the direction the conversation was taking.

The use of externalizing language in the general interactions of narrative therapy is of more importance than having to pin down *the* externalized problem. Our main point here is that we are promoting the process of externalizing conversation rather than insisting on the production of an encapsulating externalization.

Generally, it is preferable to stay with one externalized description of the problem after there has been a full exploration of the problem story and when the name of the problem plot is fitting for the client. We have found value in asking the client if the externalized name is appropriate. Even more desirable may be a discussion between the counselor and the client on the naming of the externalization. It is far more beneficial for the client to name the problem than for the counselor to do so. The collaborative nature of the client-counselor interview is strengthened when the client takes this role.

Certain problems lend themselves to a resilient externalized description. Take, for example, the work I (Wally) did with one family. Manu, eleven years old, and his father, Bill, spoke about the difficulties arising from Manu wetting the bed every morning. Both father and son were feeling particularly bad about the situation. Manu felt guilty. He hated waking up wet and smelling every morning. He had not made any progress with the problem through his life, but it had not been for want of trying. I said I would like to name the problem so that we would all know what we were talking about and asked if they could help me with a suitable name. Without hesitation, they both said, almost in unison, "Rainmaker." This became the externalized name and continued to be an apt description of the problem Manu faced. Father and son both focused on the rainmaker as the common enemy. The use of this externalization produced rapid and successful results.

Clients are not always able to produce an externalized name for their concern at the beginning of the session, unless the concern revolves around a clearly established problem. For example, some people may present with a concern that they have already identified, such as depression. The counselor can then take that description and talk about depression as the externalized problem while at the same time opening up the conversation to explore how depression entered the person's life. On other occasions, the person seeking help may comment that she does not know what the problem is, but she feels tired all the time. Rather than externalizing tiredness, there may be value in exploring her general concerns before homing in on what might be an incidental and small aspect of the problem. Counselors who attempt to quickly produce an externalized description of a problem are likely to shut down a full exploration of the client's issues.

When counselors first engage in externalizing conversations, particularly with adults, they often feel self-conscious and awkward. The counselor might be reflecting on how strange what she is saying must sound to the person she is working with. Indeed, the client might be a little disconcerted by this unusual way of talking.

More experienced counselors are not concerned by this disorientation, and it is surprising how quickly clients join with the counselor in this way of talking.

Because narrative approaches to helping do not rely on any hidden and covert techniques that cannot be shared with the client, the counselor can explain to the client what externalization is and how they will use it. For example, Tony is learning to use narrative therapy in his practice. He feels uncomfortable using externalization and decides to inform his next new client about what he is doing. In their first session, he says to the client:

"I have discovered that it is often helpful to the people I work with to give a name to the problem that is concerning them and talk about the problem as being an entity of its own and separate from them. I have found that by talking about the problem in this way, new ways of dealing with the issues are opened up that were not possible before. Is it okay that I talk in this way with you about your concerns?"

Clients are often intrigued by externalization and are likely to welcome this approach.

Mapping the Effects of the Problem on the Person

In some respects, it might seem surprising that the counselor would want to spend time looking at the effects of the problem on the client when the client is surely aware of what the problem is doing to her. After all, that is why she is seeking help. Because it appears immediately obvious why some people are seeking help, some counselors skip very quickly over the influences and effects of the problem. However, this phase of narrative work generates a large amount of information that is particularly helpful to clients. If this part of the interview is done well, it lays the foundation for the coauthorship of a new story line for the client.

We are looking here at the deconstruction phase of the interview. Deconstructive questions help the client locate the unstated assumptions produced in the client's sociocultural context. When the assumptions are named, the client can consider whether to continue taking them for granted or to reevaluate her previous involvement with the exposed discourse.

The full effects of the problem story have seldom been developed by the person seeking help. After the counselor has heard and begun to identify some of the central problem themes, he can ask the client about a range of effects that the problem has had on the client's day-to-day life. He can be interested in how it has affected the client's health, both physical and psychological, her relationship with self and significant others, with work, recreation, friendships, or the spiritual side of her life. This exploration of the problem's effects could be wide-ranging, including all of the aspects just listed plus other areas that might be pertinent to the particular client. Questions such as "What effects is this problem having on your relationship with your children or partner?" survey a part of this territory.

This part of the interview may take a whole session or be completed relatively quickly if it explores only a few aspects of the client's life. In some cases, this stage might not occur at all, as clients may be immediately ready to explore their competencies and abilities, may be open to acknowledging these in the early phase of the counseling conversation, and may have reflected to a considerable extent on the influence of the problem story.

In our experience, when the problem influences are examined, clients feel that they have been listened to and that their concerns have been taken very seriously. They typically become mindful of the burden they have been operating under and become even more active in wanting to move away from the problem's harmful effects. They may also have a greater understanding of how the problem took some control in the first place. Questions like "When did this problem first show itself in your life?" assist in the development of such awareness. The counselor's task is to help the client story the problem from its origins through to the present day. When the person decides to participate in counseling, she has often registered only some aspects of the problem. A client who can story the problem tends to have a clearer perception of it and can be made aware of what might happen if it were to continue on its present course. A question such as "If the problem continues on its current tack, what is your view on what this would mean for you in a week/month/year/five years from now?" tends to add to the bigger picture, sharpen the focus on the problem's strategies, and strengthen the client's volition toward undermining the problem's effects.

Taking this direction in the interview helps clients clearly establish and name the plot in the problem story. The naming of the plot helps draw clear distinctions between the old problem story and the more favored story that will be subsequently developed. The plot name will most likely be the externalized phrase.

The counselor and the client can then identify occasions when the problem has not completely dominated the client's life. As mentioned earlier, the problem story is not the totality of the person, although it might at first feel like that to the client.

The counselor can be curious as to whether the problem has completely taken charge or whether there are small corners of the client's life where she is in control of the problem. If the questions are framed in such a way as to identify even minuscule nonproblem domains of a person's life, the door opens for the client to become acquainted with forgotten or undetected competence. This requires persistent and finely tuned questions.

Determining Whether the Client Favors the Present Situation

The client needs to make a decision as to whether the nonproblem events are favored elements in her life. Although, again, it may appear obvious to the counselor that a client would want more of the problem-free experiences, the client is encouraged to overtly state this.

This part of the interview is often ignored by narrative counselors because they assume that domains in the client's life that are not problem-bound will be valued, and that the client will be wanting a complete divorce from the problem. However, many of us can relate to ambivalence about giving up a problem when we consider the difficulty of mounting the necessary volition to do so. Think about how difficult it is to give up problems like procrastination, perfectionist attitudes, obsessional work habits. In many cases, the counselor's volition and motivation to assist may not be matched by the client.

It is then an easy next step to assume that the client will be joining us in our exploration of alternative, apparently more favored, aspects of her life. Given our degree of investment in the process, we may find ourselves talking our clients into the alternative story that we as counselors favor. This, of course, can leave the counselor in the invidious position of arguing for an outcome that the client does not have the stomach for. For example, imagine that you are working with a couple, and that one partner has already decided to call a halt to the relationship, although this person has not yet directly communicated that decision either to the other partner or to the counselor. The withdrawing client does not want to resuscitate the relationship and is not at all invested in exploring areas of the relationship that could be strengthened. It is not uncommon for a person to have made a private decision about a course of action but, for a variety of reasons, to have not yet openly articulated it.

The counselor should check with the person seeking assistance whether the development of nonproblem areas of life pertaining to the original concern is a favored outcome. Of course, it is usual for the client to say yes, as this is in keeping with the reason that he has presented himself to a counselor in the first place. However, there is considerable value in the person making an overt statement that declares his unambiguous response to the question. We are not suggesting that clients are deliberately deceptive or dishonest. They may be constrained for a variety of reasons in their ability to state clearly and unambiguously their preferred purposes. Making an overt statement of intention or preference, and hearing oneself say it, can be a significant step in breaking free from such constraints. Clients who have reached the point at which they are ready to develop an alternative story can be invited to make a clear and unconflicted response indicating their intentions. Without such commitment, the continuation of therapy is unlikely to empower the client to address his concerns. The agenda that is then pursued may be the counselor's and not the client's.

Thus counselors can be easily seduced into becoming more and more active in advocating for what they think is an alternative, more "desirable" story as the client grows in reluctance to advocate for himself. A tug of war can ensue. This is not an uncommon development in counseling and therapy.

When the preferred intentions of the client have been clarified, the counselor can then inquire into why the client is favoring a move away from the problem and toward those competencies that the counselor has begun to help the client identify. The client has an opportunity here to outline his desires and purposes, and typically, this produces information that is newsworthy to both client and counselor. A lukewarm or conflicted response diminishes the chance that positive outcomes will occur. A clear declaration about what the client wants adds momentum to the interview and builds further motivation for the client.

Mapping the Effects of the Person on the Problem

Another aspect of the interview involves expanding and developing the alternative accounts of self that clients have started to generate. Already, the client is becoming more mindful that the problem has not completely dominated his life because he is reporting minuscule fragments of non-problem-saturated experiences. The narrative counselor and the client are ready to further identify the influence of the person on the problem.

It comes as a surprise to many clients that they have areas of competence that have been previously buried by their problem concerns. They are enormously benefited if the counselor is not in any doubt that they possess problem-managing competencies that have not yet been named and identified. This can be an exciting yet challenging part of the interview.

In some cases, the process can be as difficult as looking for buried treasure without a map. Certain clients are so disheartened and beaten down by their present difficulties that it is hard for them to believe that they have competencies to help them tackle the problem. Identifying these capabilities requires tenacity on the part of the counselor, as she could easily join with the client's despair if there is not a strong belief that the person does in fact possess memories or fragments of knowledge where the problem is not in control. Obviously, not all clients are overtaken by despair, and those who are not can, with the help of the counselor, assemble a more favored account of themselves relatively quickly. Stories in which the problem has dominated many aspects of a client's life and high levels of shame and guilt predominate also require dedication on the part of both client and counselor. The client may have to retrain himself, just as an athlete would if making a shift from long-distance running to weight lifting.

We have described this stage of the interview as the reconstruction phase. As the more favored accounts are assembled, a counterplot emerges that contrasts with the dominant plot of the problem story. It is the task of the counselor to identify any client knowledge in the form of thoughts, feelings, behaviors, and dreams that are unique and different from the problem account. The counselor is now looking for sparkling moments.

Identifying Unique Events That Stand Apart from the Problem

Recently, I (Wally) met with a five-and-a-half-year-old boy whose parents were separated. Tom visited his father once a month for twenty-four hours and was reported to be crying a lot and wanting to go home to his mother's before the scheduled end of the visit. Descriptions abounded that he was too young for such visits, that his mother was setting him against his father, that he was unmanageable, and so on. His father was leaning toward reducing visiting time "until he is older and can handle it." When I met the boy, he told me it got scary at his father's, especially when it rained, as there were giants on the roof. We talked seriously about the giants and the ways he was taming them. His teacher at school had read lots of giant stories that helped him become a specialist on giants. I also asked if he wanted to spend a little less time with his father—for example, without staying overnight—or a little more time, like two nights.

"No," he responded.

I was puzzled and asked what he meant.

"Three nights!" he enthusiastically replied. "I want to show my dad that I'm good at scaring giants."

Unique outcome questions are developed alongside the storying of the problem's effects on the person. They emerge most actively from the counselor during the stage when she is interested in the exploration of the person's influence on the problem. However, in most narrative conversations, unique outcome questioning and deconstructive questioning may take place simultaneously, as the two stages are often combined.

Therapists who are new to narrative approaches often discover unique outcomes in a distant or early period in the client's life. This happens because it is much more difficult to help clients identify recent events that defy or undermine the problem.

Although questions about distant events are not wrong, this form of unique outcome may not be so useful to the client. The client might take the view that such so-called unique outcomes are irrelevant to their present difficulties because they happened so long ago.

Michael White talks about the value of selecting an *experience-near event* as a unique outcome. Though sometimes more difficult to find, it is far more meaningful to the client. Precisely because of the influence of the problem story over the client's recent experience, the counselor needs to be persistent and creative in couching the questions. The aim is to enlist the client's concentration to isolate positive and creative acts that will serve well in the reconstruction phase of the preferred story line.

Seldom are one or two unique outcomes sufficient for the creation of a more favored story. The counselor will need to work hard with the client to assemble as many unique outcomes as possible so that there is less chance that the client can dismiss the unique outcomes as accidents or freak occurrences. An alternative story must be constructed across a range of the client's favored encounters with life. Stories are created by the linking of events into coherent sequences over time. Single valued events are not sufficient for the development of a counterplot.

The client and the counselor are now immersed in the reconstruction phase of the counseling work, and the production of an alternative and more preferred account of the client's understanding of herself is under way.

As with all storied accounts, it is important that the sparkling events are historicized so as to identify the source from which the present abilities have emerged. This is achieved by introducing a range of questions that have the client consider how she has contributed to producing a valued experience that stands apart from the problem. Some people feel so defeated by their problem that they dismiss any abilities they have marshaled to challenge it as accidental or as attributable to somebody else. The next part of the narrative interview takes us into a new field of questioning designed to elicit competence and ability.

Exploring Abilities That Have Contributed to Desirable Events

In the early 1990s, Michael White introduced the metaphors *landscape of action* and *landscape of consciousness* into the narrative therapy literature, drawing on the work of the psychologist Jerome

Bruner. These terms have proved useful in developing a line of questions that were formerly referred to as "unique account questions" and "redescription questions." Landscape-of-action questions are concerned with gathering together and sequencing a collection of unique outcomes. Landscape-of-consciousness questions invite clients to reflect on their contribution to the production of such outcomes. Both types of questions are essential to the restorying process and provide the client and counselor with the necessary information to discover numerous abilities by means of which the client has created a more desirable range of interactions.

Landscape-of-action questions focus on past events featuring favored unstoried experiences, with more recent history being initially more relevant. These questions fill in gaps in the alternative story. Questions such as "What preparations did you make for taking that next step?" and "What has been happening in your life that has given you the energy to make the kind of progress you have been making?" produce a sharper and more distinct landscape. A well-marked landscape of favored lived experiences helps counselor and client to explore the client's qualities, commitments, preferences, and desires. Landscape-of-consciousness questions are often forgotten in narrative counseling, especially by people new to the approach. However, they frequently provide the most powerful means of assisting clients in recognizing where their commitments lie and where they can gain a greater appreciation of their qualities and abilities.

These landscapes of action and consciousness figure prominently in the reconstruction phase of narrative counseling.

In the story about Peter gaining sight, I (Gerald) could have asked him, "What does this say about the kind of person you are when you can consider going to school even when your world had completely turned upside down? What does this say about what you want from your life?" Essentially, landscape-of-consciousness questions encourage clients to evaluate and reflect on how they produce the kinds of experiences mapped out in the landscape of action. Michael White points out that one landscape does not have to precede another. Each landscape inquiry can contribute to the other.

For example, Peter could have been asked to focus on the landscape of action with a question that related to the landscape of consciousness: "What other things have you been doing that tell you that you have a lot of guts?"

As people respond to this form of questioning, they gain a stronger sense of what it is like to be positioned by the alternative, favored story rather than the problem-saturated one.

Seeking an Audience to Witness Favored Developments

When clients reveal their private stories for the first time, they are often concerned about how acceptable the stories will be to others. In addition, as has already been stated in earlier chapters, significant others have stories about us that have a powerful influence in shaping how we see ourselves. Often, family and friends are the audience to the acting out of our problem stories. Sometimes it is difficult to make desired changes under their gaze, and we may feel pressured, perhaps covertly, to continue to behave in accustomed ways—ways that may sustain the stories significant others have about *their* lives.

If one audience can have significant influence in maintaining our problem, another audience can be equally potent in supporting our development within a new account of ourselves. The successful recruitment of an audience that can bear witness to and acknowledge the changes a client is making in counseling validates the person's new description of himself. An audience that can appreciate the new developments verifies the changes as real and not a figment of the imagination.

There is value in placing considerable emphasis on identifying people who will appreciate and acknowledge the client's efforts in producing changes. One concrete way of recruiting such an audience is to write a letter to a significant other or to a referring party, describing the new developments that are occurring. For example, sixteen-year-old Ian had a long association with the police and welfare authorities, mostly for stealing cars. I (Wally) worked with him for six months, and for four of those months he set a new record in being free of stealing. Together, we wrote an open letter to all those who knew and remembered Ian as a thief, recording with evidence the changes in his life. He excitedly sent ten copies to important people, including the police for their file on him. The police wrote back asking for similar letters from others.

However, the recruitment of an audience is more likely to be produced symbolically within the narrative counseling session, by means of a particular type of questioning. A very common form of narrative questioning might begin, for example, with a request that the client identify a person in his life who would be least surprised to learn of the changes he was now making. Often, clients will talk about a family member who has wished them well in their life and looked for the best in them. If a family member is not invoked, it might be a more distant relative, perhaps an important schoolteacher or friend, or a longtime neighbor.

The client can be asked what this valued person might say or do if informed about the emerging new story. The client, after reflecting on this in the counseling session or between sessions, might decide to write directly to this valued person or, if the two will be seeing each other, to show that person through an altered demeanor the changes that are occurring.

Clients can also be asked who would be most surprised by the changes now being made. This can be paradoxically effective when clients have some investment in proving to a family member that they have excelled in ways that shake that relative's preconception of who they are. This approach is particularly useful with children and adolescents, but it is of value with adults as well.

Preferably, the counselor should help the client identify more than one person who could act as witness to the evolution of more favored developments. Sometimes, it is not possible to find an available or even a living audience to the emergence of the new story. In such a case, a range of possibilities is open to the counselor. Even if the valued person has died, the client can be asked about that person and how he or she might be influenced or affected by the changes in the client's behavior. Or the client himself can be invited to become the audience to these preferred changes. A question like "When you think about these changes that you have been making, how does this affect how you see yourself in your day-to-day life?" invites the client to reflect on his new self-description in a more focused way.

Building Awareness of How Changes Affect Self-Description

As the counselor questions the client about any new reevaluations, distinctions are drawn between the person's place in the old story and the ascribed role within the new story. This reflection by the client on the meaning of the changes strengthens and helps anchor a preferred self-definition.

For example, in Chapter One, when Peter was invited to reflect on how he was able to enter into a seeing world after being virtually blind for most of his life, he began to redescribe himself as somebody who had courage to face difficult and challenging circumstances. This was prompted by questions like "Have you always seen yourself as someone with courage when you get to a really hard place in life?" Other questions I (Gerald) could have asked Peter include "If I had known you when you were little, what do you think I might have seen that would have helped me understand how you were able to demonstrate this degree of courage?" and "What do you think this tells me about what you wanted for your life?" Michael White refers to this form of questioning as *experience of experience questions.* Such questioning invites people to reach back into their stock of unstoried experiences, engaging them within a contemporary, more favored self-description.

Considering the Possible Effects of New Discoveries

Even when a client has reviewed her life and has become more mindful of the previously unstoried competencies that she has already demonstrated, the process is not yet complete. The narrative counselor needs to assist the client in bridging past competencies with the present so that these abilities are available for the management of possible difficulties in the future.

There is value in striving for coherence between the past, the present, and the future in the client's relationship with the new story. This coherence allows client competencies to be effectively storied, which in turn permits the abilities and talents to be robustly maintained in the future. *Unique possibility questions* encourage the person to gather further momentum and perhaps more focused direction toward meeting future challenges. Clients are more clearly able to utilize their alternative knowledge when they are asked questions like "Having developed these abilities, what new possibilities might they open up for you in the future?" or "What effect will these capacities have on your management of X in the future?"

Documenting Progress in Counseling

The latter part of this style of working focuses on completing and strengthening the reconstructive process. One of the more powerful methods for achieving this goal is to record on audiotape or videotape, or in letters, the progress that has been made.

It is preferable to take careful notes of unique outcomes and unique accounts during the course of the interview, instead of spending the major part of the interview recording the problem story. There is more value in recording the alternative story as it unfolds, because what gets written down tends to be given more value or weight. In Western society, considerable importance is placed on the written word. We think it is more desirable to have a record of competencies than the customary elaborate descriptions of symptoms and problems.

The Writing of Letters

There has been a considerable amount written about composing narrative letters. Some narrative counselors have suggested that a well-composed letter following a therapy session or preceding another can be equal to about five regular sessions.

Narrative letters have a particular style of their own. Usually, they are a record of a session or sessions that may include an externalizing description of the problem and its impact on the client, in addition to an account of the client's abilities and talents as identified in the session. The letter emphasizes the struggle the client has had with the problem and draws distinctions between the problem story and the developing preferred story. Here is part of a letter written to Fran and Mark that illustrates these features:

> Dear Fran and Mark,
>   We learned some important things from the two
> of you on your last visit. Some of those things were that
> your relationship has definitely had times of being a
> Partnership. One such example occurred when Fran
> returned from Australia. However, there are other
> times when the Traditional-style relationship takes over
> and wreaks havoc.

Did you notice when depression visits itself on
Fran it seems to come from a loss in confidence?
Depression grows from all those awful things in your
relationship and brings anger with it. Those awful
things that do so much damage in your relationship—
such as belittling, put downs, social comments, lack of
niceness, name-calling and Fran not having a choice
in what she wants to do. But they are an important part
of the Traditional relationship and keeping it alive and
active. I understood too that, Mark, you commented
that the financial world is run on a Traditional
base and that may also have an influence on your
relationship. It has created a conflict between the use
of "I" and "we" in conversations where I guess "I" is
Traditional and "we" is Partnership. . . .

Writing narrative letters demands considerable practice, and
at first such a letter might take several hours to compose. If you are
new to the practice, you might concentrate on recording the
sparkling moments that have been identified in the counseling sessions. After a while, you are likely to develop your own style and
will be able to craft a letter within a much shorter period.

When working with young children, you can often use cer-
tificates and awards to mark the progress that has been made in
sessions.

I (Wally) have a king tiger that sometimes interacts with children. King Tiger writes to children on an appropriate letterhead,
signed with a stamp of paw prints and a crown seal on the envelope. King Tiger shares experiences he has had and the wisdom
his grandfather or grandmother has passed on. Children often
write back, sending photos and sharing their thoughts about the
problem and their plans for finishing with it.

Another powerful way of marking positive behavioral changes
in a young person is to audiotape or videotape her account of the
progress she is making. This video or audio record can be a means
by which the young person can access newly discovered knowledge
and abilities if the old problem story attempts to resurface. Such a
record can also be used for the benefit of other young people who
are struggling with similar difficulties. Peter, in Chapter One, beat
his fear of having normal vision and went on to record his abilities

and expertise in doing this. The procedure has been described by David Epston as *consulting your consultants.*

When a client who previously felt defeated by a problem has learned how to manage it, there is value in encouraging her to give guidance to others. This is a formal way of marking the client's evolution from someone seeking help to a person who is becoming an authority both on herself and on others.

Where to from Here?

When participants in our course complete the training, they frequently ask, "When we go away from here, what support is there for us?" This is an important question, and one that we feel obliged to attend to. Many of the ideas presented in this book are contrary to the traditional forms of helping. As a result, participants often find themselves isolated and unable to tap into support from other counselors.

Where possible, we encourage participants completing their training in narrative work to form an interest group to support their ongoing development. Peer supervision has proved invaluable in maintaining momentum for this work. Increasingly, as the narrative metaphor gains recognition and becomes incorporated into therapeutic supervision, there will be more support for this style of counseling. Supervisors experienced in narrative practice are essential to the nurturance of competent and skilled practitioners.

Just Before We Say Goodbye

We have a few questions we would like to offer you now that you have read this chapter. They are similar to questions we frequently offer at the end of a counseling or teaching session.

1. Has there been anything that has struck you as helpful as you have read this chapter?
2. What were the connections you made between your own practice and experience and the ideas in this chapter?
3. We would like you to reflect on how your own experience and ideas would contribute to the development of those presented here. We would appreciate your writing to us and letting us know.

4. In what ways will this material and your responses to it be useful to you in your work in the future?

What we have presented here is merely a sample of the teaching ideas and training issues within narrative therapy. We have found the need to continually develop, expand, and modify our own learnings as we reflect on the therapeutic possibilities of narrative work. Like counselors new to this work, we have been in a perpetual state of transition, constantly developing our abilities and possibilities while acknowledging the inevitable setbacks. The rewards have been astounding. We hope that you experience, as we have done, the exhilaration of witnessing the people you work with discover their own capacities and resources for forward movement in their lives.

Notes

P. 84, *some form of disability or deficit:* Gergen, K. (1990). Therapeutic professions and the diffusion of deficit. *The Journal of Mind and Behavior, 11*(3 & 4), 353–368.

P. 87, *an identity as a professional counselor:* White, M. (1994). *The politics of therapy: Putting to rest the illusion of neutrality.* Unpublished paper, Dulwich Centre, Adelaide, Australia.

P. 93, *topics to introduce these concepts:* Davies, B. (1991). The concept of agency: A feminist poststructuralist analysis. *Social Analysis, 30,* 42–53.

P. 95, *an event or circumstance:* White, M. (1992). Deconstruction and therapy. In D. Epston & M. White (Eds.), *Experience, contradiction, narrative and imagination.* Adelaide, Australia: Dulwich Centre Publications.

P. 98, *a paint-by-numbers approach to learning:* Griffith, J., & Griffith, M. (1992). Owning one's epistemological stance in therapy. *Dulwich Centre Newsletter, 1,* 5–11.

P. 101, *rapid and successful results:* Though we had an externalized name for the problem, it was equally important that I continue with externalizing conversations to keep Manu separate from the problem. For example, I asked, "How successful have you been over this last week, Manu, in beating the 'Rainmaker' and having more dry nights?"

P. 107, *Unique outcome questions:* White, M. (1989). The process of questioning: A therapy of literary merit? In *Selected papers.* Adelaide, Australia: Dulwich Centre Publications.

P. 108, *narrative therapy literature:* White, M. (1992). Deconstruction and therapy. In D. Epston & M. White (Eds.), *Experience, contradiction, narrative and imagination.* Adelaide, Australia: Dulwich Centre Publications.

P. 108, *the psychologist Jerome Bruner:* Bruner, J. (1986). *Actual minds, possible worlds.* Cambridge, Mass.: Harvard University Press.

P. 112, *experience of experience questions:* White, M. (1992). Deconstruction and therapy. In D. Epston & M. White (Eds.), *Experience, contradiction, narrative and imagination.* Adelaide, Australia: Dulwich Centre Publications.

P. 113, *composing narrative letters:* White, M., & Epston, D. (1990). *Narrative means to therapeutic ends.* New York: Norton.

P. 114, *seal on the envelope:* Wood, A. (1985). King tiger and the roaring tummies. Dulwich Centre Review, 41–49.

Part Two

Practice

Chapter Five

Leila and the Tiger
Narrative Approaches to Psychiatry
Glen J. Simblett

Leila was Maori. Twenty-four years old. A woman. A patient. She stood in my office and handed me a drawing. Neither of us sat down. I was puzzled. This was meant to be a routine outpatient follow-up to Leila's recent discharge from a psychiatric unit. Pictures are not normally a part of that. Ten minutes earlier, I had been uncertain if she was even going to keep the appointment. We had only met a couple of times. The last time had been particularly difficult and unpleasant. She had been so troubled by hallucinatory voices commanding her to hurt herself and her family that I had coerced her into accepting admission to the hospital for further assessment and treatment. I had later heard that while there she had stopped talking, eating, and drinking. Her physical health had deteriorated rapidly. Against the advice of her doctors, she had stopped treatment and persuaded her family to discharge her from the hospital to see a *tohunga* (a Maori healer). Some incredulity had been expressed about that by the white mental health workers. They asked if potatoes in her shoes were going to stop a depressive psychosis or schizophrenia.

I was about to find out.

The drawing was an incomplete profile of the head of a tiger.

"It's a tiger," I said lamely.

She waited silently. There had been some words written beside the tiger. I could still see the erasure marks.

"Was something written there?"

Leila nodded—the slightest tilt of her head. "There was a story to go with it. I changed my mind about writing it."

I knew that I was holding something significant in my hands but did not have the faintest idea how to respond. I was outside my psychiatric training. Outside the country I was born in. Outside my culture. I knew enough to register that, but not enough to know how to proceed.

I clutched at straws.

"I really like this picture, but I don't know what it means," I said.

"Do you want to hear the story?"

We still hovered uncertainly. I noticed that she was nearer the door than I was, and the door was still open. She avoided my gaze.

"Yes, I would like to."

Leila took a deep breath. "This is a tiger. A tiger has nine lives. This tiger only has five lives left. Do you want to know what happened to the other lives?"

I did, but I didn't. Part of me knew what was coming next, and I didn't want to hear it.

"Yes, I do," I lied.

"It lost its first life in the family it was born in because of their abuse and punishment. It lost its second life to drugs and alcohol. She [sic] lost her third life in a marriage where there was no room for her hopes and ideas." She paused, for the first time catching my gaze with culturally surprising boldness. "She lost her last life when she was admitted to a psychiatric unit."

Another pause.

"She hasn't got many lives left now," Leila added.

She waited silently. Patiently. It was not an accusation. Just a statement. The way it was for her.

Where do you go from here? You begin again, maybe. I invited her to sit down. We closed the door and we talked. We tried to understand each other's point of view. We tried not to blame.

I still find it hard to understand why she gave me another chance like that, why she did not just give up on yet another Pakeha (white) doctor who did not understand. I often wonder if I would have been so generous if the roles had been reversed. The tiger drawing still hangs on the wall of my office. It acts as a gentle caution and constant reminder to me of the dangers of dominant discourse.

Since that day, I have recounted that story many times to many people. I am always careful to respect Leila's privacy with changes of name and situation. I would never wish to feel responsible for using up another of the tiger's lives. I have struggled to understand the depth of meanings embedded within the story and the range of responses it produces in people.

Some people react to the apparent abuses of inhuman doctors and nurses, using drugs to control a helpless, misunderstood patient. There could be something in that, but what about the other view? That I know I cared about what happened to Leila? That the doctors and nurses in the psychiatric unit had used radical treatment only when they thought that dramatic life-saving measures were required if she was not to die in front of their eyes? Are those the acts of uncaring professionals?

Perhaps caring is not enough.

Others look bemused at the fact that I attach so much importance to the story. It was simply a matter of misdiagnosis, they tell me. That is why Leila got better. She never had a psychiatric disorder in the first place. Yet the hallucinatory voices she had heard were as real as any I have ever come across. Her assessment and treatment had been thoughtful and careful, and second opinions had been sought, in keeping with the best available psychiatric practice.

Perhaps best psychiatric practice is not enough.

Some have suggested that the story highlights a fundamental paradox in psychiatric care: that of invisible, subtly controlling, normalizing, dominant-culturing practices versus the healing of people. It was only after I was introduced to such ideas that Leila's story began to take on a different kind of meaning for me. Perhaps within postmodernism, social constructionism, narrative and reflective practice, lie some of the answers to why I used up one of the tiger's precious lives. Perhaps within the story of Leila and the tiger lie some hints to how we might proceed in the future—proceed with nine lives intact.

Much has already been written about psychiatric practices, their historical development, and the apparent inability of the psychiatric profession to adequately address criticisms of its normalizing tendencies. Foucault has outlined the use of the silencing of protest, imprisonment within the self-referential "mirror" of observation, and perpetual judgment as subtle refinements of the asylum.

Feminist writers have spoken of psychiatry's presentation of women as stereotypes, its insidious reinforcement of oppressive inequality by those from whom women would seek help, and the damaging contradiction between psychiatry's presentation of itself as a healing profession and its unacknowledged function as part of society's systems of ordering and control.

There is little available, however, to aid a busy psychiatrist in discovering workable alternatives. It is within that dilemma that this chapter is situated. I do not aim to denigrate modernist psychiatric practices (although some criticism is an inevitable part of the process). Nor do I wish to suggest that narrative ideas and practices provide all of the answers to these troublesome questions. Life and psychiatric practice are rarely as simple as that. Instead, I offer some thoughts and ideas on modernist practices and some practical alternatives that I have introduced into my everyday work.

Beginning Treatment

Contact with a psychiatrist in New Zealand and many other countries often begins with a telephone call or letter from a general practitioner or other professional. The usual information that is passed on would be something like this:

> Dear Dr. Simblett,
>
> Please could you see Karen Casey, a 25-year-old housewife who has a depressive illness that has not responded to dothiepin [an antidepressant drug]. She has been on 150 mg. for three months. She has presented with increasing symptoms of depression, and describes sleep disturbance, poor appetite, and anxiety. She has never seen a psychiatrist before, although she took a small overdose of aspirin when she was fifteen years old. I felt at the time that this was attention-seeking behaviour. The incident was never repeated.
>
> She describes strange thoughts of suicide and hurting her husband. Her husband is very supportive, and concerned by Karen's continued depression.
>
> There is no other significant medical history.
>
> Thank you for seeing Karen at short notice.
>
> R. Shelton, M.D.

Normally, the referral would be read by the psychiatrist and then filed in the new patient's notes. It would be reread prior to the first meeting with the patient but otherwise neglected. Psychiatric training emphasizes the importance of taking a careful, objective history from patients themselves and not necessarily accepting as accurate what other doctors or professionals report. The fact that the psychiatrist holds information and opinions on the patient that the latter is unaware of, and might even disagree with, is also not considered significant. We are trained to elicit the *real* story in our own history-taking and not to allow other people's opinions to sway us from our objective assessment. Or so psychiatric training would have us believe.

To most people, information about themselves (especially information with which they may disagree) is far from neutral or unimportant. So how can we handle such information differently? What alternative practices are available to us? I have recently started to read the referral to my clients. I explain that I do not like holding in their file or in my head opinions or information on which I do not also have their thoughts. When I do this, I am aware of the possibility of opening up another professional to criticism or censure by the client. I am also aware that this action in itself challenges many professional discourses, such as the importance of presenting a united front and never challenging the views of your colleagues in the presence of the patient. By contrast, I place my action openly and explicitly in the alternative discourses of the freedom of information and consumer rights.

I then ask a series of questions related to the letter, recording the client's replies for the record:

What do you think of the referral? Is there anything there that stands out for you? Is there anything there that you disagree with?

Dr. Shelton called this problem "depressive illness." Different people seem to mean different things by that, and I wondered what you thought about it? Is it okay for us to call the problem "depression" for the moment, or would you prefer to call it something else?

As the conversation progresses, I tend to go back to the referral at times and might well pose more questions about it:

In the referral letter, it said that your husband was very supportive. What do you think about that? In what ways do you think your husband has tried to support you against depression? How successful do you think he has been? How did he discover those things—did he read a book, ask the G.P., ask you, or what? Do you know of other things he might say or do that might support you better? Does depression ever try to stop you asking for those things? Is there anything that your husband does that supports the problem, or is that too weird a way to think?

I was interested to read that your G.P. thought that the overdose you took when you were fifteen was a way of "seeking attention." What do you think about that? How much of a role did "seeking attention" play in the overdose? Did other things play a part too? Did depression play a part in the overdose back then? What about "wanting to die"? Those are both things that other people say contribute to overdoses, but maybe different people experience different things—what do you think? Do you think that people who are trapped by invisible problems ever need attention? If "seeking attention" wasn't a big part of the overdose, are you aware of other ways that you've tried to get some help and attention for these invisible problems? Did anyone notice them?

The referral mentioned "strange thoughts." Is that an okay thing to call them for now? Would it be okay to maybe write down some examples of them? Where do you think those thoughts originated from? Could they have come from depression? Why would depression want you to hurt yourself or your husband? Could it be trying to convince you that you're evil and wicked and bad through and through, or maybe want you to give up hope, or what? Why do you think it might want to do those things?

As a result of my asking such questions, the referral becomes part of the process of understanding and change. It acts as a springboard to further explore dominant and alternative stories. I also believe that it engenders an atmosphere of trust, respect, and collaboration, which are vital components of any first meeting.

The Appointment

Once a referral is received, our usual psychiatric practice would be to give out a telephone appointment or send out a standardized appointment letter. If any information at all is passed on to the client, it would usually be something like this:

> Dear Mrs. Campbell,
>   Your general practitioner, Dr. Strong, has referred you to our service. I have arranged an appointment for you to see me at Psychiatric Outpatients on Thursday, June 9, at 10 A.M. The appointment will take 60–90 minutes. Please bring a relative with you, as we might need to interview him or her also.
>   Dr. Glen J. Simblett

We might add some "consumer-friendly" details such as where to park and how to find the building, but the overall emphasis is on simple, matter-of-fact information to which no great significance is attached.

Since I learned of narrative ideas and practices, however, I feel much less confident that any communication with clients can be dismissed as unimportant or without interpretation. I now see the first contact with the person as playing a vital role in setting the stage and context within which we will work together. Small changes to letters can open up a considerably different range of assumptions, understanding, and interest. An alternative appointment letter that I regularly use looks something like this:

> Dear Mrs. Campbell,
>   I have recently been contacted by Dr. Strong, who suggested that you are having some difficulties with an eating problem at the moment. She mentioned that you were maybe interested in meeting me to see if I could be of some help. I am not sure how you feel about that. I do know from other women I have met who were struggling against eating problems that they are often not enthusiastic about seeing a psychiatrist, especially if it is a man.
>   I am afraid to say that I am both of those things, but I am also very interested in helping people claim their lives back from eating problems. This is because I have seen many women whose lives were stolen out from under them by a problem that pretended to be

their one and only true friend. I enclose some stories about people who have resisted eating problems. They might also tell something of my beliefs about such problems and the approach I use to try to support people in claiming back their lives.

Maybe you will read this and think that it would be worthwhile for us to meet and talk about this some more. I would like to say right now that I don't think that you are crazy or manipulative or attention-seeking. I have no intention of weighing you, force-feeding you, or putting you into the hospital against your will. If you would like to meet and talk, I've arranged an appointment for you on Thursday, June 9, at 10 A.M. at my offices in the outpatient department. The first appointment normally takes about 90 minutes, and if you would prefer, please bring with you a supporter or any family members you choose.

Yours forever anti-anorexically/anti-bulimically,
Dr. Glen J. Simblett

I include with the letter some "traditional" information about, and definitions of, eating disorders, including descriptions of recognized therapies such as cognitive therapy, refeeding programs, and family therapy. I make a point of putting in writing the assumptions that these methods make about the underlying psychopathology of the person or family. I present this knowledge along with the alternative knowledges of the anti-anorexia/anti-bulimia leagues and some of the assumptions that underlie narrative-informed therapies.

Such an appointment letter has produced varied responses. Because it is filed with a client's notes, it has occasionally been seen by my colleagues. Some of them have expressed surprise at my willingness to put in writing that I would not force someone with anorexia nervosa to enter the hospital against their will. They have wondered if I am opting out of my responsibility to use the Mental Health Act—the New Zealand statute that mandates treatment when individuals are mentally disordered and a serious danger to themselves or others, or seriously diminished in their capacity to care for themselves.

I believe this to be a valid criticism. I do indeed use the Mental Health Act in the circumstances described. I am also aware that there is a dominant assumption in the psychiatric profession that "anorexics" also fall into this category. There is even a strong research base indicating that profound cognitive changes are produced by starvation and anorexia nervosa. This research can be used as incontrovertible evidence that starving "anorexics" are physiologically incapable of making rational decisions.

Because of previous experiences with other clients, I have developed different assumptions. I assume that a person fighting anorexia or bulimia would be physically moribund, and probably unable to keep an appointment with me, before being mentally incapable of making informed decisions about her life, safety, and treatment. The explanation for these differing assumptions lies, I believe, in the manner in which questions are posed and the climate of therapy itself.

When I view a client as in rebellion against the problem of anorexia rather than as a passive victim, or even an active anorexia collaborator, I help construct a climate capable of appreciating resistance. Within *this* climate, I often find that the client allows me to witness her stand against the problem—a stand I might neglect if I viewed it in other ways. Acknowledging the client as a vital ally against the problem tends to emphasize and document occasions of informed, rational choice and agency. These elements of behavior are, by definition, not present when people are mentally disordered to the degree required by the Mental Health Act in New Zealand. Simply put, if you are willing to look for evidence of clarity of thought and action against the problem, you usually find it. If you cannot find it, then utilizing compulsory treatment statutes may well be a rational alternative to consider.

Another practical reason for writing a letter like the one I have quoted is that compulsory admission to the hospital is a real fear of clients fighting eating disorders. Many have told me that the problem may use that legitimate fear to prevent them from seeking help of any kind—and especially the help of a psychiatrist. I also assume that people are better at freeing themselves from problems when they feel confident about seeking help from professionals. This is why I phrase my appointment letters as I do.

I received a different kind of feedback from Sarah, as we were collecting together her story for the anti-anorexia/anti-bulimia leagues' archives.

"I wondered what you thought of that first appointment letter," I said. "Other women had told me that the first appointment was really hard, so I designed it to try to interest them in coming despite anorexia/bulimia's protest. Do you think it works, or needs changing?"

"I came, didn't I?" Sarah replied.

She did.

Taking a Psychiatric History

The importance of doctors taking a systematic, systemic history is emphasized from medical school onward. It is widely accepted that accurate diagnosis is more likely to come from history-taking than examination. Indeed, it is through the patient's history that we come to focus on relevant areas of examination. This rubric holds as true for psychiatry as for any other branch of medicine. Psychiatry, in fact, prides itself on being the only medical discipline to take a thorough history of the person's life.

For me, this is one of the key narrative strengths of psychiatry. It gave me my first clue to the importance of people's stories.

Clients often experience the relating of their story as a highly significant event. Many of the linkages and observations that they make during this telling have never occurred to them before—or if they have, they have rarely been shared with another human being. This in itself is significant, although the therapeutic nature of storytelling is rarely alluded to in standard psychiatric texts.

At first, a student may feel clumsy and gauche at taking a psychiatric history. A novice is required to learn a list of headings and standard questions, beginning with so-called open-ended questions and moving toward more specific, closed questions. The aim is to record an accurate, objective history that is repeatable by different practitioners at different times. In practice, I suspect that there is not a junior doctor in the whole world who has not felt the heart-dropping horror of a patient relating a totally different account of problems or events to his or her consultant when the latter asks the same relatively standardized questions. The fluidity of people's stories in everyday practice is dismissed as an artifact of doctors' differing skill levels or patients' altered perceptions (influenced by factors such as pathological mood or manipulation) rather than understood as inherent in the very nature of storytelling.

Once psychiatrists become more familiar with the process of history-taking, they tend to identify particular themes within a person's history. The appreciated themes lie, almost by definition, within the perceptions of the questioner rather than the experience of the questioned. Those that are noticed and subsequently developed tend to depend on the training and theoretical interests and beliefs of the psychiatrist.

For example, psychiatrists impressed by the strong research base for the biological causality of psychiatric disorder would diligently search for evidence of family (and by assumption, genetic) history, birth trauma, and accompanying somatic symptomatology. A psychiatrist with a belief in the importance of psychodevelopmental factors would tend to assist the patient in acknowledging and expanding on the traumatic experiences of childhood.

Although arguments rage and theoretical themes come and go with shifts of fashion and the impact of scientific breakthroughs, one of the great narrative strengths of psychiatry has always been an open acknowledgment that psychiatric disorders are complex beasts—illnesses that require biopsychosocial exploration if we are ever to understand them fully. The development of increasingly complex, multiaxial classifications, such as the *Diagnostic and Statistical Manual of Mental Disorders (DSM)* and the *International Classification of Diseases (ICD)*, is an attempt to quantify such complexities. Since much of the etiology of mental ill health remains uncertain, these classification systems remain obvious social constructs. They have been noted to simply consist of "a way of seeing the world at a point in time" or "a consensus of current formulations of evolving knowledge."

Problems may arise when, within a modernist framework, a psychiatrist assumes that these classification systems are progressing toward an objective scientific truth. This tends to be a tacit assumption of those who use these classification systems in everyday clinical settings. The emphasis on the scientifically provable also tends to draw attention away from neglected alternative "axes," such as the spiritual, political, racial, and gender. Under a social constructionist view of problems, the constructs on the alternative axes have the potential to produce profound effects on people.

The underlying, culturally based assumptions of these classification systems are often left unstated. For example, it is accepted that people of "other" cultures can develop "culture-bound syndromes" as well as syndromes that are not culture-specific (such as schizophrenia). The possibility of culture-bound syndromes in dominant white, Western culture tends to be ignored or unresearched. It seems to be assumed that more "developed" cultures do not engender or exhibit such conditions. The underlying assumptions and beliefs common to the community and culture of psychiatric experts who develop these "ways of seeing the world at a point in time" are also left undisclosed.

Because the coconstructed elements of psychiatric classifications are often neglected in their everyday use, it is hardly surprising that the coconstruction efforts of the psychiatrist in the development of patients' stories are also ignored. There is an assumption that a psychiatric history taken with sufficient skill will avoid the pitfall of the psychiatrist "corrupting" the development of objective truth.

A postmodernist view of history-taking, by contrast, accepts that this process is always subjective, always coconstructed. Rather than being admonished to avoid subjectivity, I am encouraged to understand, appreciate, make plain, and use these inevitable characteristics in the battle I undertake with the patient against the problem.

The traditional schema for the psychiatric history contains the following series of subheadings:

Presenting complaint

History of the presenting complaint

Personal history of patient

Family history of patient

Previous psychiatric/medical history

Drug history

Narrative practices enable me to follow such a schema while also exploring and deconstructing/coconstructing clients' dominant and alternative stories. The following examples offer some ideas for using the schema in different ways.

The Presenting Complaint

This is one of the few parts of the psychiatric history where psychiatrists are trained to record the patient's words verbatim. Note that it is the complaint that is traditionally recorded, not the problem. In the modernist psychiatric interview, it is the psychiatrist who is charged with the responsibility of naming and defining the problem, in the form of a diagnosis. Defining the presenting complaint can easily be transformed into a process of collaboratively naming the problem.

Jane was a student in her early twenties who referred herself to me with the stated problem of depression. In our first meeting, I briefly introduced myself and then explained that it was important to me to see problems as separate from people. I suggested some ground rules for our interaction, such as her having the right not to answer any of my questions. She thought that would be okay. I went on to say that my experiences with other clients had suggested that asking certain questions could sometimes make problems protest and complain, so I would sometimes check with her to see if she would like me to change the subject. I made it clear that if she ever did want to change the subject, that would be fine with me. After getting her agreement to these "ground rules," I asked whether she thought the problem was still around, and if so, what she now thought the problem or problems were.

Jane thought about this for a while, and then replied: "I feel a lot better now, but I know it will come back. That's the way it usually happens. Last year, I was depressed for over a year."

I asked her if it would be okay for us to call the problem "depression" for the time being, and whether she would mind if I asked her some questions about it. She agreed to this process.

History of the Presenting Complaint

Normally, the next step would be a semistructured interview eliciting the historical origin and progression of the complaint. A psychiatrist's language and paths of questioning would usually begin to change at this point and would already reflect certain assumptions about the problem or diagnosis. These days, I prefer to be a little more careful about making assumptions and try to open out the questioning in an externalizing, deconstructing manner.

With Jane, I asked whether it would be okay if I wrote down some of her replies while we spoke, because it was unlikely that I would be able to remember them all. She agreed to that, and I went on to indicate that I was really interested in how depression had entered her life.

"Jane, I was interested in you calling it 'depression.' Have you always called it that, or did you originally call it something else?"

Jane did not seem to find the question difficult. "I didn't know it was depression originally. I first noticed losing interest and avoiding people when I was fifteen."

"How did things go from there?"

"My parents split up after that, and I was fine. I went to England a few years ago, and that's when I got depressed."

"So if you didn't call it depression in the beginning, what did you think it was?"

Jane hesitated, and I decided that the question might be too confusing. "I mean, did you call it something else, or did you notice a reaction to it in some way, or what? What did you notice?" I added.

"I don't know. I just knew that I hated it."

"Okay, so maybe you just thought of it as 'I hate it' at first. Did other people call it depression, or did they think it was maybe something else?"

Jane seemed to be warming to my style of questioning and the way I was recording her answers, with occasional checks that I was understanding them correctly.

"Yeah, other people called it laziness."

"What do you think about that? Do you think it was laziness?" I knew, even as I asked, that such a question played into the dominant cultural discourse of the negative nature of laziness. I also suspected that it might support a common depressive discourse of worthlessness. I asked the question despite these thoughts because I felt it was important to elicit Jane's own thoughts about laziness.

"Maybe it was laziness. I *am* a lazy person." She began to look troubled, so I figured that I had indeed activated a depressive discourse.

I decided to try deconstructing Jane's ideas about this a little further.

"What are your thoughts about laziness, Jane? Is it ever something that you enjoy?"

She nodded. "I enjoy being lazy sometimes, but I wish I could get things done when I need to get things done."

I recorded that answer, making a mental note to come back to it at a later session. I decided to begin asking some questions to elicit the breadth and depth of the effects of depression on her life and health.

"So how did this depression thing creep up on you? Did it happen quickly, or sneak up on you slowly, or what?"

"I think it happened quite quickly. I know that I hated school in England from day one. I didn't enjoy it. It wasn't a nice place. I started being horrible to Mum."

"So should I write that it happened quite quickly?"

She thought about that, then said, "It probably crept up on me over the first few weeks."

"Okay, I'll write that, too. So did you notice anything else?"

"I lost weight . . . I was lazy . . . I snapped at people, and I'd cry at any given moment."

"Anything else?"

"In England, I lost concentration, I stopped reading books, I even saw a hypnotherapist about it. I'm not sure about that, though. I've always left things until the last moment. I'm a terrible procrastinator. I can find anything to do except what I need to do."

Jane again became quiet, and I made a guess that the problem of depression was taking advantage of her description of herself as a procrastinator to hide from our explorations. I decided to try to expose the gap between depression and other discourses in Jane's life.

"So tell me, is losing concentration different from laziness or procrastination?"

"Mmmm, yeah, it is."

"So would it be okay for me to record, 'Losing concentration seems different from being lazy and procrastinating'?"

"Yes." She also agreed that losing concentration was something we could blame depression for, rather than laziness or procrastination.

"Jane, was there anything else?"

Although at first sight this seems a dull, repetitive process, I find that it is important to explore beyond the first two or three answers to questions—to persevere in the belief that people have a bottomless fund of knowledge and answers available to them.

Jane answered: "I gave up on life . . . I started existing . . . I stopped going to college . . . I stopped crying . . . There were times I didn't leave the house for days . . . Depression affected everything, it got in the way of pretty much everything."

The questioning continued in this vein, and we slowly drew together a list of some of the things that depression had affected or taken from her life. When depression was around, she slept in late, did not get dressed, ate the same food constantly, and watched TV without really enjoying it. "I was a walking *TV Guide*," she commented.

"It took part of my personality. I was eager to fit in. I used to be really different, but I changed my image in England—I don't think I liked it better. Depression made me accept the mainstream, I lost any quirkiness. By the time I left England, I was beginning to enjoy being like everyone else."

"Assumptions about how I *should* be may have helped in me losing myself. I still kept hold of some of myself. I still had an interest in music, for instance. That may have made depression's job easier—I didn't reinvent myself, I just smoothed out the edges to be more acceptable."

We agreed that this process had made her vulnerable to depression and had made it easier for depression to begin to define her in its image.

"Sometimes I'll feel I'm a nice person, sometimes I'll think I'm really horrible—why do I have friends?"

We had clearly moved into considering how external cultural pressures can influence people's ideas of self. Because I shared with her my experience of currently living in a country where I was not born, we talked about the differences between English and New Zealand culture. I asked how depression had managed to follow her here.

Jane said: "It's a lot better here in New Zealand where I've got friends around me. That helps. Sometimes I like being by myself, but it can make me feel more secure being myself with friends. Coming back here was a good move."

I decided that this was an opportune time to begin to record the story of Jane's resistance to this depressed description of herself.

"That sounds like you've made some progress against depression since moving back to New Zealand. Is that right?"

Jane agreed, and I continued, "Looking back at all of the things that you noticed depression stole from you, what have you managed to get back?"

"Now most of me is back, but now and again I can slip back into it and think, What am I doing?"

She paused, and seemed to be struggling to think of other things. I read out to her the list that we had initially recorded of the things depression had affected. She agreed that currently

- Her sleeping was okay.
- She had "no appetite."
- Her concentration was "terrible."
- She could "feel happy."
- She was still tearful at times.
- "Everything's still a bit of an effort."
- She was still irritable and bad tempered—"I can go over the top."

After defining the areas where she felt that she had made progress against depression unaided, I began to question her about what she might prefer in her future, if this success at claiming her life back from depression were to continue.

"I want to get control of my life again. I don't want to feel horrible. I want to do my work, manage my time, be sensible about things, to stop ignoring things that I know won't go away. I have problems with my identity now. I can never settle on who I am. Sometimes I think, 'My God, that's ugly, what am I trying to do?' I want to become the old me, a better person. Sometimes I think it's so easy, other times it's like a roll of sticky tape that you can't find the end of."

Family History

The recording of a person's family history is another important part of the standard psychiatric history. It is evidence of psychiatry's acceptance that people are not solitary individuals but exist within a network of relationships. There are, however, a number of unstated assumptions within this process and the way it is conducted.

For example, there tends to be an emphasis on white, Western concepts of the nuclear family: the history is usually limited to first-degree relatives (parents and siblings) or to relatives living in the same household. Broader family, historical, and sociopolitical contexts tend to be neglected. Although this emphasis may be defensible on the basis of time limitations, such a narrow context tends to emphasize the importance of upbringing, nurture, genetics, and parenting at the expense of other aspects of people's experience. This process in itself reflects psychiatry's current theoretical positioning.

To broaden the narrative much beyond the usual psychiatric practice is clearly an impossible task in a single session, so I make a point of coming back to it in later conversations—broadening, deepening, and illuminating the stories that people carry with them. In Jane's case, we established that she was one of several children and that her parents were divorced. The dominant story of her relationships with her parents she related as follows:

"I've always got along with Mum, but we've never been close. We got closer when they broke up. She would tend to make me feel stupid and unimportant. When she got remarried, I didn't want her new husband around. I didn't want to accept him."

"I see Dad a lot. I guess I was a daddy's girl when I was a kid. We were pretty well off. He's now remarried, and his new wife is like a big sister."

In later sessions, we broadened these stories. For example, Jane pointed out that there was still a temptation for her to be "Daddy's girl." This surfaced when her father suggested that she return home because of her depression.

I decided that this cultural invitation for her to be a "good little girl" might be relevant to the experience of losing her preferred self, and I encouraged her to consider the "good little girl trap" that I had heard other women comment on. Did she have any thoughts about that? Did she know what they were talking about?

She seemed to recognize it. "There's been a pressure to be a good little girl from very early on. I seem to have been trapped into the good little girl thing since I came back to New Zealand. Why is it a trap? It's a trap because there's no way I can get out of it. If I try to get out of it . . . other people criticize and make fun. . . . Things that I really believe in and hold really strongly become a joke. Over the last few months, I've been really doubting myself. I've been saying to people, 'I'm wrong, I'm gonna change,' so I don't know what to believe in any more. I would like to change, but I don't know why. I don't know if it's for the wrong or right reasons. Yeah, it's important to me to be sure about that."

She also agreed that she had noticed evidence of the "good little wife" trap in her mother's life, and she had become aware of a change in her mother after her parents' separation. I asked whether this "good little wife" trap had affected her own thoughts about relationships.

"It's made me cynical about relationships between men and women. I see everything as a potential disaster."

"Do you think men play any part in the good little girl, good little wife, good little mother traps?"

"Yes, they do. They do it by appearing to make assumptions—like I'm a prude, or I'm real sensitive, or old-fashioned."

"Do you think that you're real sensitive?"

She thought about that some. "I can take offense, but I react back. There's a real fine line between being a good little girl and being looked down on. I'm not striving to be a good little girl."

"Is it just men who seem to make those assumptions?"

"No, it's like when I'm out with a lot of guys, I'm not seen as an individual, I'm seen as someone else's girlfriend, and I'm not. I wish people would know I'm Jane. I guess I do that, too, but I don't think that the same assumptions are made about the guy. It's like I become invisible to people outside, or a part of a guy. People seem to assume that I belong to someone else."

"Do you think that sort of thing makes it harder for a woman your age to develop a sense of personal identity?"

"Yes, I do."

"You said in the first session that trying to fit in had made it easier for depression to sneak up on you in England. Do you think that some of this might help explain how depression followed you here?"

"Possibly." Jane looked troubled and seemed to be having difficulty thinking. I sensed that we had probably taken that particular story as far as possible for that day.

"Maybe we should think about that some more some time?"

"Okay."

Personal History

The recording of historical events in a person's life can be transformed into a process of identifying and recording dominant and alternative stories. In Jane's case, we quickly established that she had lived in a small village until she was twelve years old. In her early teenage years, she had noticed that she retreated to her room to eat her meals and often felt separate from her family. There was thus a history of isolation in her life. I asked whether depression might ever have taken advantage of isolation, and she agreed that it had.

Thinking back to her childhood, she said: "When I was a kid, I was permanently scared. Dad had a bad temper, although we get along fine now. Since then, we've sorted out a lot of stuff."

She later added, "I was a horrible child."

I elected not to follow up on that particular description of herself because it was likely to further encourage depression's discourses of guilt, self-blame, and unworthiness.

She recognized that moving to New Zealand after her parents' divorce had been part of a story of "making a new start." I suspected that this story could be used against depression's tactics of sameness and boredom, so I made a point of noting down that description for future reference.

I asked Jane about her relationships with boyfriends, and she told me that her first relationship at the age of sixteen had "ended in tears when he ran off with my best friend."

We spoke of how upsetting that betrayal had been for her, while also acknowledging the commonness of such events during teenage years. Thinking about more recent relationships with men, Jane noted that when she had returned to England, "it was a shambles, I got really wimpy. I just compromised a lot of my beliefs. I used to ring up and try to sort things out when he'd been a beast."

I asked her for some examples of beast-like behavior, but decided against pursuing her ideas about men receiving a training in treating women in a beastly fashion. She already seemed relatively free of self-blame on this topic. If she had shown evidence of being seduced by these experiences into believing that she deserved such treatment, then it would have been very important to deconstruct these ideas further. To ignore them would have left unchallenged discourses that had rendered her potentially vulnerable to depression.

She had also noticed that she "had a tendency to want someone to be around." On her return to New Zealand, this tendency had led her to go out with a close male friend despite her recognizing that "we were totally different. I think we decided to get back together without thinking about it." She paused, reviewing these relationships in her mind. "I always end up choosing the wrong person."

It would have been tempting at this point to explore a dominant story of Jane choosing the wrong person. This story line would usually lead psychiatrists to conclude that her experiences as a child had led her to repeat a learned pattern of seeking men who would treat her badly, or to even conclude that she was "codependent." The task of therapy would then have become "assisting" her to accept and change these aspects of herself.

I decided to avoid such internalizing explorations and instead posed a question that had the potential to open up some different contexts.

"Jane, it probably doesn't surprise you that I've heard lots of women say something like that. I have also come across a few different explanations. Some people say that women seek out men who will abuse them because that's what they've come to desire and expect. Others say that women have to work pretty hard to find a man who isn't going to treat them that way. Maybe there are other explanations, too. What do you think?"

Jane smiled. "Yeah, the second one is pretty true. Although not everybody is like that. I've never had a serious relationship. I don't get serious about someone who isn't right."

"So are you saying that despite choosing the wrong person, you somehow become aware that they aren't right for you?" She nodded. "So what happens when you figure out that they aren't right and this isn't serious?"

"I usually end the relationship."

So much for codependency.

By posing questions that opened up several contexts for the story of 'choosing the wrong men,' we were able to identify an alternative discourse that included Jane's wisdom, her resistance to being fooled, and her ability to act on her discoveries. Such a discourse seemed to offer her more opportunities to resist her relationship with depression than one of "codependency" or "repetition compulsion."

Previous Psychiatric History

Normally, this is a relatively straightforward process of asking the client if she has had previous contact with mental health or psychiatric services and if so, what diagnosis was made and what treatment offered. I attempt to broaden this information-gathering exercise into a more productive narrative. The following examples drawn from a series of clients who had previous experience of psychiatric services illustrate the process.

Sarah was eighteen years old and had been struggling against anorexia for about eighteen months. She had already received "traditional" treatments for anorexia, and this excerpt from a letter that I wrote to her conveys some of her views and reflections on her previous treatment:

Dear Sarah,
    . . . Your intuition had also suggested to you that a psychiatric hospital was not the right place for you to beat anorexia. If you had stayed there then, the anorexia would have succeeded in getting you alone again. I asked you if anorexia was easier to fight alone or together. You seemed pretty clear that it was easier to fight it when someone was not telling you what to do, and it was important that people understand this dilemma and avoid using force.
    You also thought that deciding not to stay in the psychiatric unit for eating disorders was a radical decision. Although you seemed clear that anorexia had contributed to that decision, you thought that it was only a 50 percent contribution. You pointed out:
    "It made me feel like I was crazy. It did not feel like the way that I wanted to fight anorexia—it was more for it than against it." When I asked if you could explain that, you added: "It was for it because it didn't let me be myself, it made me feel like a child, and it used force—so if you didn't eat then they would take something away from you and it would feel like they were forcing you to eat and bribery."
    These observations had led you to ask, "Do I want to live in those circumstances?"
    I asked what you meant by that and you told me: "It took you out of the real world. You were living in a make-believe world where you didn't get to make any choices in the way of eating."
    I asked if people might interpret your objections as anorexia seeking the freedom to make its choices

without supervision, and you replied: "You have to make your own choices. To learn how to fight it yourself. For me, personally, I don't care about weight. It's not what I'm fighting. I'm fighting to love myself. To be happy. That's why I don't think scales and trials work. They don't measure the person inside you or your happiness. It's not possible to be happy with the person that you are and be anorexic. False happiness goes with the territory, though. An example of that is when I started riding horses again. That was false happiness. I wasn't happy with myself, I was happy because I was doing something I wanted to do, and anorexia wasn't hassling me because I wasn't eating."

Not only does this process provide important and clinically relevant information, but it also reduces power gradients, enabling clinicians to consult their clients. A valuable reference source for other clients to reflect on is also produced. It soon became clear that Sarah was not alone in her views.

Over a series of sessions, Julie, a twenty-eight-year-old woman who had fought anorexia for about eight years, had the following observations to make about her previous and current treatment:

Dear Glen,
    When I first saw a Clinical Psychologist for treatment of an eating disorder she treated it in the traditional manner. She asked me to keep a diary of the food I ate and when I vomited. At first it seemed to help. (I went from vomiting every day to once a week.) But anorexia was just letting me go for a while knowing that it could come back later. It knew that one day they would tell me I was okay and that I didn't need to come back again. It also knew that I didn't need to write in the book every time I vomited and that they would never know. Also the eating diary helped anorexia keep a track on what I was eating. It still wouldn't allow me to eat certain foods or too much of anything. Anorexia used the diary to calculate calories eaten in a day. Too many meant a long run the next day.
    I guess this just shows me again that the tapeworm [anorexia] can't be killed by chopping off its head. It just grows two more and comes back with vengeance.

Instead, I need to feed myself information that tells the truth, i.e.:

• that happiness does not depend on size

• that my healthy weight and shape are right for me

• that the effort required to remain at this artificially low weight is just not worth it

• that staying at this weight makes me dependent on the tapeworm and therefore makes the tapeworm strong.

. . . Anorexia tapeworm doesn't like being disowned as it is telling me it is part of me and I can't destroy it without destroying myself. But I know what is going to destroy me and how, but it isn't going to because I'm not listening.
            Anti anorexia 4 ever
            Julie

Simply obtaining the when and how of previous psychiatric contact does not yield the richness of detail that these narrative techniques provide. Furthermore, the therapist would miss the benefit of hearing the client's unique observations and insights.

It is all too easy to dismiss such powerful testimonies as subjective, anecdotal, and hence invalid—or to be so overcome by what appears to be doctor-blaming that the message of change goes unheard. When we have been so thoroughly trained in confusing the problem with the person, it is all too tempting to switch tracks and confuse the problem with the therapist.

Drug History

In modernist Western culture, there is a marked polarity between the psychological and the physical. This, along with a strong emphasis on the importance of individuality, self-control, and avoidance of mind control, has contributed to the preference of the general public for talking treatments over medication. On the other hand, psychiatry's reductionist scientific emphasis on the biological origins of mental illness has tended to elevate the clinical importance of physical treatments.

These discourses tend to produce a tension of differing desires and beliefs between psychiatrist and client. The client is likely to want talking treatments, and the psychiatrist scientifically proven, effective physical treatments. The psychiatrist can easily come to believe that her task is to educate the client in the biological origin of the diagnosed mental disorder and to persuade him to accept physical treatments. The client is usually under a social expectation to comply with the psychiatrist's expert knowledge in these matters or risk being described as "resistant" or even "personality disordered."

Narrative beliefs and practices allow me to consider different views of problems and their effects on people. The virtual space created by externalization and the complexity and rigor of deconstruction allow us to identify the scope of the problem's influence and its effects on body, mind, spirit, relationships, family, and society. Instead of trying to marry dichotomy and difference, I use an alternative metaphor that views experience as an ecological system, with each part dependent on and influenced by the other. This metaphor allows each social construct to be approached with equal importance and value. The biological and biochemical are neither ignored nor overemphasized.

I asked Jane if she had ever been prescribed medication for her problems. She thought about that and replied: "When I was fifteen, my mum took me to see a G.P. who gave me some little pink tablets." We laughed about that some, and she continued, "They told me that they were vitamin tablets, but I think they were antidepressants. I didn't take them for very long."

I asked her if she had experienced it as helpful not to be told what the pink tablets were. She replied that she would have preferred to be told what people thought was wrong and what the tablets were for. We had a brief discussion about this and decided that if I were to prescribe medication, it would be important for me to explain to her the reasons why it might help and let her make the final decision about taking it.

Later in the interview, I asked her if she had noticed these problems affecting her body. She was not quite sure what I meant by that, so I elaborated: "Well, some people have noticed that depression can affect things like sleeping, eating, how much energy they feel they have, things like that."

"Yes, I'd either not get enough sleep or too much. In England, it was chronic insomnia. It would take two to three hours to get to sleep. Everything would go through my head."

"So when was the last time that you noticed it affecting your sleep?"

She considered this. "Over the last six months, I've had maybe three sleepless nights."

"Did you notice it affecting anything else about your body?"

"Mmm, I'd go days with one meal a day or I'd overeat lots. At the moment, I'm not really eating."

"So what was the connection between depression and eating?"

"Overeating was part of the depression. If anything happened, I'd go straight for food as comfort. There was also a constant fear of getting fat. For the last two-and-a-half years, I've been constantly dieting."

We noted that depression had currently taken her appetite and led her to the edge of an eating disorder's trap.

There seemed to be enough effects on her biological functioning to consider the use of antidepressant medication, so I decided to explore this further with her.

"Jane, there's a view of depression that suggests that when it begins to affect things like sleeping, appetite, concentration, and energy, as well as thoughts and feelings, it's worth considering pills. Not that pills cure depression just by themselves, but that people are made up of biochemicals as well as hopes, wishes, thoughts, feelings, and spirits. Maybe depression can have effects on *all* of those things. Do you think it might be worth us considering how to fight depression at the biochemical level as well?"

She agreed to consider this further, so we talked in depth about the possible risks, options, and benefits of antidepressant medication. We agreed to a trial of antidepressants in which she would pay particular attention to the areas in which depression had been affecting her body. She was concerned that the antidepressant might cloud her thinking, so we agreed that if that proved to be the case, we would need to change the medication or stop medicating altogether. We both recognized the importance of clear thinking in freeing a person from depression's grip.

Using this approach, I have found that the prescription of medication can be transformed from a process filled with potential misunderstanding and conflict to one of shared ideas, informed co-research, and client agency.

Reflections

I firmly believe that reflexive practices are one of the key strengths of my narrative approach to psychiatry. Because of that belief, I have attempted to build a myriad of reflexive loops into my work. These encompass a number of spheres of influence. Reflexive loops are not new to psychiatry, but one of the unique facets of the narrative approach is the explicit inclusion of the client in their development. This activity works against the traditional flow of power in the therapist-client relationship. It helps create an atmosphere of respect and a real valuing of the client's knowledge and abilities.

I seek constantly to ask questions to which I genuinely do not know the answers. These are the areas where I assume I am most likely to learn new ideas and practices from the client, and I am rarely disappointed. This process is, I believe, fundamentally different from both modernist psychiatric practices and strategic approaches to therapy. In the latter, the client is claimed to be the expert, but the therapist (usually in private consultation with other therapists) actually determines the value and "correctness" of that expertise, using selective attention and "reframing."

I am aware that my practice is open to accusations of subjectivity and anecdotalism—two aspects of knowledge viewed as highly suspect and unscientific within modernist research medicine. Paradoxically, within a postmodern, narrative framework, the subjective and anecdotal nature of knowledge is seen as one of its greatest strengths. The more subjective and anecdotal the information, the nearer it tends to come to a client's lived experience—and it is within the client's vast repertoire of lived experience that unique accounts and outcomes are assumed to be most likely to originate.

Because of this assumption, I try to saturate my work with reflexive practices. This shows itself first in the very structure of the questioning and recording during the therapeutic session. I strive to check and cross-check, questioning the client on whether I am recording their stories accurately and in the manner that they would prefer. Fortunately, no one has ever objected to the recording process.

The Reflexive Alliance

After a session, I write an account of the conversation, including any questions that have occurred to me later, and send it to the client to consider further. This is not a traditional psychiatric practice. Usually, the patient's history is recorded in his file, and occasionally a copy is sent to the general practitioner. The psychiatrist's conclusions are also recorded in the file, to be considered by other psychiatrists who might come into future contact with the patient. Those conclusions would then be measured against the prevailing standards of best psychiatric practice. The patient is not usually privy to these expert musings, unless he makes specific application to read his file.

Narrative-informed psychiatric practice expects psychiatrist and client to work in alliance against the impact of the problem on the client's life. If I take this perspective on my interactions with clients, it would be foolish of me to keep my ally in the dark. In Jane's case, I sent her a copy of the history I had recorded and asked her to consider it before we next met.

At that next session, I asked, "Jane, what did you think about the history I sent you? I am sorry there was a bit of jargon in it, like 'syndromal major depressive episode (nonpsychotic),' but my profession insists that I record things like that. I hope it didn't put you off." She shook her head, and I continued, "If you would like me to explain any of it, I would be happy to." Again, a shake of her head. "Well, what did you think? Was there anything there that was wrong, or anything that stood out in particular? Anything we should maybe look at further?"

She reread the copy that I handed to her and replied: "There were a few bits that surprised me, I couldn't believe that I had said them. There are things there that I know are true, and some things that hadn't occurred to me before."

"What sort of things are you thinking of?"

"It was weird to see that I'd said things like 'I'm horrible,' and that bit about boyfriends. It's like it's a significant part of my life, and I try not to see it that way. At first, I read it and went 'Urgggh.' It was quite disturbing. Then I thought that it was a good idea."

"So what bits made you go 'Urgggh'?"

"Well, a lot of it appeared a bit harsh. I thought what a complete mess it all is. All of it is true, but it looks such a big deal when put all together. It was good to get it, though, because when you come out after seeing you, you can't remember what you said, and reading this allows you to decide if you are on the right track, or have said anything untrue."

"After reading it, is there anything that you think doesn't ring true, or needs changing?"

"Yes, the bit about 'when I was a kid, I was permanently scared.' That's not right. And I don't think that I was a 'horrible child.'"

We talked about that some, and I agreed to record: "When I was a kid, I wasn't permanently scared. I had a happy childhood. I was scared when I got into trouble. I was spoilt rotten. I don't think it was as bad as me being a 'horrible child.' I would push and push, and I still do that sometimes, although I'm often not aware of it."

"Did I get the boyfriend bit out of perspective, maybe?"

She shook her head. "It's a messy part. I never saw my relationships as affecting my behavior, because I don't see myself as very experienced. I tend to think, 'I don't know what to think, so I'll shut up.'"

Her comment reminded me of how in both socially constructed therapist-client and male-female relationships, there were pressures on the client or woman to be silent. I asked, "Jane, do you think there's any chance of that showing itself here, in our relationship?" She looked puzzled, so I added, "I mean, if you don't know what to think, you might just shut up?"

"Yes, it might. Sometimes I'll talk all around it and annoy everyone, and sometimes I'll just shut up."

"Would it be okay if we paid some attention to that if we ever found it happening? I would hate for you to think that you had to be silent here, just as I would hate you to feel that you had to answer all of my questions."

She agreed to our doing that, and we went on to discuss how she had progressed in her struggle against depression since we last met.

A further reflexive loop is created when reflections themselves are recorded and forwarded to the client. Reflections on reflections are then invited, until the client is satisfied that her preferred histories are being accurately recorded.

This is an extremely rigorous process, which stretches the current accepted standard of psychiatric history to a new limit. One advantage of the postmodernist concept of coconstructed reality is acceptance that a person has many histories, of many selves. All these histories are worthy of exploration and expression. The goal is to assist people in developing the self-descriptions they prefer (rather than those descriptions defined by problems such as depression). We should not be surprised if it takes a while to achieve that.

Communities of Concern

A further reflexive loop is formed when I seek clients' permission to discuss any of their questions or discoveries with other clients who might be struggling against similar problems. Many clinicians would express grave concern about such a practice, pointing out the dangers of breaching client confidentiality. I am always very careful to seek the client's consent to these uses of personal material. If the client does give his consent to being involved, I am also careful to ask if he would prefer to be known by a pseudonym. Surprisingly, everyone to whom I have put my request has granted it in one form or another. There is a particular willingness to do so when clients discover that stories of other clients' experiences are valuable to their own quests.

Such activity works quite differently from standard psychiatric practices that emphasize comparison of the patient with standardized norms and large research cohorts. I find it can assist many clients in breaking through the terrible isolation created by the problems they face. The sharing of discoveries also offers evidence of clients being able to help others as well as themselves—an experience usually denied them within traditional individual therapies.

Over a period of time, it becomes possible to create around therapist and client a virtual group or community of people committed to seeking freedom from similar problems. This group can then act as both a synergistic and an appreciative audience for the process of change.

It is hard to overemphasize the importance of this activity in my everyday practice. Inherent in social constructionism is the belief that a social community needs to be available to assist a person in the development of preferred stories and ways of thinking, acting, and being.

I introduce a client to these communities of concern in a number of different ways. I have slowly developed an archive of written material from the process of narrative-informed therapy. This archive consists of letters, writing, and poetry, and I make a point of inviting each client as she ends therapy to edit her own story as drafted within our correspondence. I then offer her the choice of keeping it for herself or entering it into the archives, altering and removing parts that might infringe on her boundaries of privacy.

When something a client says triggers a connection for me, I often find myself muttering, "Hold on a minute . . . ," rushing over to the file cabinet, pulling out a wad of papers, rustling loudly and dramatically through them, then reading aloud something I believe of relevance. Often, the client also finds the words relevant, and I then invite her to consider this discovery in relation to her own developing stories. Eventually, many of these reflections will in turn join the archive.

I also try to draw on other narrative archives (such as those of David Epston and the Vancouver Anti-Anorexia/Anti-Bulimia League) in order to broaden the knowledge base. This sharing of archives is also an attempt to dilute my own effects on the coconstruction process. I firmly believe that the wider and richer the stories and shared experiences available within the communities of concern, the greater the opportunity for people to discover elements both similar to and different from their own. Important discoveries lie in both. This process of what has now become a global sharing stands in contrast to dominant cultural and professional discourses of hoarded knowledge as power and of competitive research practices.

Written archives take time and energy to develop and may lack the freshness and spontaneity required to capture the constantly changing patterns of everyday unique outcomes. A more immediate reflexive loop is formed by seeking permission to pass on material orally; this can permit very rapid interchanges of ideas from day to day.

Professional Supervision

A further, less contentious reflexive loop that I have worked to develop is one of professional supervision. Finding a narrative supervisor is no easy task, but I am fortunate to be working in a small city with a group of practitioners who have embraced narrative with commitment and passion. I have found it essential to my work—and also to my personal well-being—to attend both personal supervision and a regular narrative interest group. My experience of supervision in this manner is fundamentally different from that found in other therapeutic models. I experience it as a central example of "walking the narrative talk." Cooperation, mutual discovery, creative synergy, respect, and sharing are implicit aspects of the supervision process. Sometimes we struggle to pin down who is supervising whom; most of the time, that question is just plain irrelevant. A community of concerned therapists and counselors has become essential to my own process of choosing my preferred description of myself as a narrative psychiatrist.

Personal Transformation

When I first introduced narrative practices into my everyday work, I remember thinking that I was entering unexplored territory that could easily be subject to considerable interpretation and criticism. It was a territory with a language and cultural practices that were new to me. Only after satisfying myself that these practices had a strong ethical and moral basis did I feel comfortable employing them at all. The opportunities for abuse, and for using knowledge of coconstruction to dominate and distort rather than to liberate and heal, seemed enormous.

These ideas were just so "right," so "experience-near" to my own experiences, that they seemed unavoidable. They opened up possibilities of tackling problems that had in the past deeply frustrated and disheartened me. Nevertheless, with the benefit of hindsight, I think I was naive in failing to appreciate all the subtle but profound changes that postmodern ideas would introduce.

My first reaction was to recoil in horror at how easily some of my training in modernist practices had led me to unknowingly silence the people seeking help from me and to coconstruct their view of themselves as flawed, pathological, or powerless. I had been taught, for example, that patients with problems like anorexia or self-mutilation were "manipulative" or "personality disordered." According to this view, they had chosen their self-destructive lifestyle in preference to the "normal" lifestyle that "proper treatment" would have provided for them. It had never occurred to me before that the "proper treatment" might *in itself* contain elements of domination, coercion, control, and normalization—elements that supported the problem and dominant power hierarchies rather than the person. Such elements, despite their good intentions, stood in the way of people seeking self-agency, freedom, and true responsibility.

When the full impact of those discoveries struck me, I seriously considered leaving psychiatry. I (along with the vast majority of students entering medicine) had set out to help people, not abuse, dominate, or blame them. What, I raged, had been done to me? This was one of the few occasions when I was glad of the length of time involved in medical and psychiatric training. After so long in the business, it was difficult to figure out what else I might be qualified for!

So I decided to stick with it, to try to understand how this paradox had come about, and to attempt to fully realize medicine's stated aims of healing and relief of suffering. I remain glad that I did. Over time, I have been able to acknowledge how medical and psychiatric training equipped me with skills and knowledge that can equally well stand against processes of pathologization, domination, internalization, and abuse as for them. I try to remind myself that the rampant medicalization of human distress is also an attempt to stop blaming victims—an attempt to relieve them of the crushing responsibility for their own suffering.

There are always alternative stories.

Doing No Harm

One of medicine's founding maxims, "First do no harm," remains a keystone of practice. But if you are not to harm, you need first to have your eyes open to the harm that you do—even that harm done with the best of intentions.

Narrative has shown me the harm implicit in many everyday, accepted psychiatric practices—even "best psychiatric practice." For example, it is expected that staff meet together at reviews to talk about and analyze patients, their histories, and presumed pathologies. The patients themselves are excluded from this process, except when further questions need to be asked of them or when doctors want to communicate diagnoses and treatment plans.

The person's exclusion from the history sharing and speculation is viewed as either necessary (because it is assumed that distress would result) or of no particular relevance. I now believe that such exclusions are both relevant and potentially harmful. They set a boundary between patient/disease and experts/solutions rather than between people and problems, which is the more helpful distinction.

Reviews of this type strongly contribute to objectification and allow little possibility for the person herself to be a part of reflective process. In such a setting, it is also all too easy for the staff's conversation to turn to descriptions of the patient as "manipulative," "attention-seeking," "personality disordered," or just plain responsible for her ills. This is especially likely to occur when the problem is not responding to treatment in the expected, accepted manner. Such assumptions clearly have profound effects on how staff treat clients. It is not that such assumptions are necessarily right or wrong, but rather that they are less likely to develop when clients are intimately involved and valued in the assessment and treatment process.

Simply having the client present at reviews does not solve all problems of exclusion, however. Professional conversations can simply move behind closed doors. It is also easy, because of the considerable power differential between staff and client, to silence or inhibit any alternative views that the client may hold and to leave her feeling silenced and isolated among powerful, all-knowing professionals.

What seems to be required is staff committed to separating people out from problems and to working in a culture that pays more than lip service to valuing people, cooperation, and mutual respect. Developing and maintaining such a culture is in itself a considerable challenge.

Collegial Reactions

Introducing my colleagues to these narrative ideas and practices has produced some interesting and surprising experiences. Not all of them have been pleasant. I have been accused several times of being "too involved with the client," the implication being that I have joined with the client in his pathology. This is particularly likely to occur when I have supported a client in speaking out against traditional aspects of the medical system that seem unhelpful to him. Interestingly, none of my clients have ever suggested that they feel I have become overinvolved in their problems. On the contrary, they often support me in recognizing my own limitations. Many of them have indicated that if I do become overinvolved, and the problem begins to dominate me, I am unlikely to be of much use to them. I think they have a good point.

More recently, I have been accused of being too dogmatic and inflexible, too dominated by this narrative business to consider *other* methods of treatment. I find this criticism particularly perplexing. I wonder how it is that my passion and excitement are sometimes experienced as dogma. I wonder if it is possible to introduce these ideas from a position of privilege in a hierarchical system without eliciting just accusations of abusing power. I wonder how it is that I have explained these ideas so clumsily that staff interpret narrative as just another eclectic method rather than a postmodernist perspective put into practice. I have occasionally doubted my own sanity and thought back wistfully to the "good old modernist days" when everything seemed a lot simpler. But only occasionally. I remember speaking to Julie two days after attending a seminar by David Epston and the Auckland Anti-Anorexia/Anti-Bulimia Leagues. Prior to the seminar, I had been about to launch into a family-based refeeding program with her, which she had already shown some reluctance to enter. I had been assuming that it was her family circumstances that were making her anorexic. The seminar had suggested that different assumptions were possible.

I explained that I had just been to this amazing seminar and gave her some of the Auckland Leagues' archives to read.

"What do you think?" I asked, hardly waiting for her to finish the first page.

She hesitated, and looked at me appraisingly. "It looks interesting."

I wondered what to do next, then remembered a psychotherapy supervisor who had once advised me that when in doubt, explain the dilemma.

"Look, Julie, I think I was just about to launch into something that would have been a big mistake. Here I am believing that you and your family are the problem, when anorexia is. It never occurred to me that people fighting anorexia might experience my asking them lots of questions about food and weight, and constantly expecting them to be weighed and measured when they can't say no, as abusive and supportive of the problem. That kind of shocked me when I heard it, and I really don't think I can use that approach any more.

"Now, I know that changing tacks like this is probably going to make you wonder if I know what I am doing. You might decide that you don't have any faith in me any more, and that would be okay. I can refer you on to someone else if you want, but I really think that we should give this other approach a try. But I guess I need to warn you that it is kind of new to me and maybe we are both going to have to learn along the way. What do you think?"

Julie nodded. "Okay."

We are both still learning.

Notes

P. 123, *refinements of the asylum:* Rabinow, P. (1984). *The Foucault reader: An introduction to Foucault's thought.* London: Penguin.

P. 124, *systems of ordering and control:* Penfold, P. S., & Walker, G. A. (1983). *Women and the psychiatric paradox.* Montreal, Canada: Eden Press.

P. 124, *discovering workable alternatives:* Tomm, K. (1989). Externalising the problem and internalising personal agency. *Journal of Strategic and Systemic Therapies, 8*(1), 54–59.

P. 125, *doctors or professionals report:* Maguire, G. P. (1983). The psychiatric interview. Chap. 11 of *Companion to psychiatric studies*. London: Churchill Livingstone.

P. 128, *narrative-informed therapies:* Epston, D. (1991). *Personal correspondence of Auckland League archives*. Auckland, New Zealand: private publication; Vancouver Anti-Anorexia/Anti-Bulimia League (1995). *The undead*. Vancouver: private publication; Madigan, S. (1994). Body politics. *Family Therapy Networker, 18*(6), pp. 27–29.

P. 128, *Mental Health Act:* New Zealand Department of Health. (1992). *Mental health (compulsory assessment and treatment)*. Wellington: New Zealand Department of Health.

P. 129, *starvation and anorexia nervosa:* Pirke, K. M., & Ploog, D. (Eds.). (1984). *The psycho-biology of anorexia nervosa*. Berlin: Springer-Verlag.

P. 130, *from medical school onward:* Kaplan, I., Sadock, B. J., & Grebb, J. A. (1994). The doctor patient relationship and interview techniques. Chap. 1 of *Synopsis of psychiatry*. Baltimore: Williams & Wilkins.

P. 131, *at a point in time:* Sartorius, N. (1992). *The ICD-10 classification of mental health and behaviour disorders—clinical descriptions and diagnostic guidelines*. Geneva: World Health Organization.

P. 131, *formulations of evolving knowledge:* American Psychiatric Association. (1994). *Diagnostic and statistical manual of mental disorders, 4th ed.* Washington, D.C.: American Psychiatric Association.

P. 138, *other aspects of people's experience:* Mid-Island Tribal Council. (1993). *In search of a "just therapy": The Mid-Island Tribal Council context*. Dulwich Centre Newsletter, (1), 15–20.

P. 147, *most likely to originate:* White, M. (1989). The process of questioning: A therapy of literary merit? In *Selected papers*. Adelaide, Australia: Dulwich Centre Publications.

Chapter Six

Countering Alcoholic Narratives

John Winslade
Lorraine Smith

Counseling for people experiencing problems with alcohol and other drug use is an area of professional specialization that has been somewhat isolated from the developments of ideas in related fields. We do not think such isolation is useful. Therefore, in this chapter, we want to argue for the relevance and usefulness of narrative thinking in the domain of alcohol and other drug counseling and to demonstrate some applications in practice.

It is not our purpose to critique treatment practices or to suggest that there is not much that is valuable and useful in the current bodies of knowledge regarding the "problems of alcohol." Rather, we want to pose some questions that arise from the narrative metaphor and to illustrate the application of a narrative approach to work in this area. However, some introduction to the rationale behind the narrative approach is necessary, because we are aware that we are proposing some things that will be quite foreign to those familiar with the established practices in this field of counseling.

The language typically used in the literature about alcohol counseling has a distinctly modernist ring about it. It is laced with medical metaphors (diagnosis, assessment, treatment, recovery) that connect it with the kind of scientific discourse by which knowledge has become validated in many fields of psychology in the twentieth century. One of the results of this has been the establishment in the public mind of the concept of alcoholism as a "disease." Many of the approaches to helping people experiencing problems associated with heavy drinking have been premised on this idea. But the notion that the desire to drink is a medical condition is relatively recent, and it has been contested from a number of quarters. Nevertheless, even many of those who criticize it continue to use some of the terminology that locates alcohol counseling within a medical discourse. For example, they still use the word *treatment*. Now, we do not say that this idea is wrong, and we would certainly acknowledge that for many people it has been a life-saving idea that has helped them bring about significant changes in their relationship with alcohol. What we would dispute is the extension of a useful idea into a statement of universal truth.

We regard the established ideas of alcohol "treatment" as valuable stories that have achieved a certain dominance in a particular culture at a particular time in history. But like many other dominant stories, they can prevent other stories from seeing the light of day. It is our purpose here not to dispute the value of the "alcohol as a disease" metaphor, but to propose some alternative metaphors that might lead to different kinds of knowledge about the ways of alcohol. This effort is inspired by our belief that innovative practice develops out of the interplay of many kinds of knowledge rather than out of the quest for singular truth. In the field of alcohol counseling, we would expect the "one size fits all" approach to leave many people struggling with their problems, unassisted by the available alternatives for counseling.

One of our guiding principles has been the desire to avoid the language of personal deficit that has become so prevalent in much of modern psychology. Kenneth Gergen has explained the gathering momentum of the tendency in the twentieth century to accumulate a series of technologies with which to ascribe psychological deficits to people. From his social constructionist perspective, the term *alcoholic* is an example of a description that has the potential to transform a person from a responsible subject to an object of medical-psychological practice. It marks a person as different from others, as occupying a particular category of personhood. It creates a "nonideal" identity for the person that, because of the power that lies behind the technologies that create the term, tends to perdure across time and situation.

Gergen points out several results of this trend. One is that the deficit language serves to undermine local, familial, or personal knowledge about how to deal with alcohol problems and to grant privileged status to the knowledge of the professional who has been trained in the established truth. In this way, it shores up the position of the professional in the counseling relation and requires the client to submit herself to a professional process. Such submission leads to an enfeeblement of the person rather than an empowerment. We do not want to imply that practitioners of conventional alcohol treatment processes have no desire to empower their clients, but we do want to promote conscious attention to the ways in which discourses position us in disempowering relations that we might not otherwise choose.

In advancing a narrative style of working with alcohol problems, we are endeavoring to avoid such deficit language altogether. We also seek to foster and call forth alternative and local knowledge about how to deal with alcohol problems rather than rely narrowly on the stories and metaphors that have been favored by their establishment as scientific truth. In the process, we want to render transparent some of the cultural norms and social conventions around alcohol that, if left unexamined, are always likely to become implicated in the professional practice of alcohol counseling.

The advantages we see in using the narrative approach in this area of counseling include the opportunities to explore

- The many conflicting messages about alcohol that circulate in various communities
- The implication of discourses about race, gender, and class in the construction and maintenance of "alcohol problems"
- The effects of the normalization of alcohol and the effects on people of the definitions of "normal" patterns of alcohol use
- The impact of commonly held notions, such as "alcoholic," on the counseling process itself
- The opening up of space for descriptions of self that are not subsumed by the description that "alcohol trouble" brings
- The opening up of space for the development of lifestyles that are preferred over an "alcohol lifestyle"

General questions that might guide our collaborative inquiry (with our clients) in this area include the following:

- What purpose does alcohol serve in our social contexts? Who benefits? Who suffers?
- What are the tactics alcohol uses to seduce or overpower its subjects?
- How does alcohol recruit people into an alcoholic lifestyle?
- What might the career that alcohol has planned for people look like?
- What does alcohol convince other family members and associates about those who become its "injured parties"?
- What does alcohol have to convince its victims about in order to gain and maintain power?
- What does alcohol have to blind its admirers to in order to enjoy its continued influence?
- If I were alcohol, how would I set out to defeat a counselor or convince a counselor that I was not the problem?
- What circumstances in a person's life might alcohol exploit for its own purposes?
- If I were alcohol, how might I tempt a counselor into cynical indifference toward, or disrespect for, my loyal subjects?

Reflecting on Personal History

Some of the ways of speaking about alcohol that circulate in both lay and professional discourse seem to suggest that there are particular categories of persons for whom the kinds of questions we have just asked might be relevant. However, we believe that their relevance might apply much more widely than to the category of person labeled "alcoholic" by conventional assessment processes. To illustrate this point, I (John) will present some aspects of my personal history.

I have never seen myself as having any particular problems with alcohol or other drugs. Although I enjoy a drink from time to time, alcohol has never been something to which I have committed myself in a big way. I thought it would be useful to engage in some personal reflection on why this might be.

What I recognized was that there were influences in my life that I could connect with a sense of identity and a set of social relations that did not feature alcohol in a pivotal way. The social circles in which I have mixed have given me plenty of stories of sobriety or moderation with which to fashion my own thinking and social practices. I have naturally absorbed these moderating influences; they have become part of my habitual patterns of thought and behavior. You might even say that I have become dependent on them or addicted to them, in the sense that I do not, for example, remake my consciousness of them in every social situation where alcohol is available. They have become more automatic than that. In fact, I can get to the end of a social occasion and notice, on reflection, how I have kept my own alcohol consumption within quite moderate bounds without a lot of deliberate decision making.

But I can also look at my personal history in quite different ways. You might have inferred from what I said in the previous paragraph that there was no tradition of drug problems in my family. But this is not quite the case. I can think of half a dozen close family members for whom drug use has led to death, arrest, disease, emigration to escape police detection, and other major effects. All of these events that have happened to people around me are woven into the fabric of the family from which I have drawn important aspects of my identity. In contrast to my initial assumption that drugs have not played a large part in my life, I have in fact been substantially influenced by these personal histories. I have been charged with the task of defining myself in relation to them. But it is worth noting that the awareness of the influence of drugs in my family was not immediately available to me when I started thinking about this topic. My own stories about myself were not strongly bound up with stories about drugs as important influences.

What does this mean? I don't think it means that I am "in denial." This is a concept that has quite a following in the drug and alcohol counseling field, but to us it often seems quite dangerous, because it speaks of counselors "knowing better than" rather than "knowing with" their clients. The denial concept can serve to excuse practitioners from entering into dialogue about their clients' experiences and therefore lead them into communicating a message of superior knowledge and status.

What my history does say to me is that it is not really possible for us to live in the present world without our lives being affected in some way by drugs, even if the effects come indirectly through people we care about or who have a shaping influence on our lives. But it is also worth remembering that there are always other influences, other stories on which we can base our sense of self. There are always stories in our lives that provide counterplots to the adverse influence of drugs. Far from being a feature of denial, my usual lack of attention to some of the more problematic stories in my family history may be one of the reasons why I have not gotten into problems with drugs.

From a narrative perspective, stories come to have an influence in our lives as we devote our attention to them. Devoting our attention to stories of heavy drinking leads to different kinds of thinking and different kinds of daily practices from those that develop when we devote our attention to stories about moderation or sobriety. And if change is about shifting our attention from the ways we are positioned in one set of stories to the available positions we may take up in another set, then as counselors, we need to develop and elaborate on the conversational moves that facilitate such shifts in clients.

All of this suggests a way of thinking about how people get drawn into a lifestyle that strongly features alcohol or other drugs and leads to problematic or dangerous patterns of usage. The new thinking differs sharply from the assumptions that lie behind some of the more usual responses to alcohol problems. There is no reference to any inner essence or character of the person with the alcohol problem, whether this character is thought of as genetically determined or developmentally cast in concrete. Nor do we use the metaphors that see people as machines with faulty parts that can be fixed through reprogramming. Rather, we are interested in the postmodern emphasis on the *discourse* about alcohol—that is, the set of ideas that circulate in social and professional contexts and that define the limits of thinking about and relating to alcohol. These cultural scripts determine how people develop their relationships with alcohol.

The Problems of Totalizing Descriptions

The language we choose to use in relation to alcohol and to people who are experiencing difficulty with it is crucial. There are some ways of speaking about alcohol's influence that require people to adopt as an article of identity the statement "I am an alcoholic." This sounds like a totalizing description of a person's identity. It leaves little room for other descriptions of self as it invites the person to organize a sense of self around alcohol as a problem issue. Revising the statement to "I am a problem drinker" does not make things any better.

From a narrative perspective, we would call statements like "I am an alcoholic" *internalizing statements*. They locate whatever problem the person has been experiencing deep in some unchanging aspect of the individual's nature and therefore make it hard to change. They reify the problem—which has only ever been a social construct anyway—into some kind of biological reality. They generate an internalizing discourse that makes invisible the many social practices that promote, sustain, and nurture the life of the problem. They lead to the categorization of people, to marking them off as different from others. And when people are marked off as different, they can easily be discriminated against.

Language of Disability

There are other areas of life where this kind of thinking has been challenged more strongly than it appears to have been in relation to alcohol. Take, for example, the field of disability awareness.

Disability activists have been arguing in recent years that people with disabilities are marked as different by the labels they are given and, as a result, treated as second-class citizens. They have been pointing to the common language practices by which this oppression is achieved. They argue for respectful ways of speaking about people—for example, saying that someone is a "person with a disability" rather than a "disabled person".

The problem with the dominant way of talking that places the disability first is that it invites people with an impairment to develop their identity first and foremost around their "disability" rather than around any other talents and abilities they might have. Other family members, friends, associates, and employers are then invited to think in the same way about them. In this way, limited thinking gets built into limiting relations that restrict the person's quality of life. It is all too easy to go along with the assumption that it is the impairment that produces the limitations rather than the social context in which the impairment is defined as a disability.

Sexist Language

Consider also the feminist critique of sexist language, which has woken us up to ways in which the possibilities and opportunities that life offers have been systematically limited for women in ways they have not been for men. It has been in taken-for-granted linguistic assumptions that gender-based power relations have been established. As a result of the feminist critique, one hears less often the kind of statement that used to be common on quiz shows when a woman introduced herself: "I'm just a housewife."

Like the self-description "I am just a housewife," the statement "I am an alcoholic" reads to us as a declaration about a social role or position that is being used to define an aspect of identity. Moreover, neither statement was invented by the people who make it: both are comments learned in the language community where they originated, and then adopted as self-descriptions. We believe that, as they are uttered, they place the person who utters them into a subjugated social position.

"Alcoholic" Identity

We also believe there are real consequences that follow when the first statement a person makes about his or her identity concerns a problem. For example, such a statement promotes counseling practices that give great precedence, weight, and power to the problem story. Counselors are directed by the statement into detailed assessments and evaluations that focus both on the person and the problem. A word like *dependent*, as it is used in relation to alcohol, also serves as a powerful totalizing description, giving precedence to the problem story and implying moral weakness, lack of maturity, powerlessness, and reliance on others to "fix" the problem.

A statement like "I am an alcoholic" might blind both the counselor and the client to other interpretations of the client's lived experience, especially those aspects that do not fit within the description of "alcoholic" but can easily be overtaken by such a categorical and all-encompassing definition. Labels like "alcoholic" can also lead the counselor and the client to ignore or minimize the impact of social discourses about gender, race, and class on drinking practices and the powerful cultural pressures and expectations in favor of drinking. They also serve to locate problems with alcohol in individual psychopathology and mask the wider context in which the vast industry of alcohol thrives.

A Narrative Approach to Alcohol Counseling

After training in narrative therapy, I (Lorraine) began to work with a number of clients who were experiencing alcohol problems. Because I worked within a social constructionist framework and from a narrative perspective, I was uncomfortable with the implications of many of the specialized knowledges in the drug and alcohol counseling field.

I did not want to invite my clients, in our conversations together, into medicalized, deficit-oriented notions of their identity that might accompany the use of words like *treatment, recovery, remission, relapse, addiction, dependency, tolerance, substance abuse disorder, alcoholism, assessment, psychiatric diagnosis, alcoholic, problem drinker,* and *addict.* Such terminology suggested illness or disease. It implied a condition requiring specialized treatment from an expert in possession of knowledge to which the person with the condition needed to submit in order to "get better." Furthermore, such language did not seem to fit with a narrative emphasis on collaborative conversations in which the client plays a full part in the naming of the problem and in deciding the direction of therapy. It seemed to foster a therapeutic relationship based on a power relation to which I did not want to adhere. I wanted to develop ways of speaking about the problems people face in relation to alcohol that were more in tune with narrative thinking.

Inviting clients to join in the process of researching both the influence of alcohol and the influence of these conventional ways of speaking about alcohol has generated conversations that differ significantly from those involved in standard approaches to alcohol treatment. A common practice in narrative therapy is to write a letter to the client after a counseling session that is intended as a record of the session and also as a means of building on the developments that have occurred during counseling. The following excerpt from a letter I wrote after a counseling meeting with

Greg is one example of this kind of story-building and illustrates the language uses we are exploring.

Dear Greg,
   . . . You explained to me that taking a long hard look at alcohol and the trouble it brings brought you to the conclusion that this trouble is no longer acceptable, that you are no longer willing to put up with "alcohol trouble" in your life.
   Greg, was this the first step in protesting against "alcohol trouble" and the beginning of your rebellion against the troubles of an alcohol lifestyle? I'm remembering that you explained to me that it seems as if you almost inherited an alcohol lifestyle because it has always been such a big part of normal life. So how come you've been able to look alcohol in the eye and say, "No more!"?
   You told me that in your opinion alcohol tries to convince people, especially men, that it will increase their mana [ability to command respect] but that now you have come to the conclusion that alcohol actually steals mana. Has this discovery helped you to stand so staunchly against alcohol so far? Do you think that, as the influence of alcohol decreases in your life, pride in yourself will increase? If this is true, is your protest against "alcohol trouble" about taking back your mana? Is it sort of like recovering stolen property?
   You explained that at times alcohol has made some decisions on your behalf (decisions that do not fit with what you value and believe), and that actions and behaviour inspired by alcohol have often led to trouble and shame. Greg, am I right in guessing from this that you trust your own decision-making ability more than alcohol's decision-making ability? Am I right in thinking that this means that you trust your plans for your future more than you trust alcohol's plans for your future? Is this what you mean when you tell me you want to be more your own man than alcohol's man?
   I noticed that you had sussed [figured] out a lot about the ways of alcohol and that you were putting

this knowledge to use in your protest against alcohol trouble. As you continue to be so staunch are you finding that you are seeing even more clearly through the tricks and empty promises of alcohol?

I'm looking forward to meeting with you next week so you can catch me up with developments.

Lorraine

Externalizing Alcohol

It will be obvious from this letter that Greg and I had been engaged in an externalizing conversation about alcohol. Although alcohol is already an entity external to the person, it is our experience that the impact of alcohol is often "life-encompassing," and that it defines the person's self-perception as well as his view of relationships. Therefore, the externalization speaks not just of the bottle of beer but of aspects of a person's life and identity that have been storied by alcohol. The purpose of the externalization of "alcohol" is to disrupt the effects of internalizing descriptions such as "dependency," "alcoholic," and "addiction." By not using these words, we avoid taking on board the baggage that these descriptions bring with them—for example, shame, blame, weakness, helplessness, and loss of control, not to mention social stigma.

Clients often initiate an externalizing conversation with statements like "Alcohol's causing me grief." Although such statements can be helpful in terms of developing an externalization and often pave the way to mapping the impact of alcohol, we believe that an externalizing conversation also needs to be deconstructive of the *relationship* between the person and alcohol.

This way of speaking, if sustained, helps to separate the person not just from alcohol the chemical but from the many internalizing ways of thinking about alcohol that are commonly available to people like Greg. In this instance, we developed a conversation around the notion of "alcohol trouble." Other clients have come up with many other descriptions of the problem, such as "the great destroyer," "treacherous friend," "a bad buddy," "the trouble maker." They have also had much to say in response to inquiries about

- Some of the tactics alcohol employs in recruitment and selection
- Some of the ways in which alcohol attempts to overpower, to dominate and have control in their lives
- Some of the tools of entrapment and captivity that alcohol employs
- What alcohol promises, or gives away as free samples
- How alcohol dupes, swindles, and defrauds
- What alcohol demands in return

On the other hand, clients have also spoken of the ways in which they have managed to

- Put alcohol in its place
- Stand up to alcohol's dominating ways
- Retrieve what was rightfully theirs from alcohol's clutches (for example, dignity, esteem, money, hope)
- Protest or rebel against alcohol's regimen
- Strike out on their own without alcohol for company
- Free relationships from the influence of alcohol

Alcohol in Context

What might happen if we started to pursue these kinds of inquiries? What might we discover if we began to seriously think of alcohol problems as located in the social context in which we live rather than in individuals? What might happen if we were to let go of some of the humanistic or modernist assumptions about alcohol?

The narrative metaphor leads us to look at the alcoholic narratives circulating in our language communities. It suggests that, as individuals, we are given a series of positions that we can take up in relation to the discourse of alcohol lifestyles. These are hard to step out of, because they are made up of the assumptions that we take for granted in the linguistic and social worlds in which we live. Among such assumptions are the fixed nature of the word *alcoholic;* the principle "Once an alcoholic always an alcoholic"; the dynamic of codependency; the need for individuals with alcohol problems to "bottom out" before they start to improve; and the moral judgments behind the assertion that people must "admit" that they have a problem before they can be regarded as being on the road to "recovery."

If, however, we start from the assumption that alcohol lifestyles exist outside of persons, as part of the social discourse that surrounds us, we may start to notice some of the subtle ways in which we are invited every day to introduce the habits of alcohol into our lives.

We were reminded of this phenomenon on a trip to Australia. The reward we were offered for having traveled across "the ditch" from New Zealand was the privilege of buying some duty-free products. Ninety percent of these products were alcohol. Thus the message we were being given was that alcohol was the most valuable product we could take away with us as travelers.

Another example is the social conventions governing the use of glasses when we drink. We save the best and most expensive glasses for drinking alcohol, whereas if our friends ask for a glass of water, we tend to hand them a glass we bought at the thrift store. A message of value is given in each of these situations.

Take as another example the narratives that are told around alcoholic poisoning. I have drunk enough to make myself sick a few times in my life. It wasn't pleasant. But notice the difference between alcohol and other drugs. Take enough sleeping pills to poison your system and you are said to have overdosed, probably with suicide in mind. (Of course, because the person who took the pills is part of the language community that adheres to this discourse, it often *is* a suicide attempt.) But take enough alcohol to poison your system and we—especially men—say things like "Must have been a good night," tell boastful stories about it, laugh and wink and joke about it. The difference in meaning made around events that are physiologically similar points to the role of culture and discourse. The sense we make of the event— suicide attempt or good night out—is achieved by reference to the norms of culture rather than to the properties of the chemical itself.

There are a hundred other linguistic and social practices surrounding us every day that train and cajole us into alcoholic lifestyles. Think of the social expectations of reciprocity when someone buys you a drink. If several people are involved, one drink may become three or four drinks as a result of the implicit social obligation.

We were struck once by how several clients were speaking about a party they were going to as "a keg," giving the impression that "a keg" was a ritual in which alcohol was the guest of honor. From a narrative perspective, we would be curious about how alcohol came to achieve this status and what such status might mean in terms of the requirements of other guests to pay their due respects to the guest of honor.

At a conference of alcohol and drug workers, a man spoke about how secret drinking had taken over his wife's life, and when he had discovered the extent of the problem, secrecy had extended its tentacles to include him as well. We are interested in the underlying and unspoken statements about the meaning of drinking in our society (perhaps specifically women's drinking) that may have contributed to the "need" for secrecy. It is unlikely that they were invented by this couple.

A Personification of Alcohol

We could personify the alcohol lifestyle and call him Al. We say "him" not out of sexist exclusion, nor out of any neglect of problems women do face in relation to alcohol and other drugs, but because we think the historical and the current patterns of alcohol lifestyles have been largely male-defined in our culture.

We can all ask ourselves, if we care to, how Al has sought to befriend us over our lifetime. Al has always been made out to be a vibrant personality, a convivial companion, a teller of tall tales, a good mate. Al can also be a confidant in times of trouble, a solace when we are in pain. And what about Al the connoisseur, the man of the world, of fine taste and distinction? Or Al the high priest conducting initiation rites into adulthood, especially for young males?

Over time, we have all met Al. We can't avoid him. And he offers us no choice but to relate to him. We are offered several different kinds of relationship according to how we respond to his recruitment drives. Some of us are a little resistant at times. In any recruitment drive, there are some reluctant recruits—the half-hearted tipplers, the occasional social drinkers, the teetotalling party poopers.

Incidentally, the notion of resistance is best used to describe these people who resist Al's influence rather than to describe those who do not respond to "treatment" in the ways that counselors expect. As William Miller and Stephen Rollnick have shown, the latter use seduces counselors into ascribing to clients internal motivational traits, or their absence, rather than seeing motivation as the result of interactions between counselor and client. The problem is that the idea that resistance is located in the individual with a problem leads us back into deficit thinking. Resistance is usually ascribed to the client as a personal deficit. The idea of resistance in the counselor's mind can then set up a relationship built on a contest to overcome the resistance. Usually implied in such a contest is the assumption that authority and superior judgment lie with the counselor. We would recommend reserving this word for those who fail to be impressed by the requirements of the alcoholic culture in which we live. Such discipline in the use of language would help us avoid deficit ways of thinking. Miller has argued cogently against counselors ascribing resistance or lack of motivation to the client; he prefers to see this lack as part of a relational phenomenon. We support this stance, and would add that when discussing difficulties in the counseling relationship it may be productive to initiate an externalizing discussion about the restraints operating on the counseling.

But there is more to say about our personification of alcohol discourses. Al is a major mythical/cultural hero, as important to the day-to-day lives of New Zealanders (we can't speak with authority about other cultures but would invite readers to question their own social traditions in this regard) as Santa Claus is to six-year-old children. In New Zealand, we are told by advertising that Al stands behind the successes of our All Black rugby team and our yachting heroes. Such influence must be taken seriously, we inevitably conclude. If the assertions are true, we cannot but admire those bright-eyed enthusiasts who model themselves so wholeheartedly on the heroic Al. These people should not be regarded as sick or disturbed individuals whose genes prevent them from noticing when they are causing danger to themselves and others.

No, these individuals are the successes of a society that gives Al such a prominent place. They really take Al to heart. They adopt his mottoes. They speak his lines. They commit their passionate youth to worshiping his dogma. They participate every week in Al's rituals of consumption and regurgitation. Heroically and selflessly, these neophytes and converts blithely ignore their own and their loved ones' safety in the pursuit of Al's rewards. The more zealous of these youthful believers eventually mature into Al's stalwart faithful, who serve at his altar for many years. The rest of us, meanwhile, are examples of mediocre zeal toward (or outright resistance to) the culture in which Al seeks to hold sway.

Some of us are recruited into positions in the selling of alcohol. We are not villainous people. We do care about the damage that alcohol does in society. We are not members of any conspiracy. We are simply earning our living and catering to the needs of people—the needs that Al has trained us to think and feel that we have.

Some of us are recruited into positions of policing alcohol consumption. We may have official roles as police officers or schoolteachers, or we may simply take on policing responsibilities as friends and family members of people who give themselves selflessly to Al's service and drink tirelessly in his honor. Al can even recruit counselors into this role.

Some of us are recruited into roles in which we deal with overconsumption. We become helpers, rescuers, advisors, interpreters of danger. Al, of course, is quite concerned any time we do these jobs overzealously and in ways that interfere with his recruitment drives. So he has learned to live with and accommodate and even fund us on certain conditions. These conditions are that we pay attention to him when he makes "helpful" suggestions about the way we should think about alcohol problems. Al needs us just as much as he needs the sellers and providers. He needs us to help him hide the skeletons in his closet. Every year, for example, he has a few thousand deaths to pretend are not his fault. He has a lot of violence to project onto other causes. Al is a thief who steals money and health from people. And sometimes he is a two-timing "friend" who steals partners from people who trusted him. All these skeletons need to be protected.

What he needs from us are ways of thinking about alcohol problems that blame the person in the middle of the problem rather than Al himself. So he sponsors the tireless search for the gene that will predict which people are going to go over the top in dedicating their lives to his worship. If the rest of us can be reassured that we don't have the gene, we won't be tempted to revolt against Al's influence. Al promotes the idea of alcoholism as a disease, and he is prepared to sacrifice some of his most zealous disciples to this cause, because he knows that in this way he can more easily reassure thousands of others that it is okay for them to continue to indulge heavily. Al likes treatment programs that focus on the individual and explain alcohol problems solely in relation to the internal dynamics of the psyche or the faulty programming of the human computer or the dysfunctional family. Such modes of treatment distract the attention and energy of the helpers from the social narratives by which Al continues to recruit and maintain commitment among his followers. As long as a deficit can be found in the person, Al is happy, because attention can be diverted from his influence.

We hope we have said enough to indicate what we mean by alcohol lifestyles. We have mentioned only a few of Al's tricks and strategies. What we would suggest is that people who work with those who are influenced by Al can learn more by questioning their clients directly. Those who have suffered greatly at the hands of Al know many more of his tricks.

Getting a Divorce from Al

Daniel was one such person, who came to me (Lorraine) for counseling. Together, we generated a conversation around the influence of Al in his life. In response to my questions, Daniel developed the metaphor to the point of understanding his relationship with Al in a deconstructive way. He was reaching the point of deciding that he wanted to arrange a "divorce" from Al. The following is a letter I wrote to Daniel after a counseling session. It serves as a record of the exploration of the problems he was struggling with in counseling and also as an example of how a new story can be developed from a narrative perspective.

Dear Daniel,
    I have been thinking about our meeting today and thought it would be useful to both of us if I put into writing some of the things we talked about. If there are

things I have got wrong or that you feel I need to understand more fully it would be great if you could let me know next time we meet.

Daniel, when we first met, you explained that you've had a long and troublesome relationship with alcohol (Al) and that over the years "Al" has stolen away more and more of your self to the point where, at times, it has seemed as though you were more "Al's man" than your own man. Over the years "Al" has persuaded you to hate yourself, stolen away your ability to love others and convinced you that you were going nowhere. Also, at times, "Al" has taken over your memory [blackouts] and made decisions about behaviour and actions that do not fit with your values and desires for your life. You explained that for these reasons you have had a gutsful of your relationship with "Al."

Daniel, you told me that "Al" endeavours to demand all your attention, commitment and passion, attempting to drive everything else out of your life, have complete control over your present and your future, to be in the driver's seat and at the controls, leaving you little space to be your own person. You agreed that "getting a divorce from Al" was a good description of where you are at in this relationship.

Daniel, I am very curious about how, over the last month, you have managed to resist "Al's" demands for you to return to the relationship. I understand that this stand has been far from easy and that, like many divorces, it has at times seemed like a mine-filled battlefield. I can't help wondering what "Al" has not managed to steal away from you that has assisted you in this separation, that has enabled you to not only survive, but also be 100 percent successful in maintaining this separation for over a month? I wonder what you have kept from "Al" that has enabled you firstly to decide that "Al" playing havoc with your life is unacceptable and secondly to believe that you have a right to something a little different and better for your life? You explained the frustration you feel about your unfulfilled potential. Do you think it's possible that "Al" never managed to completely steal

away your sense of your personal talents and abilities?
Is it possible that this knowledge of your unfulfilled
potential, as well as opening the door to depression,
is also assisting you to stand so powerfully against the
demanding battering of alcohol? You also told me that
sheer determination to reclaim your right to be your
own man rather than "Al's" man was keeping you
going in this mission. Is determination a quality that
"Al" has blinded you to in the past? I mean, did you
know that you possessed such gutsy determination or
has it come as a surprise to you?

Daniel, as you continue to stand against the
demands of alcohol, is it possible that you will retrieve
other "stolen property" that will assist you to "stay
divorced" and assist you also in the creation and
development of a lifestyle that is more suited to you
than one dominated by "Al"? If this is so, do you have
any ideas or suspicions about what this stolen property
might be?

I really liked that story about "Al" battering on
the door. It kind of fits with your other story about
"Al" being like a demanding and abusive lover. And I
am very curious about how you not only managed to
get "Al" outside the door but to lock it as well! I'm
remembering how quickly you told me the door was
locked and that you had the only key. Where do you
think you found the key?

You explained how depression was attacking you
and attempting to wrest the key away and open the
door to "Al." Daniel, I understood you as saying that in
the past depression always invited alcohol in and they
worked together to strengthen each other's place in
your life. I was thinking how, even in our meeting,
depression attempted to convince both of us that
alcohol was the only remedy available for formidable
cases of depression, almost as if depression was a
poison and alcohol was an antidote. From your
experience, do you think it's true that alcohol is a
remedy for depression? Do you think that over the
years alcohol and depression have worked together to
strengthen each other's place in your life or worked
together to assist you to develop your full potential?

You explained some of the methods depression uses to increase its power: for example, keeping you in bed all day, isolating you from other people. Does your awareness of these methods and of their effect sometimes assist you to rebel against the rule of depression? For example though depression tried hard to persuade you to miss our meeting today, you somehow managed to disobey this instruction. Is this rebellion more in keeping with you being your own man or more consistent with you being ruled by depression? Have you had some other practice at rebelling against the rule of depression or are you just beginning to put this knowledge to use in this way? If your familiarity with depression and its tactics of control does provide you with some knowledge for successful rebellion, is this knowledge also useful or important in your mission to divorce "Al" and become your own person?

The image I had in my mind after our last meeting was that you were becoming your own freedom fighter. Daniel, as you put more ground between yourself and "Al," do you think that you will discover more and more weapons with which to resist the onslaughts of alcohol?

I have many more questions but am hoping I haven't already overwhelmed you. If any of these thoughts or questions are interesting to you, we can discuss them more fully when we next meet, or if you feel inclined to write some responses that would be great.

Yours in allegiance against the tyranny of "Al,"
Lorraine

Responsibility

In the conversation I had with Daniel, I was not asking him, in a typical humanistic way, to "take responsibility" for the problems that he was experiencing. From a social constructionist perspective, this is nonsense. We are not individually responsible for the discourses that operate on our thinking, and if we take on such responsibility, we can become paralyzed by consciousness of personal deficiency.

None of us can claim to have invented Al's way of speaking (and neither did the brewery bosses or the media moguls). At the same time, we are all collectively and continuously reinventing him whenever we use his language. Al's social conventions of tomorrow are what we are all forming today as we perpetuate or alter the conventions of yesterday in our practices and our words. So it makes sense to speak in ways that place Al outside of ourselves. This way of speaking gives us a position from which to deconstruct his effects on our lives, and as Daniel was doing, to claim our lives back from Al's control.

The kinds of conversations Daniel and I engaged in developed from asking questions that invited a separation of the person from the demands of alcohol and a tracing of the effects of alcohol in the life of the person. Some examples of these kinds of questions are

- Can you tell me some of the things that alcohol has been robbing you of?
- How would you describe your relationship with alcohol? How much power does alcohol have in this relationship, and how much power do you have? How would you prefer the power to be divided?
- How does alcohol want you to relate to your family? To your partner?
- Do alcohol's ways of living require any energy from you that you would prefer to devote to your work? How do they persuade you to give up this energy?
- How does alcohol trick you into getting into trouble with the law?
- What does alcohol convince you of in order to get you to do things that you know aren't safe or healthy for you?

And we can ask of other family members who may be part of the counseling:

- How has alcohol's influence over your father affected you and your relationship with him?
- What sort of role has alcohol got you into the habit of playing as it has taken over more and more of your husband's/wife's/father's/mother's/son's/daughter's life?

- How did your family get recruited into alcohol's lifestyle?
- What do each of you think alcohol has stolen from your family?

Implicit in all of these questions is a respectful recognition that the person is not to blame for the problem. However, as the letter to Daniel illustrates, we would also want to offer serious invitations to take up a position of responsibility in the relationship with alcohol. Daniel is given openings to think of himself as an actor in his own life, not just a puppet of alcohol. He is asked to explore the possibilities of agency against the problem. He is invited to take responsibility for solutions to the problems alcohol has drawn him into rather than responsibility for the problems themselves.

Reclaiming Agency

Renee's story further illustrates the importance of promoting personal agency. Renee was twenty when her probation officer suggested she meet with me (Lorraine) because she was in trouble with the law. She was also five months pregnant. She expressed despair and hopelessness about ever being able to get the better of alcohol and described herself as having no hope that she could stop drinking. She also spoke of being overtaken by guilt about the impact of alcohol on the health of her unborn baby. She was being beaten by her boyfriend for drinking while pregnant.

I asked Renee whether she thought guilt supported a close relationship with alcohol or supported her in her desire to put some limits on that relationship. Renee was clear that guilt and shame strengthened the power of alcohol. I did not want to strengthen the position of guilt in her life, but I also did not want to participate or collude in the minimizing of the disastrous effects alcohol was in all probability having on the development of her child.

An externalizing conversation enabled us to map out in detail the effects of alcohol on unborn babies. We explored Renee's ideas about why guilt was so strong, about the possible effects of alcohol on her baby, and about existing medical information on the effect of alcohol on the unborn. This sort of conversation could have played into the hands of guilt, but separating the person from the problem and consistently speaking in an externalizing way served to place the blame on the shoulders of alcohol rather than on Renee.

In subsequent conversations, Renee spoke about this conversation as a turning point in her relationship with alcohol, saying, "It got me thinking about what alcohol was doing to me . . . that alcohol was trying to get my baby off me . . . that alcohol wanted to be the mother even . . ."

I wrote the following letter to Renee after our first meeting. It serves as a record of the way I was attempting to coauthor with her a narrative that would disrupt the narrative that might be supporting alcohol.

> Dear Renee,
>
> I have been thinking about our meeting yesterday, about you and your battle against "alcohol destruction" in your life and in the life of your baby. I couldn't help wondering what squarely facing alcohol as an enemy says about your courage and determination to refuse to let "alcohol destruction" claim your baby as another of its victims.
>
> I am wondering who, out of alcohol, your friends, your boyfriend, your baby and yourself would most value and understand the strength it takes to face up to "alcohol destruction?"
>
> I am wondering who, out of alcohol, your friends, your boyfriend, your baby and yourself would most value and understand the cost of, and the difficulty in, looking alcohol in the eye and limiting its destructive power in your life?
>
> Who out of alcohol, your friends, your boyfriend, your baby and yourself would most support you in your battle to take control of your life back from "alcohol destruction"?
>
> Renee, I guess some of these questions may not be easy to answer, so I just want to let you know that I think of them as questions to ponder on and wonder about rather than as questions to which you will necessarily have quick, easy answers. So I'm hoping that you will bear with me because I have a few more on the tip of my tongue.
>
> Who do you think out of alcohol, your friends, your boyfriend, your baby and yourself cares most

about your baby? How do they show this? If you have
friends who expect and encourage you to drink and say
it's OK, I wonder if they are experts on the effects of
alcohol or if they just want you to get drunk with them?

Renee, do you think alcohol supports violence
and abuse in your life? Does your boyfriend support
(perhaps unintentionally) violence and abuse in your
life? Do your friends (perhaps unintentionally)
support violence and abuse in your life? Does your
baby support violence and abuse in your life?

Do you think that you're entitled to better support
and understanding than you get from your boyfriend,
your friends, and from alcohol?

I wonder, if we could know, what your baby thinks
of you for looking alcohol in the eye and standing up
to the destruction it brings? I wonder if, in years to
come, when your baby grows up, she will be thankful
to alcohol for trying to persuade you to drink or
thankful to you for trying your hardest to make a
better life for her?

Lots of questions for you to think on, Renee.
One more. How come you've wised up to the lies of
alcohol? For example you told me that you used to
think that alcohol brought happiness and good times
into people's lives but that you have discovered that it
really brings destruction. How come the good feelings,
good times promises of alcohol don't convince you
any more?

Good luck in your mission. Looking forward to
catching up with you next week.

Lorraine

As a postscript, Renee immediately limited alcohol to one
"stubbie" (can) of beer on Saturday night for the remainder of her
pregnancy and began to question and monitor the abuse and violence in her relationship. We explored the hows, whys, and significance of these outcomes at subsequent meetings. However, Renee
did not manage to completely save her baby from "alcohol destruction" (fetal alcohol effects), as her decision to cut back on her consumption was made some months into her pregnancy.

The Discourse of "The Alcoholic" and Its Blinding Power

One of the difficulties we suspect many people face in naming Al's effects on their lives and deciding that these effects are negative is that discourses about drinking and alcoholism actually get in the way. Bill's story illustrates this point.

When Bill came for counseling, "alcohol trouble" had been influencing his life for some time. Heavy drinking had led to his notching up a series of convictions for drunken driving. These had resulted in the loss of his driver's license and the considerable legal expenses that accompanied his court appearances. He had also been suffering from blackouts and had been subject to "hassles" on the job about the fact that his drinking was affecting his work performance. He was weighed down by worry, not so much about the drinking itself but about its effects. Now that "alcohol trouble" was affecting his freedom (through driving disqualification and the threat of imprisonment if he was caught again for the same offense) and his employment, Bill was beginning to consider that the problems alcohol was causing in his life were unacceptable to him.

I expressed curiosity about how alcohol had tricked him into allowing it to exert this influence without ever being held accountable for its effects. One of the reasons Bill put forward was that he did not believe he was an alcoholic and therefore could not possibly have a problem with alcohol. From a narrative perspective, we might say that the discourse about alcoholism had been blinding him to its effects in his life and relationships—effects that he might name as problems if he could see them. For an extended time, common perceptions about what an alcoholic person is like had served to mask the impact of alcohol on Bill's life and perhaps prevented him from confronting and protesting against this influence. For him, "alcoholic" was such a powerful and totalizing definition of identity that it did not fit with the many other aspects of his lived experience. He did not drink every day, or even every week. He had always had a job and a home and paid his bills. Quite justifiably, and without any deficiency in personal courage that the notion of denial suggests, he had rejected the word *alcoholic* as a description of himself.

But he had not had available to him any other ways of speaking that might help him identify alcohol as having problematic effects. To the contrary, he had lived in a world in which "hardout drinking" was a taken-for-granted part of family, work, social, and sporting life for as long as he could remember. Heavy drinking was a way of life for people in his cultural milieu. He was not naive or stupid but had simply accepted his unwitting recruitment into a lifestyle in which alcohol played an important role. In contrast with a more humanistic approach, the one I took in our conversation avoided any implication that he had volunteered for recruitment into an alcoholic lifestyle. I did not ask him to "take responsibility" for his drinking. But we did discuss how alcohol had not obtained his informed consent to its consequences in his life, and how it had hidden some of the costs of what it had been offering him.

Reclaiming Competence

Once we have established that Al is having an effect in a person's life, and we have begun to have an externalizing conversation about it so that the client begins to separate himself from a close identification with alcohol, we are in a position to talk about fighting back against Al's influence. This separation opens the door for discussing the person's "relationship" with alcohol. Ongoing metaphors can then be developed about features of this relationship. Is it a close relationship? Was it more distant at some other time? Have you managed to introduce more distance this week? Has alcohol sought to move back closer to you? Is it an abusive relationship?

But dealing with problems that have been defeating people requires a process through which they can build a sense of competence to overcome the problem. In narrative therapy, we seek to help a person or a family discover and use the knowledge they already have about how to deal with the problems alcohol has introduced into their lives rather than to teach them about knowledge we have as counselors. In this way, we seek to minimize the dangers of professional colonization of clients.

This kind of conversation often does not come easily at first, either to counselors or to clients. Al's ways of speaking are much more familiar, involving blame of others or oneself rather than Al. And Al does not give up without a fight. We find that narrative questioning requires courage and confident persistence on the part of the counselor because it entails a break with social convention.

But the narrative approach is characterized by an unshakable belief in the incomplete nature of all oppressions. Al seems to have a lot of influence, but he is never in total control. There are always parts of a person's life that are kept separate from Al's influence. There are days when a person has managed to stay sober or drink moderately and safely. There are aspects of family life that have not been completely taken over by Al's influence. There are elements of hope. There are resources for dealing with the problems that Al is talking people into—resources that may be temporarily overlooked but that can be drawn on. There are always the sparkling moments in the story of despair and blackness.

Typically, these resources, these sparkling moments, these events that would not be predicted on the basis of Al's powerful influence in a person's or in a family's life, these minor achievements in the face of the problem, are currently not given much weight or attention. They are not being taken seriously enough. They are not being storied in a way that allows them to come to speak for a person's identity. They remain isolated pockets in the person's or the family's consciousness. But it is through the recovery of these resources, through the recognition of what has remained unrecognized, through the building of new stories around these events, through the gradual process of performing rituals of identity around these new stories, through the forging of relationships that utilize previously underused resources, that changes are brought about and problems with alcohol overcome.

In order to elicit these *unique outcomes,* as Michael White has called them, we use a style of questioning that brings them to conscious attention. For example:

- Can you tell me how, despite the powerful influence of alcohol, you made the decision to come here today and ask for some help? How did you persuade yourself to do that?
- Which are the areas of your life that you have not allowed alcohol to take over? How have you managed to prevent a complete takeover?
- How have you prevented alcohol from completely wrecking your marriage?

- If we were to go back over the last week, could you tell me about the successes you have had, even for a few hours, in saying no to alcohol's demands?
- In the past, in what ways have you worked together with other members of your family against the effects of alcohol?
- Has there been a time in your life when alcohol was not in charge as much as it has been recently? What were you doing then that helped this state of affairs to exist? What difference did it make to your partner/family/friends and work when alcohol did not dominate?
- Who are the people in your family who might serve as models for you in the task of overcoming alcohol problems?

Insoo Kim Berg and Scott Miller suggest asking about changes that might have happened between making the decision to ask for help and getting to the first appointment. They suggest that many important things happen in this time that might be building blocks for the new story. They also propose the value of asking coping questions for people who are having difficulty identifying areas of their lives that alcohol has not taken over. For example: "In view of all that alcohol has done to you, how have you coped? How have you survived? How have you maintained a sense of yourself apart from alcohol?"

Building the New Story

Establishing these points of difference between the dominant story and certain lived experiences is still not enough, though. There is a need to story them in such ways that the person sees them as meaningful plot developments in their lives rather than as random asides. A story needs to be developed of successful protest against the influence of Al, of turning away from risky behavior, of dealing with the problems that alcohol was hiding from the person's attention, of respect for one's health, and of relationships freed from the domination of a drug.

Narrative counseling approaches exude a kind of optimism that can be infectious to clients. But there is also sometimes a danger that counselors can run on ahead of their clients as a result of this optimism. In this regard, it is useful to remember that alcohol can be a formidable foe and that there is a strong need for counselors to respect alcohol's strength. The following story illustrates this point.

Joe initiated counseling saying, "Alcohol's no good for me" and "Alcohol is causing me heaps of trouble."

He predicted that, without alcohol under control, his life would be from "the inside looking out" (a reference to being in jail). Joe was clear that he would prefer to be his own man rather than alcohol's man and clear about why this was preferable. However, he also very much appreciated "the gifts of alcohol" and attributed many of the good things in his life to alcohol. He also expressed a belief that no matter how much he tried, he could never win over alcohol.

James Prochaska and Carlo DiClemente's wheel of change would suggest that Joe was at the "contemplation stage" at this point. Joe and I (Lorraine) discussed areas in his life that alcohol had not managed to take over. For example, alcohol had not managed to ruin his reputation as a "good worker." We wondered how this could be. We developed a strong externalization of alcohol as a "bad buddy." I asked what the "bad buddy's" plans for Joe's future might be and how they might fit with Joe's own plans. The conversation was hard work, and there was little evidence of any possible shift. Alcohol's power seemed to be invincible. Moreover, as the counselor, I was beginning to feel defeated by alcohol as well.

However, a turning point came when Joe and I had a conversation about the game of Indian arm wrestling. This was a game that Joe described as involving two forces battling it out. What it demanded was muscle strength, as well as strength of mind. It was a pastime Joe had some experience with. He told me that, of all his friends, he could always hang out the longest. He described how he had learned that the first sign of weakening in his opponent was the first slight quivering of the arm. After he felt this quiver, nothing would make him give up.

Joe also described how he and his buddies had the habit of "playing chicken," with two cars speeding straight toward each other. This, he said, was a "game" initiated by alcohol. Again, in this game he had the reputation for hanging in the longest before he swerved away. (Again, I felt affected by the power of alcohol's demands. They seemed overwhelming.)

I asked Joe what he thought might happen if he turned this stamina and strength of mind on alcohol, or if it suddenly started working against alcohol instead of for alcohol. Joe replied that he thought it would be "a battle to the death." After some serious thought, he added that he thought that alcohol would probably win.

I was disappointed. I agreed that alcohol was a formidable foe and asked Joe if he was in the process of making up his mind whether to take on a warrior of such strength and such powerful reputation.

Though this language might sound dramatic, I believe Joe had come to see me because he knew that alcohol was posing a real threat to his life. Despite comments like "Oh well, you have to die sometime" and "I don't really want to get old anyway," he was not totally convinced that he wanted to give his life completely to alcohol. I was left with the chilling thought that, left unchecked, alcohol would probably take Joe's life or someone else's life via Joe's hand.

At the time of writing, Joe is engaged in "arm to arm" combat with alcohol and is beginning to notch up some victories. These victories are summed up by Joe in the language of the arm wrestling metaphor: "My arm was one centimeter from the table," he said. "Right now, we're both holding even, but I'm not even sweating yet."

This is not a story of dramatic, startling, or rapid change. But it is a story of change—a story of a person asserting himself over the demanding appetite of alcohol for his time and energy. As a coauthor in storying this change, I have needed to be patient, to have great respect for the power of alcohol, but to resist the invitation to feel defeated or overwhelmed by this power. At times, though, it seems like alcohol has demonstrated to us that it is not going to be budged an inch. This power can set counselors up to dismiss the client as either too deeply captured by alcohol to ever escape or too morally weak to do anything about it. Alternatively, they may decide that they are inadequate counselors.

One way of demonstrating respect for the power of the foe is to take seriously the significance of the very smallest of achievements in the face of the enemy. I asked Joe how he knew he had made his mind up to take on alcohol. His response was that he knew this when he spent a night drinking without tipping his head right back! This seemingly small change first alerted him to the possibility of getting the better of alcohol. His next success was drinking without tipping his head right back and leaving a party "before the bitter end."

To avoid rushing on ahead of Joe, I thought it was very important to celebrate the victories, no matter how small, by accounting for them in minute detail. It also felt very important to offer support through the not-so-victorious times by planning and strategizing and looking for more weapons (resources and knowledges) that can be deployed in the battle. The warlike terminology reflects Joe's words. For him and for some others, coming out from under the influence of alcohol is often akin to a battle in which the counselor is an ally. In this context, withdrawal symptoms can be likened to weapons in alcohol's arsenal.

Although it took some time before Joe decided to start the battle with alcohol in earnest, we want to emphasize how the process allowed Joe to stay in charge of rearranging his relationship with alcohol. Because the timing and pace were under his control, he was able to take the full credit for beginning to bring alcohol under his control. The time taken to story in careful detail his use of his own resources and abilities in the battle with alcohol serves two purposes. It encourages him to use these resources in the present battle, and it also identifies resources he can envisage using in other areas of his life as well. In this way, Joe begins to develop a counterplot to the story of alcohol. Meanwhile, alcohol is still recognized as a mighty warrior who continues to win some battles. In fact, recognizing it in this way builds a realistic context for the making of meaning about both backward slips (they are predictable) and victories against such powerful odds (they are even more amazing).

Building an Audience for the New Story

The social constructionist perspective teaches us that the stories from which we build our self-concepts are stories that have been told and retold in the linguistic contexts of our social networks. If this is true for the problem stories about alcohol, it also needs to be made true for the new stories of competence, of protest, of agency in the social conditions of our own life. A good story needs an audience before it can be appreciated as a good story. A counselor may be the first audience. But there is a need for the deliberate searching out of wider audiences.

This is where other family members and friends and support groups can be of real help. The challenge in family counseling is to engage each of the family members, as well as the person who is central to the life of the problem, on the side of opposition to alcohol's influence. Some narrative questions that might elicit this kind of development might be

- What might these occasions when you have taken aspects of your life back from alcohol say about the qualities that you have inside you to call on in tough times?
- Who else in your family might have noticed that you have these qualities?
- Can you think of other occasions when you have seen these qualities in him?
- What does it mean to you that she is taking fewer risks with alcohol in the last week?
- What confidence is there in the family or among friends that he can keep these changes going? In what ways can other people support this?
- Who else might it be worth surprising with these new developments in taking your life back from alcohol?

Some excerpts from the letter that I (Lorraine) wrote to Renee and have already cited provide examples of the process of recruiting an audience for the new story:

> . . . You tell me that your boyfriend, your sister,
> your mother and your friends have all noticed and
> appreciated your startling turnaround. Did your
> success surprise these people or do they know
> something about you that would have led them to
> expect that you would be so successful so quickly in
> your battle against alcohol and the destruction it
> brings? What sort of things did they notice that first

alerted them to your success? I'm wondering what
sort of difference this success has made in your
relationships with these people? I'm also curious
about what they appreciate most about this change?
. . . What would you guess that your baby would
be thinking now about your ability to be her mother?
What do you think your baby might be feeling now
about her future life with you?

With some widespread problem issues, narrative counselors
have engaged their clients in sharing their stories of success against
oppressive narratives with other people who are struggling with the
same issues. For example, David Epston and others have been
active in developing an investigation into the methods by which
anorexia and bulimia have operated against the best interests of
many young women. This investigation has engaged such young
women as co-researchers in the process. Armed with an understanding of how the prescribed body images of women invite many
people to internalize oppressive notions about their worth as
human beings, these people have been able to build identity
around a protest against the damaging discourse. In doing so, they
are taking a political stand against the oppressive social conditions
that have contributed to the problem in their own lives.

It does strike us as a little odd that there are not more groups
of alcohol-oppressed people engaging politically against its influence. Perhaps an antialcohol league is a possible development for
narrative therapists to foster. We are not implying a return to pro-
hibitionist thinking or other structuralist solutions. Nor are we wanting to deny the positive contributions of alcohol in many social
situations. But we do think that those who have suffered at the
hands of alcohol may be in the best position to tell us about the
tricks that alcohol plays in our discourse. This would help us all to
participate in the development of ways of speaking that promote
healthy moderation and sobriety and are less inviting of alcohol
trouble. And if we think in the way narrative ideas teach us to think,
perhaps the people affected by alcohol are already telling us these
things. Are we paying the kind of attention that allows us to hear?

In the end, though, we do believe that there is a need for
deconstructive work in this field of counseling, particularly on the

therapeutic discourses that might be said to collude with alcohol's ways. We suspect that the doctrinaire equation of the desire to drink with biological disease does not well serve the development of alternative stories about alcohol. Although many may have found this equation personally satisfying, there are many others— such as Bill, part of whose story we have told—who have not. As professionals, we are in the position of being keepers of and privileged contributors to the kinds of power/knowledge that influence the experiences of many lay people affected by alcohol. This means that we need to take care to be reflexive about the language in which we discuss alcohol and how it positions us in relation to our clients. We would prefer not to participate in the ongoing repetition of internalizing language that continues to convince many people affected by alcohol that they are sick or weak. Such language subjects individuals to professional discourse and also renders them politically docile.

Rather, we are eager to promote the narrative metaphor as a potentially powerful tool in the elaboration of alternative stories in the combat against alcohol trouble. The stories we have presented here have illustrated how the narrative approach can gently disrupt taken-for-granted thinking, lay and professional, about alcohol. This approach encourages the growth of local, indigenous knowledges about ways to defeat alcohol. It also respects the persons who are the source of such knowledge as heroes in their own lives rather than as victims of a disease that requires their willing subjection to professional discourse.

Notes

P. 159, *premised on this idea:* Fingarette, H. (1986). Alcoholism: The mythical disease. *The Public Interest, 19,* 3–22.

P. 159, *a number of quarters:* Berg, I., & Miller, S. (1994). *Working with the problem drinker: A solution-focused approach.* New York: Norton; Fingarette, H. (1986). Alcoholism: The mythical disease. *The Public Interest, 19,* 3–22; Marlatt, A. G., Larimer, M., Baer, J., & Quigley, L. (1993). Harm reduction for alcohol problems: Moving beyond the controlled drinking controversy. *Behaviour Therapy, 24,* 461–504; Park, J. (1992). Interested parties: A discussion of public statements in the alcohol arena in New Zealand. *Australian and New Zealand Journal of Sociology, 28*(3), 351–368.

P. 159, *psychological deficits to people:* Gergen, K. (1994). *Realities and relationships: Soundings in social constructionism.* Cambridge, Mass.: Harvard University Press.

P. 163, *totalizing description of a person's identity:* White, M. (1995). *Re-authoring lives: Interviews and essays.* Adelaide, Australia: Dulwich Centre Publications.

P. 164, *internalizing statements:* White, M., & Epston, D. (1990). *Narrative means to therapeutic ends.* New York: Norton.

P. 164, *rather than a "disabled person":* Hadley, R. G., & Brodwin, M. G. (1988). Language about people with disabilities. *Journal of Counseling and Development, 67,* 147–149.

P. 164, *defined as a disability:* Oliver, M. (1990). *The politics of disablement.* New York: Macmillan; Winslade, J. (1994). The social construction of disability: Some implications for counseling. *New Zealand Journal of Counselling, 16*(2), 44–54.

P. 166, *after a counseling session:* White, M., & Epston, D. (1990). *Narrative means to therapeutic ends.* New York: Norton.

P. 168, *an externalizing conversation about alcohol:* White, M. (1992). In Epston, D., & White, M. (Eds.), *Experience, contradiction, narrative and imagination.* Adelaide, Australia: Dulwich Centre Publications.

P. 172, *lack of motivation to the client:* Miller, W. R., & Rollnick, S. (1991). *Motivational interviewing: Preparing people to change addictive behavior.* New York: Guilford.

P. 177, *this is nonsense:* Gergen, K. (1985). The social constructionist movement in modern psychology. *The American Psychologist, 40*(3), 266–275.

P. 179, *promoting personal agency:* Davies, B. (1991). The concept of agency. *Postmodern Critical Theorizing, 30,* 42–53.

P. 184, *the incomplete nature of all oppressions:* White, M., & Epston, D. (1990). *Narrative means to therapeutic ends.* New York: Norton.

P. 184, *as Michael White has called them:* White, M. (1992). Deconstruction and therapy. In Epston, D., & White, M. (Eds.), *Experience, contradiction, narrative and imagination.* Adelaide, Australia: Dulwich Centre Publications.

P. 185, *getting to the first appointment:* Berg, I., & Miller, S. (1994). *Working with the problem drinker: A solution-focused approach.* New York: Norton.

P. 186, *wheel of change:* Prochaska, J., & DiClemente, C. (1982). Transtheoretical therapy: Toward a more integrative model of change. *Psychotherapy: Theory, Research and Practice,* (19), 276–288.

P. 188, *the linguistic contexts of our social networks:* Fairclough, N. (1992). *Discourse and social change.* Cambridge, England: Polity Press.

P. 190, *the best interests of many young women:* See works cited in Chapter Five notes.

Chapter Seven

Therapy with Male Sexual Abuse Survivors

Contesting Oppressive Life Stories

Tim Harker

Narrative therapy is about stories. Stories about problems and stories about breakthroughs. But most of all, it is about acknowledging and working with the life stories that people bring to counseling that form the plot of their lives and identities.

The world around us provides the social narratives from which our life stories are drawn. These narratives are the individual and cultural context from which our sense of who we are is derived. When people come to me for therapy, they bring with them the meanings and perspectives they have gleaned from their family, their community, and their contact with the wider world.

As a therapist, I carry my own set of meanings and values, my store of memories, understandings, and experiences, that have been interpreted through the cultural lenses I wear and that have become my own life story. These narratives make up my sense of self and my perspective on others and the world around me. They form the basis from which I "do therapy."

This chapter is a story, too—a story about sexual abuse, the meaning of which comes out of the social narratives that form our world of meaning. It is a story about men, about the men I have met in therapy, about myself as a man and a therapist, and about the stories of masculinity that circulate and are lived out in our communities. For me, it is most of all a story of liberation, of people breaking free from oppressive meanings and life stories.

My Story

First then, a little of my own story and how I "came to" narrative, so that you might better locate me and my therapy approach. As a white, middle-aged male with a university education, I am in a relatively privileged position in New Zealand society. However, as a boy and young man, I sometimes struggled painfully to live up to the models of male identity that I saw around me and to which I aspired. The images and icons of manhood demanded an invulnerability and sense of power and control that were often far from my own experience. The doubts and fears I felt, and the hurts and indignities that I suffered, had little possibility for expression and acknowledgment in the context of the call of manliness to be stoic and tough.

As I grew from "boyhood" to "manhood," my story of self and life was written and rewritten. A constant thread was the struggle both to be a "man of the world" and yet to find some expression for the story of emotion and sensitivity that was so much a part of my lived experience. As I grew into adulthood, the constant rewriting or restorying of my self became a search for a perspective that could resolve the fundamental contradiction between my lived experiences and the dominant prescriptions for being male.

It is perhaps no surprise, then, that the fledgling men's movement attracted me in the early eighties, for it provided a restorying of masculinity that allowed some congruence between those formative stories of caring relationship and being male. I began to understand that "normality" was little more than a cultural tale, and that it often prescribed ways of being that brought unhappiness and distress.

Community work reinforced an understanding of the importance of community and social context, cornerstones of the narrative approach I now embrace. The power of discourses of justice and compassion that were a significant part of my family and church origins led me to seek understandings in the texts of socialism and critical theory. Close encounters with a fundamentalist cult engendered in me a skepticism about claims to absolute Truth.

As I moved more into therapy work, I attempted to incorporate this sociopolitical and questioning stance. Feminist contextualizing of psychological difficulties provided some fit with my questioning of gender and power relations. But it was the discovery of the narrative approach being developed by Michael White in Australia and David Epston in New Zealand in the late eighties that opened up a whole new chapter for me in my therapy praxis.

Narrative immediately appealed to me because of the way it took account of social context and power relations, because of its questioning of the "taken-for-granted," and because of its critique of the normalizing tendencies of dominant social practices and discourse. It acknowledged and validated alternative knowledges of manhood and personhood that provided greater coherence for my own life story and experience. Incorporating this approach into my work and general perspective has been both very challenging and very rewarding.

My Approach to Therapy

I work in private practice at a community counseling agency. A large proportion of my casework is with men who are seeking to rid their lives of the oppressive effects of childhood sexual abuse. Situating these men's stories within their social and discursive context forms the basis of the narrative approach I use, and I believe this approach is liberating and healing.

The focus of this therapy practice is a process of *deconstruction*. I seek to situate the problems that people bring to therapy within the world of meaning. Deconstruction is the process of taking apart or looking beyond the taken-for-granted meanings and commonsense explanations related in male survivors' stories, to locate their origins in the social context.

The deconstructive process can be facilitated by a form of questioning similar to that described by White and Epston. The questions invite the reexamination of meanings from a perspective that asks, Why does it have to be that way? Other questions follow:

- Where does that particular interpretation come from?
- Are there other meanings that might provide more valid and preferred interpretations?
- How do these new meanings disrupt and challenge the oppressive abuse story?
- What alternative stories of self and the world then become possible?

To me, this is what "externalizing the problem" is all about: situating the interpretations of the abuse event within its context of meaning. What does sexual abuse mean to this man? What particular meanings are being experienced as incoherent, contradictory, or oppressive by this person? What specifications of manhood are being lived out here, and how are they shaping the experience of the abuse?

As I understand it, the process involves a careful listening to the story the male abuse survivor is telling of his life. However, this is listening with a very particular ear—listening for how meaning is being constructed and related, and identifying the action of oppressive discourse. It requires a special kind of curiosity—a curiosity about what discursive meanings and frameworks lie behind the experience being described and a constant vigilance and active seeking for exceptions to the dominant abuse story. These exceptions, or *unique outcomes,* provide opportunity to develop an alternative story not dominated by the abuse. For abuse survivors, this story is often one of courage and resourcefulness, as they struggle to make a life for themselves in the face of the oppressive meanings and experience of the abuse.

Therapy in this context is about challenging dominant notions of normality and right and wrong that are so influential in shaping these men's lives. It is about calling into question the taken-for-granted assumptions that we live by and that construct our experience of the world. It involves seeing beyond the individual to the discursive context he is framed by. The abuse-dominated problem story becomes only one possible version of a life.

I seek to introduce a spirit of curiosity and critique into the therapeutic conversation. I am not so much questioning the individual as interrogating the social and cultural meanings that have shaped the man's abuse story. Questions are aimed at unearthing alternative preferred accounts of the man's life that are not dominated by the oppression of the abuse. I invite the man to join with me in considering questions like the following:

- What forces have acted to produce this particular story of this life?
- Which dominant specifications of manhood are at work here, and with what effects?

- What interpretations of the abuse events are adding to this person's pain and distress? (Often, interpretations that produce shame, guilt, and inadequacy.)
- What evidence is there of alternative preferred stories that run counter to the oppressive story of the abuse? (I am especially alert to qualities of courage, determination, resourcefulness, dignity, and the like, that often go unrecognized in abuse survivors' accounts.)
- How can these be given the "air play" they need to become viable alternatives, to be made real in a person's life through action and acknowledgment?
- What community of people might support this preferred life account?

These questions are shaped by the issues that are of importance for the man in his life and evolve for me in the course of our conversation. My experience in working with other men who have been sexually abused alerts me to common meanings and experiences among abuse survivors. However, I am most interested in the unique experience of each man and seek to shape my therapeutic questions accordingly.

A Case Example

Let me turn now to a story coauthored in therapy with Dean, who came to therapy to deal with the ongoing effects of childhood sexual abuse. I have chosen to focus on the impact of masculinity on the experience of sexual abuse, as I see gender as one of the key frameworks by which we make sense of ourselves, our world, and our experience. In a society where "being male" is one of the most significant bases of identity, it is inevitable that discourses of masculinity will be powerful shapers of men's lives and experience. As a critical part of the social fabric that we live in, the ideas and practices of masculinity are key elements in men's sense of self and world.

Masculinity provides an important lens through which males abused as children interpret and reinterpret that experience as they grow up. There are many other discourses that impact on male survivors that I will not be addressing here. It is my hope, though, that the story that follows might serve to bring to life some implications of this narrative framework for therapy with men abused as children.

A Transparent Lowlife

"You know, I guess, that those childhood feelings were taken away from you because of the abuse. You weren't a child any more. Suddenly you're something else. But it was figuring out what that something else was."

Dean was sexually abused by an older brother and a minister over a number of years into his teens. He arrived at my door one day wanting to "sort out his life." He complained of lacking self-confidence and of a feeling of not knowing "who he was" or "where he was heading in life."

When Dean first came to see me, he talked about himself as he thought others were seeing him: "They just see me as shit, Tim."

"In what way like shit?" I asked.

"Well, it's like they're up there looking down on me . . . like they can see right through me."

"What is it you think they are seeing?" I asked.

His reply was striking: "I think they just see a lowlife, a person going nowhere." Dean talked about feeling like he could look no one in the eye and described the way he was often plagued by fears in public places.

Two things stood out for me in Dean's statement: the experience he was describing of feeling degraded in the eyes of others and a sense of transparency.

The sense of transparency to others' gaze and the associated assessment of degradation was a constant theme in the story Dean told of his life. This "being seen through" reminded me of the notion of "the Gaze" as discussed by Michel Foucault and picked up strongly by Michael White in his more recent discussions of narrative therapy. This gaze is one means by which dominant norms about how to be and act exert a policing effect in people's lives.

One of the ways this occurs is through people monitoring each other, policing the norms of acceptable behavior and thought. This "surveillance" is so effective that it brings people, like Dean, to police their own behavior, thoughts, and feelings.

I did not see the experience of degradation and transparency as pointing to damage or disorder within Dean's "psyche." I viewed his experience as the result of being positioned outside of social norms by the sexual victimization he suffered as a boy. As will become clear, Dean's positioning within "macho" masculinity provided only one interpretation of that abuse—that it was shameful, disgusting, and degrading, and threw doubt on his identity as a man and a person of worth. But I digress.

Dean talked about the difficulty he had "connecting to girls" in a sexual sense during and after the period of abuse. The feeling of transparency was already evident: "It was as though the girls knew what had happened to me. It's like that thing we've talked about when people can see through you—I always thought they could just pick up on it. I always felt not as good as them."

Here again is that sense of transparency before the gaze of others. The power of dominant social norms is at work here, bringing Dean to assess himself as a male and a person in the eyes of these girls. The fact that it was most unlikely that they did know that Dean had been abused did not, in the end, matter. The meanings of manhood in which Dean was immersed took on such power that Dean felt constantly judged in the eyes of others. Foucault has referred to this as "normalizing power" and points to the processes of assessment and classification as key mechanisms for this power. Dean's experience can be seen as one of feeling assessed against prevailing norms—and found wanting.

In my experience, it is common for people who have suffered sexual abuse to feel intensely this transparency and a sense of inferiority to others. The powerlessness of the abuse situation combines with the shame and guilt about an experience that all too often carries meanings of being responsible for terrible wrongdoing. In Dean's case, I understood these meanings as being shaped significantly by the context of being male.

I was, then, particularly interested in the knowledges that were informing Dean's assessment of himself in the eyes of others. My purpose in exploring these further with Dean was to deconstruct the abuse story that was still dominant in his life and to create some breathing space for alternative meanings and knowledges. What were the meanings inherent in his world that were constructing this experience of self as transparent, guilty, and shameful?

Deconstructing the Abuse Story

Dean accepted my invitation to explore more fully where such an assessment might have come from. We discussed the way in which, when he was a boy, the abuse story had come to dominate his life and self-concept. Dean described feeling "very vulnerable to anybody and anything . . . and no matter how old I got, I still had that small feeling. There were a lot of people that could kick you around."

Dean is describing what I believe is a common experience of sexual abuse. This experience is fundamentally one of powerlessness—the powerlessness of a small child confronted with an adult using his greater understanding, physical size, and adult status to take sexual advantage of the child. As Dean put it, "I guess I was scared of what might come back on me—like he [the abuser] might give me a walloping, or that he might do something worse the next time." The distress is compounded by the framework in which it occurs—a context in which all too often a child is disbelieved, or even blamed for causing the abuse or allowing it to go on. Dean again: "Even if I had spoken out about what was happening, I felt no one would have believed me."

We explored how that feeling of smallness was "put on" him by the abuse and the actions of the abuser. This allowed us to begin to situate the abuse in its context of power—the domination of the abusers and the power that prevailing interpretations of the abuse had to cause such distress. Questions like the following oriented our discussion:

- How do abusers take advantage of children like you?
- What powers of persuasion and manipulation might they use?
- What part might threats play in this?
- How is secrecy enforced?
- How do others' interpretations of abuse (for example, their blaming of the victim) play into this?
- How come kids end up being the ones feeling guilty and inferior?
- Other people's stories suggest to me that abusers are using their power to off-load their own problems onto kids. Do you think the guilt and shame belong with those kids or with their abusers?

- How has the abuse tricked you into feeling that you were to blame?
- How were you talked out of your innocence?
- In what ways do you still protest your innocence and resist these condemnations (at least to yourself)?

These questions were intended to begin to contextualize Dean's childhood abuse within the power relations inherent in that experience and to begin to disrupt the power of the abuse story to instill self-blame and guilt. I discussed with Dean how the power dynamics and interpretations of the abuse were contributing to the transparency and degradation he was still experiencing.

As this conversation continued over a number of sessions, Dean began to separate himself from the interpretations that had been put on him by the abuse and the context in which it occurred. As that happened, we were able to begin to consider together the alternative story of who Dean was apart from this abuse-defined self.

He-Man Masculinity

As therapy progressed, it became increasingly clear that the conceptions of manhood that had been most influential in Dean's life were highly instrumental in shaping his ongoing experience of distress about the abuse. I decided to invite Dean to consider more directly how his experience of the abuse was affected by being male.

"I'm aware that these experiences you have been describing to me of feeling like people can see through you, and feelings of shame, disgust, and inadequacy, are similar to what many men I have worked with have talked about. How much of the way the abuse affected you do you think was about being a boy, that you were male?"

His answer was striking: "Because I was a male, it was like a big kick in the guts—you were sort of bending over trying to catch your breath. And you don't feel as strong as the next person . . . you know, you don't feel as good."

Like many men I have worked with to overcome the legacy of childhood sexual abuse, Dean struggled to reconcile that event with being male. His attempts to deal with the "kick in the guts" of the abuse led him to turn to images of masculinity that promised power and strength. The "he-man," the icon of manhood within his peer group, provided an image that he strove to live out through his teenage years.

When Dean first talked about this he-man masculinity, I was interested to know what it meant to him.

"What was that like? What did it mean to be a he-man?"

Dean's reply was graphic: "You had to portray a tough character . . . like smashing up, getting violent with things, furniture, cars, people. Like we were always beating something up . . . we always had scruffy clothes, long hair—you had to portray this being tough. It was like living life in the fast lane—we don't need fueling up. We can run on empty . . ."

Dean's portrayal of the he-man fits well with a "macho" conception of masculinity with its emphasis on power, being in control, and being tough and rough.

For Dean, the he-man narrative was the lens through which he came to interpret his world and thus his experience of the sexual abuse. How he experienced that childhood event, how the abuse came to be storied and restoried into his life, would be significantly shaped by the he-man philosophy.

It was with this in mind that I set out to explore with Dean what this conception of manhood meant to him, both during his growing up and currently. He looked to these images of power to counter the powerlessness and the feeling of being "small" that the abuse had left.

"Because the abuse had happened, you were sort of looking around for heroes," he said.

I was immediately interested, for heroes are laden with meaning and significance, particularly for males.

"Who were your heroes during your growing up?"

His reply was full of he-man imagery: "Men with muscular bodies and big swords and beautiful ladies at their sides."

I was struck by the contradiction between this image of power, strength, and invulnerability and the "feeling small and vulnerable" that Dean had described before.

"What was it like," I asked, "aspiring to be a he-man with this power and strength, knowing inside that you had been abused and feeling so vulnerable underneath?"

"Well, they looked so perfect, and I knew that the abuse would not have happened to them. So you were kind of telling yourself lies . . ."

These specifications of manliness raised significant contradictions for Dean in making sense of the childhood abuse he had suffered. His feelings of powerlessness and vulnerability made a mockery of his attempts to live up to the perfection and power of his heroes, and this only intensified his feelings of inadequacy.

We were beginning to see more clearly how Dean had been positioned through his growing up within frameworks of masculinity that stood in contradiction to the experiences of sexual abuse he suffered. The narrative of the he-man—merely a more dramatic version of a patriarchal masculinity based on images of power and control—clashed violently with the powerlessness, vulnerability, and implied homosexuality of suffering abuse from another man. He was caught up in conflicting meanings and experiences for which he struggled to find resolution.

Rather than experiencing the power and strength promised by "he-man" masculinity, Dean was left feeling tired, scarred, and powerless:

"So you had to, like, deflect your armor to face what was out there. And I guess each piece of violence was just another piece of armor to fuel up on. It's like going through a war, trying to portray this image . . . and ohhh, after those wars and wars, there's just a tired person with a massive amount of scarring, whether it be emotional or physical. And it just pulls you down."

Fears of Homosexuality

Masculine images not only emphasized Dean's sense of powerlessness, but they also provided an interpretation of the abuse as implying homosexuality. When abuser and victim are of the same sex—and especially when they are male—it is common for the abuse to be seen as having such implications. This tendency demonstrates the power of heterosexist masculinity and its denigration of homosexuality.

The inference of homosexuality reflects also a lack of understanding of the power dynamics of sexual abuse and the confusion of sexual victimization with sexual orientation. It is well known among those working in the field of sexual abuse that most such abuse is in fact perpetrated by heterosexual men. Popular discourse all too often assumes that the sexual abuse of boys by men is a homosexual problem, both for the abuser and the victim.

Combined with the strong prohibitions in dominant masculinity against homosexual behavior, the linkage between abuse and sexual orientation often results in confusion and distress for male abuse survivors. This is particularly so if the young person experienced any sexual pleasure in the abuse, which promotes confusions among power, pleasure, and sexuality.

Dean and I had already discussed some concerns he had about sexuality as a result of the abuse. When inquiring about these concerns with men, I am very aware of the homophobia that dominant conceptions of masculinity engender. In my experience, many men who have suffered sexual abuse are left with fears or confusion about their sexuality. Most find this very difficult to talk about because of the shame created by homophobia and the fear of being discounted as homosexual. Although I think it is important to invite men to discuss these concerns, I make a point of reassuring them that this is a common concern experienced by many male abuse survivors. I had this in mind when I addressed the subject with Dean.

"Many men who I have talked with about their experience of sexual abuse have talked about confusions or fears it has left them with about being gay or being seen as gay by others. Has that been a thing for you at all?"

Dean's reply was emphatic: "Yeah, yeah, yeah, that was exactly it, you know. You felt gay because you had been in bed with men. It's disgusting . . . I've never wiped that feeling away, you know."

"What was it like, then, to be a he-man, knowing that you had been abused and thinking that you might be gay?" I asked.

"It was terrible because . . . there aren't any gay he-men out there, are there?"

There was no place in this "he-man" masculinity for experiences of sexual victimization, with its implications of homosexuality. With no viable alternative frameworks to refer to, Dean was left having to live an interpretation of the abuse that said he was or would be seen as gay. Within the world of the he-man, the only possible response to this was the disgust and dread Dean experienced.

The denigration of homosexuality was conveyed in the talk of the locker room and in the taunts of the school yard. Cries of "Sissy," "Homo," or "Queer" carry implications of shame, the threat of violence, and alienation from the realm of acceptable masculinity. The heterosexist assumptions of this macho masculinity define any sexual act with another male—whether abusive or not— as constructing an identity of homosexuality. The common misapprehension that sexual abuse is about sexuality rather than power contributes to this thinking. Dean's references to "being in bed with other men" has similar connotations.

In light of the abuse, the world of the he-man labeled Dean homosexual—an identity that that framework defined as disgusting and terrible.

"In terms of the he-man, what sort of a man are you if you're gay?" I asked.

"Yeah, well you're not a man," Dean replied without hesitation.

I shared with Dean my support for homosexuality and my belief that it has much to offer men generally, with its challenge to the limiting prescriptions of what it means to be a man. For me, this is an important part of where I "come from" as a therapist; such a stance opens up "space" for the valuing of homosexuality. Dean was happy in his heterosexual relationship, but I always consider the possibility that men addressing issues of sexuality might be struggling with the knowledge that they are gay or bisexual and might be too afraid to acknowledge it to others—and possibly to themselves.

We discussed how the discounting of homosexuality is not restricted to "macho" masculinity but is all too common in our society. Dean's disgust and feelings of inferiority can be seen in this context as understandable and congruent responses. Dean was reassured to know that other men I worked with had often expressed similar concerns about sexuality.

Dean conveyed to me his ongoing confusion about the implications of the abuse for his sexual orientation. He identified as heterosexual but found that he also had sexual feelings and thoughts about men at times. He did not think he was homosexual, because he felt strongly attracted to women and enjoyed his relationship with his woman partner, but he also had feelings of attraction for men that did not fit with the norms of heterosexuality.

Deconstructing Sexual Identity

I set out to deconstruct these ideas with Dean. Our discussion was oriented by questions I put to Dean, such as

- How did the abuse convince you that it could define your sexuality?
- Where do ideas that sexual abuse defines sexuality come from?
- In what ways do you think that the confusing of power and sexuality in abuse contributed to these confusions you have been left with?
- How did the homophobia that prevailed among your he-man peers add to this?

As we explored this problematizing of the taken-for-granted meanings of the abuse, it became clearer to Dean that abuse was about power, and that even though it had gone on for a long time and he had experienced pleasurable sexual feelings as part of it, it did not *make* him anything. By situating the interpretations of the abuse event within the world of discourse and meaning, we identified the way in which particular perspectives—such as that of the "he-man"—constructed identities that seemed natural. Understanding these interpretations as just one way of seeing things freed Dean to consider other possibilities.

It seemed important to me to deconstruct the whole notion of sexual orientation and the way different sexual identities are defined and constructed. Questioning again provided the means for me to invite Dean to reconsider the dominant meanings that added to the distress of the abuse story. These questions evolved for me as our conversation progressed.

- Is it possible for people who identify as heterosexual to have sexual feelings for others of the same sex?

- How do we account for the fact that many men relate that they have, at some stage in their life, had a "homosexual experience"?
- How might we explain that all the major studies of men's sexuality show that a significant proportion of heterosexually identified men have homosexual fantasies or feelings?
- Might it be that there is a confusion between sexual acts and sexual identity?
- Could it be that the boxes we put around these categories are not as solid as we sometimes think?
- Why does there seem to be such a compelling need to police the boundaries of heterosexuality?
- What difference might it make if we saw sexuality more as a continuum than as a set of rigid categories?
- If you were able to stand apart from abuse's definitions, what possibilities might arise for your sexual orientation?
- Which of these might have a fit for you?
- In what ways have you already been living from that preference or those preferences?

We discussed the issues raised by these and other such questions on and off over a number of sessions. Dean began to consider an alternative description of himself as a man—a description that did not fit the dominant conceptions of manhood.

Reconstructing a Life of Worth

Through the process of questioning I have described, Dean's experience of the abuse was situated externally within the frameworks of knowledge and meanings it was produced by. We thus began to loosen the hold that guilt and shame had on Dean. In the conceptual space opened up by this questioning process, Dean and I explored together the possibilities for an alternative account of his life and identity that was not dominated by the definitions of the abuse and he-man masculinity. Tracing the destructive effects of the abuse to masculinity (among other significant discourses) began a process of deconstruction that allowed us to coauthor a new and preferred identity.

Creating a New Story

As we deconstructed the prescriptions of the abuse and the he-man, alternative ways of being that were already gaining some currency in Dean's life began to take on new meaning and significance. These alternative perspectives provided different and preferred possibilities for Dean as a man, with their greater valuing of intimacy, caring, and connection with others.

This process of reconstruction is based in the realization that there are many possible stances available within the web of discourses that make up the world of knowing. Different positionings within this web bring with them very different life experiences. Out of Dean's story, we discovered evidence that as he grew older, he came into greater contact with alternative discourses of manhood—discourses of relationship and of caring that resonated with the caring and compassion of his mother. Experiences of intimacy with a woman partner and getting a steady job brought different expectations of personhood that required a revisioning of the he-man narrative.

It became clear to me as we engaged in the process of deconstruction that when Dean came for therapy, he was already in the process of reviewing the influence of the he-man discourse in his life and was seeking alternatives that had a better fit with his current reality. Dean's life experiences offered numerous opportunities to explore alternative conceptions of manhood that provided a more fitting account of his experience of childhood abuse.

While discussing the new home that he and his partner were building and their plans to have a child, Dean commented that he felt pretty good about what they were doing.

"That's a bit different from the smashing things up sort of idea of those he-man days!" I commented.

"Oh, for sure," Dean replied. "I suppose I feel pretty good about what we've been able to build up at home. I feel like I've begun to make a home again where I can feel warm and secure."

We talked more about those achievements and what they meant to him—how he had held down a job for a number of years, and now held a responsible position in his company; the steady relationship he was now in; the home he was building; and the way he was working in therapy to rid his life of the effects of the abuse.

I was very interested to know more and focused our discussion with questions like

- How have you been able to achieve so much despite the feelings of inadequacy that the abuse has put on you?
- What sense of value and worth have you been able to resurrect that has enabled you to believe in yourself enough to not only keep on but "get ahead"?
- What have you had to draw on within yourself?
- How is that different from the way you think others see you?
- Is it possible that they might not think that way at all?
- Is it possible that you do not have to be subject to their judgment?

As Dean came to recognize and acknowledge the achievements he had made in his life, and the qualities those achievements spoke of in him, he began to redefine and revalue his sense of self.

Dean had already talked about his mother, to whom he had felt really close before she died when he was in his teens.

"You've talked about your mum and how much you admired her—her strength, her caring, her reliability. What do you think your mum would make of what you have managed to achieve in your life?" I inquired.

Dean paused and reflected for a few moments. "I think she would be rapt, eh Tim! Yeah, I think she would be really proud," he said with feeling.

We considered what a different account of his life this was from the abuse-dominated story of his being a "shit" and a "lowlife." Bringing Dean's mother into the conversation began to widen the audience of people who might value and validate this alternative story.

As we focused more on this new story, Dean was able to separate more and more from the descriptions of himself that the he-man and the abuse had coproduced. The process opened up space for Dean to tell a different story of his life. At our next session, he commented that talking about everything he had achieved had "really got me thinking. Before, I couldn't really picture my life and what I *had* achieved, until we talked about it. Then I could see it more clearly."

He told how his family (apart from his mother) had often predicted he would "grow up bad," but that he had always resisted this idea. Even when he was caught up in the world of the he-man—"living fast and running on empty"—he aspired to a life that he could feel good about and take pride in. Dean began to talk about his life as something that *he* had made, despite everything, and how he was beginning to like the way it was turning out.

The Implications of Reconstruction

As our discussions continued, I was eager to draw out more fully Dean's story of his resistance and of his determination not to be defined by others or by events such as the abuse. He began to gain new appreciation of what he had achieved in his life and of his own value as a person. As he put it: "You're surrounded by so much shit, you don't really appreciate yourself, what you've done and what you've achieved. It's not until you talk these things out that you really become aware of yourself and what you've achieved."

Not only did Dean begin to experience his life differently in the present, but his history as a person was being rewritten as well. The story of the lowlife, of the "bad sheep of the family," changed dramatically as he looked back from this new and preferred perspective. He now began to understand his history as one of courage and determination in the face of very difficult circumstances.

As this reconstruction developed, we explored more fully some of the implications for his conceptions of himself as a man.

"How do you see yourself as a man now, Dean?"

"Today, now, I'm a lot stronger man," was Dean's reply. "I can face things a lot easier."

I was interested to explore the difference between this conception of strength that was coming out of his growing sense of achievement and the kind of strength prescribed by the he-man discourse, with its implications of violence and invulnerability.

"What is that being stronger, Dean, that being able to face things? What kind of a strength is that?"

"It's not strength as in muscular strength. . . . It's more of a personality strength," he replied.

Dean expanded on this at a meeting at the end of counseling: "I feel like I have achieved things to build up that personality strength. . . . The armor that I wore back then is now transformed into a house. And the sword that I once carried is transformed into a job I've held for five or six years, and being the foreman there."

Although Dean seems here to be speaking out of normative prescriptions for manhood—having a responsible job and building his own home—he is valuing these things as achievements that stand in contrast to images of himself as a lowlife and a no-good. When I explored this more with him, it became clearer that he was valuing these things in ways that the he-man prescriptions of tough and rough would never have allowed.

I commented on this: "When you talk about your house, it's like this is not just a house, a structure—there's a whole lot more coming through . . ."

"Yeah, true, Tim, it's like I've made a home again, like I was always searching for that before. It's a real good feeling—warm and secure." He went on to talk about the connection he was feeling now with "the wind, the hills . . . nature." Dean's sense of relationship with others and the world stands in contrast to the destructiveness of the he-man discourse.

As Dean took on this new perspective of himself and his life, he no longer felt exposed to the judgment of others.

"That is being strong . . . being equal—not letting people see through you" was his comment. His newfound sense of strength and the coherence it gave to his self-narrative provided a counter to others' critical gaze. As Dean came to value himself and his life more, he experienced himself as "more real" and of greater significance in his world.

The deconstruction of sexuality described earlier spawned other perspectives and explanations regarding Dean's sexual feelings. Our deconstruction of the straitjacket of heterosexuality gave legitimacy to Dean's experience. Challenging the he-man's definition of normal heterosexuality opened up other possibilities. Our discussions of the fact that men do not generally talk openly about experiences that do not fit within dominant prescriptions of masculinity led Dean to theorize that other men probably had their secrets, too. Dean talked about his belief, which came out of our discussions, that there was "a secret, a secret thing in all of us, whether it be a sexual secret thing or hobbies or whatever . . . and hey, let's look at men [sexually]—well, so what, I say. It's no big deal!"

Questioning the confusions of power and sexuality in sexual abuse freed Dean to define his own identity in his own way. He began to talk in terms of the sense of choice that acknowledging his sexual feelings for both men and women allowed. In reviewing this at the end of counseling, he said: "Like for me today to feel those feelings [of attraction to other men]—I feel it's good, eh. Because today at my age, I can choose, you know—I've got the power to choose . . ."

His revised conception of strength was important here, too. It enabled him to feel secure in his difference from masculine norms. No longer did he worry if he felt different from others.

"I feel like today I've got the strength to stand up and say, 'Well, I'm a bit different and you've got your thing and I've got mine, and if you don't like it, well, too bad!'"

One of the ways dominant conceptions of manhood hold their power is through the isolation of men from each other's lived experience. In counseling, Dean found an opportunity to talk with another man about other ways of being that were not acceptable within the he-man narrative (and most other dominant forms of masculinity). He reflected on this at the end of counseling: "I'd never really talked with anyone except you, because I see you as a man I can talk to and relate to. Like I can't exactly talk to one of the guys at work about it!"

I hope this story of therapy has demonstrated that our "talk" was a particular kind of talk, with a very clear intention: to deconstruct dominant frameworks of meaning that produce experiences of self resulting in distress and pain, and to reconstruct preferred life stories that bring relief from that suffering.

Dean's rewriting of his life story was not something that I believe happened only in therapy. Rather, I see this writing and rewriting of self as an ongoing process throughout life. In simplified terms, Dean's experience of sexual abuse produced a rewriting of the identity that, because of the dominant frameworks of meaning available to him in his social context, brought him ongoing distress. As he grew from childhood into adolescence, his life was written and rewritten by the changing nature of this context. The he-man became a major constructing force, only intensifying the shameful and degrading meanings of the abuse. As Dean grew into early adulthood, his context changed, bringing with it further rewritings of his identity.

These new frameworks of relationship and responsibility brought into question the assumed narratives of the past. His dream of making a life for himself became more attainable. In therapy, I sought to pick up on and develop this restorying process.

Dean's own reflection on this chapter led him to "update himself" on the point he had reached in his life. This was a positive process for him—a reminder, as he put it, of "what I've come through and where I've got to." It reaffirmed for him the reality of the new story being written in his everyday life—of Dean as a person of worth and value, no longer defined by the oppressive interpretations of the abuse and the he-man.

It seems appropriate to end this chapter where I began. My own story, too, has been influenced by my encounter in therapy with Dean. Deconstructing notions of sexuality and manhood has raised new and interesting questions for my own life and therapy practice, and has contributed to the ongoing process of writing and rewriting my identity and life story.

Notes

P. 194, *written and rewritten:* Mark Freeman talks about the self being written and rewritten constantly throughout life. Freeman, M. (1993). *Re-writing the self: History, memory, narrative.* London: Routledge.

P. 195, *a process of deconstruction:* I owe much to the work of Michael White for my understandings of discourse and deconstruction. White, M. (1989). The externalising of the problem and the re-authoring of lives and relationships. In *Selected papers.* Adelaide, Australia: Dulwich Centre Publications, pp. 3–21; White, M. (1992). Deconstruction and therapy. In Epston, D., & White, M. (Eds.), *Experience, contradiction, narrative and imagination.* Adelaide, Australia: Dulwich Centre Publications. Other theorists have broadened this understanding: Foucault, M. (1981). *The history of sexuality, vol. 1: An introduction.* Harmondsworth, England: Pelican; Foucault, M. (1979). *Discipline and punish: The birth of the prison.* London: Penguin; Weedon, C. (1987). *Feminist practice and poststructuralist theory.* Cambridge, Mass.: Blackwell.

P. 195, *male survivors' stories:* I find the term *survivors* unsatisfactory because of its implications of "mere survival." Although *survival* captures some aspects of living through and beyond sexual abuse, it fails to account for many of the qualities of these people's lives. I use it here with this qualification to maintain readability.

P. 197, *in therapy with Dean:* This is a fictitious name to protect the man's identity.

P. 198, *picked up strongly by Michael White:* Foucault, M. (1979). *Discipline and punish: The birth of the prison.* London: Penguin; White, M. (1991). Deconstruction and therapy. *Dulwich Centre Newsletter,* (3), 21–40.

P. 199, *"normalizing power":* Foucault, M. (1991). The means of correct training. In P. Rabinow (Ed.), *The Foucault reader.* Harmondsworth, England: Penguin Books.

P. 200, *the actions of the abuser:* See Kamsler, A. (1990). Her-story in the making: Therapy with women who were sexually abused in childhood. In M. Durrant & C. White (Eds.), *Ideas for therapy with sexual abuse.* Adelaide, Australia: Dulwich Centre Publications. (An interesting discussion of some mechanisms that abusers use to shape the abuse story.) White, M. (1995). Naming abuse and breaking from its effects. In M. White (Ed.), *Reauthoring lives.* Adelaide, Australia: Dulwich Centre Publications. White, M. (1993). Men's culture, the men's movement and the constitution of men's lives. *Dulwich Centre Newsletter* 3–4. Jenkins, A. (1990). *Invitations to responsibility: The therapeutic enagement of men who are violent and abusive.* Adelaide, Australia: Dulwich Centre Publications.

P. 202, *being tough and rough:* See, for example, Connell, R. W. (1987). *Gender and power.* Cambridge, England: Polity Press.

P. 203, *denigration of homosexuality:* Kaufman, M. (1987). The construction of masculinity and the triad of men's violence. In M. Kaufman (Ed.), *Beyond patriarchy: Essays by men on pleasure, power, and change.* Toronto: Oxford University Press.

P. 204, *sexual victimization with sexual orientation:* Dimock, P. (1988). Adult males abused as children: Characteristics and implications for treatment. *Journal of Interpersonal Violence, 3,* 203–221; Lew, M. (1990). *Victims no longer: Men recovering from incest and other childhood sexual abuse.* New York: HarperCollins.

P. 204, *power, pleasure, and sexuality:* Lew, M. (1990). *Victims no longer: Men recovering from incest and other childhood sexual abuse.* New York: HarperCollins.

Chapter Eight

School Counseling in a Narrative Mode

John Winslade
Aileen Cheshire

"I'm really worried about Sam—he's so shut off from everyone. I wish he'd come and see a counselor."

This statement over a cup of coffee in the staff room had a familiar ring to it. Teachers had been concerned about Sam ever since he had arrived at the school three years earlier. He appeared isolated, depressed, and unhappy. Always dressed in black, he walked the corridors and sat in class with his long hair covering his face, unwilling to make eye contact with anyone. In his second year at the school, he had teamed up with another student and together they sent out strong signals that they did not want anything to do with other people. Other students saw them as "heavy metalers," and there was concern about the dark side of their talk.

Some teachers had made an effort to connect with Sam and his friend but had not seemed to succeed. Small disciplinary incidents had resulted in Sam's mother coming to talk to his year-level deans, but little hope had been generated for the possibility of things being different for Sam. The concern continued. Teachers saw Sam as an "at risk" student and felt they had tried everything they knew to "break through" to him, without success. Frustration and growing concern were beginning to dominate every occasion on which his name was mentioned.

From a narrative perspective, we would hear a description of a student as "at risk" as a statement that could be pivotal to the establishment of a discursive position. It is the kind of description that can set up a power relation between educational professionals and students. Therefore, we would suggest approaching it with some concern for the effects of its use. There is always the possibility of its becoming a step in the process of marginalizing a person, especially if its use suggests an internal deficit of some kind. This word of caution is not meant to cast doubt on the genuineness of the expression of concern about Sam but merely to illustrate how words are not innocent. They can shape our thinking and set up relations. When teachers use such words in ways that are dangerous for students, we would seek, as counselors, to deconstruct the usage by asking about the events that had led to the labeling and would then seek ways of talking that sound less like "professional speak."

Several teachers had made openings for Sam to come for counseling. Year-level deans and classroom teachers had made suggestions about counseling, and as a counselor, I (Aileen) had sent him letters of invitation. He had rejected all approaches. Then, early in his fourth year at the school, he walked into the counseling area and asked to use the phone. When he had finished, I chatted with him about how his year was going, and one of his replies prompted me to say that it sounded like he wanted to talk some more about what was going on for him. He agreed, with a sigh of relief.

The Wall

When Sam returned for his first appointment, I was curious about what had brought him to counseling. He answered by talking about his fears of being "blocked off" from other people. A turning point had come for him at the end of his third year at high school, when he had begun his first serious relationship with a girl, Annie. What he feared was that he was so shut off from others that he was going to "stuff up" the relationship, but he desperately wanted it to work. I began to ask questions about Sam's metaphor of being "blocked off," with the thought that this could provide a way of having an externalizing conversation around what he saw as the problem.

"Is feeling 'blocked off' a bit like having a wall around you?" I asked.

Sam responded enthusiastically to this description, which fitted closely his sense of isolation. We went on to explore what the wall looked like, what it felt like, its color and texture. Clearly, this was no ordinary wall.

"What's this wall like, Sam?" I asked. "What's it made of?"

"Concrete," Sam replied immediately. "It's hard and grey and cold, and it feels incredibly thick."

"How high does it come up?" I inquired. "Does it tower above you, or can you sometimes look over it?"

"It's pretty high. Far too high for me to see over, and I sure couldn't push it down. It surrounds me, really. It's like I can reach out and touch it, and that's all."

Separating the Person from the Problem

In the very act of description, Sam was objectifying the oppression that had been experienced by him as an internal deficit. He was starting to take up the position of subject and turn the tables on the oppressive problem that had been describing and defining him.

I went on to ask if this was a solid wall or if there were any blocks missing. Had he taken any down, or had anyone managed to mount an outside attack? His girlfriend had been the first to make a breakthrough, Sam said. As he described her persistence, we wondered if she had made a study of attacking medieval castles, as she seemed highly skilled—although we noted that Sam had weakened a few blocks to give her a hand. As we talked in this way, Sam's voice grew in energy, and he increasingly talked about "I" and "the wall" as two different things.

I asked him how it was for him to have some blocks removed from the wall, and if this was a process he wanted to continue. Sam replied that he had never let any blocks be taken out of the wall before, but he now wanted to try taking down a few more, although that was scary because the wall had been there a long time. As Sam's story is developed, we can start to see these questions about differences from the oppressive experience as deconstructive of the wall itself.

We went on to explore the history of the wall, as I was interested in whether it had always been there, and when and how it had arrived there. Such exploration of history can also serve the purpose of deconstructing the inevitability of the problem. If the problem has developed through events in time, then selecting different events for emphasis, or different constructions of events, can allow its inevitability to begin to crack and fragment. The most difficult histories to deconstruct are those that stretch back into childhood beyond the reach of our sense of history. Still, the historical search can start to disrupt assumptions about ourselves that have come to seem fixed. As Sam talked about his childhood, we came to see that the wall had served a very useful purpose. Sam had experienced severe physical abuse in his childhood, and this, combined with other trauma, had left him feeling very alone and confused.

What he could now see was that in order to survive, he had cut himself off from others so that he could not get hurt any more. The wall had been built by him as his protection, Sam said, although he had never thought about it like that before. We looked at different ways in which children and adolescents cope in difficult situations, and he decided that, as he could have chosen a criminal lifestyle, or drugs as a friend, his building of the wall was perhaps useful. Here, the *news of difference* (Gregory Bateson's term, discussed in Chapter One) relates to perspective. I had invited Sam to break down a simple, monolithic view of the wall into a fragmented, more complex understanding, simply by viewing it with other possibilities in mind. It was another way in which the totalizing effects of the wall on his identity could be deconstructed.

I asked if he was interested in breaking bits of the wall down slowly. He was, and I made it clear that he was in charge of the demolition job and therefore could set its pace. As breaking down a wall often revealed unexpected things behind it, we thought it a good idea for Sam to call rest times. I wanted to make it clear that he was in charge of the schedule, not me. I am aware through past experience that one of the dangers of counseling is that the counselor's eagerness to witness the development of alternative stories can rush ahead of the student's comfort with and commitment to those alternatives. If this was to be an exercise in coauthorship, I needed to trust his authority on the issue of pace.

We also talked about how it might be for him to experience feelings the wall had kept out, and that sometimes this could be painful. A useful starting point was to look at the resources Sam had to build up his strength for the demolition job.

Thus far, I had deliberately focused my attention on developing the single extended metaphor of the wall to familiarize Sam with the principle of externalizing conversation. The wall had been objectified and consistently talked about as something outside of the person rather than linked with some internal dynamic of Sam's. The extent of his oppression by the wall was cause for taking a narrative counseling process slowly and carefully. There were many aspects of the wall's relationship with Sam to explore. I have found that many students in high school obtain much relief from this externalizing way of talking that locates problems outside of "self." They feel respected and valued, and they can start to imagine a life without the problem. Sam could start to envisage life without the wall.

I ended this first meeting by asking Sam what might have happened to the wall during our conversation, as it seemed that there hadn't been too much of the wall around while we were talking, and I wondered how he had been able to achieve this. The question seemed to get Sam thinking that the wall had not been very present as we spoke, and that maybe it was not as strong as he had thought. This was a first step in the building of a counterplot, or alternative story, to the story of the wall. I could have asked questions much earlier in the session about the times when Sam had managed to open chinks in the wall in his relationship with his girlfriend. However, I had chosen first to anchor Sam's growing sense of being separate from the problem, and this was done by building up the externalization of the wall, its history, and its effects. At this stage, the sense of separateness from the problem seemed to be a more important "unique outcome" in Sam's experience of himself than any that might have been discovered in his relationships with others. Significantly, it was a unique outcome that was immediate to his experience. I had a strong sense that the unique outcomes in others' attempts to break through his isolation might not be valued by Sam until he experienced the wall as separate from himself.

Gaps in the Wall

Sam and I agreed that we would meet for four sessions, then review how things were going. At our next meeting, Sam's awareness of the fact that the wall was oppressing him was growing. He had had enough of it. I asked if coming to see me was a bit like beginning to muster his forces against the wall. Sam agreed that it was. He had gotten glimpses through the gaps in the wall of how life might be without it, and in his relationship with Annie, he was beginning to see possibilities of preferred ways of being. Meanwhile, in his life behind the wall, depression was his only friend.

Annie came with Sam to our third meeting. I welcomed her presence, because she provided opportunities for Sam to develop his sense of himself in relation to others. Any development in this direction would be deconstructive of the isolation that had been the effect of the wall in Sam's life. We began to build on the ways in which his relationship with Annie offered him an alternative story of himself. She was able to widen the audience of those who were beginning to see changes in Sam for the first time. Other students were beginning to notice Sam's smile and conversations. Teachers, too, began to notice a change. These different impressions of Sam became both a source of strength for a new story about Sam and a consequence of it.

Of course, there were also times when the responses of a fellow student made Sam question whether life behind the wall wasn't easier. Building an alternative story is not necessarily a quick or simple process, and my response was to describe these times as "rest times" or "time out," acknowledging that the wall was built for a protective purpose and that it might still be needed for a while. Sam said that these descriptions were helpful.

I was glad that in our first session, I had predicted that such times might happen, not for any strategic purpose, but to realistically acknowledge the process of challenging dominant discourses. Sam was able to identify certain strategies that assisted him at such times, some of which involved his "touching base" with people he was beginning to trust in school. One of his main sources of strength was the academic ability he was beginning to deploy. This ability enabled him to find a "place" in the classroom because he saw and felt that it was valued.

Extending the Audience

As Sam began to experience new feelings, he also began to reexperience memories of abuse from his childhood. These memories became so powerful that it was now the memories themselves that began to oppress him rather than the direct effects of the events. He began to experiment with cutting himself, to test whether he was "more real" than the memories. At this point, I talked with him about involving an outside therapist in his growing support system. I openly discussed my feelings of inexperience in exploring the effects of abuse in his life, and I asked whether he might have a preference for working with a male therapist. There was also the limitation of time in working in a school situation, and this, combined with my absences for training, meant that bringing another person into his support system would have advantages.

Sam said he felt okay about seeing someone else, and thought a man might be good. He said he would trust me to find someone who would not tell him he was mad; he had grown to appreciate the way of talking that located the problem outside of himself. I referred Sam to David Bullen, a clinical psychologist who works in a narrative framework. Sam thought it would be useful for me to go to the first session with him, which I did. Together, we were able to bring David up to date on Sam's stand for himself against the wall and also on his current concerns. As we walked out, Sam turned to me with a grin and said, "That guy doesn't seem like a shrink at all—he asks questions just like you do!"

Sam worked with David over several months. During that time, the ending of his relationship with his girlfriend precipitated a crisis for him. My role with Sam became more one of a support person or witness. He dropped by regularly to bring me up to date on new developments. In his relationship crisis, I was part of his safety system as he dealt with his pain. It is part of our code of practice within the school that when a student is working with an outside therapist, the school counselor steps back from a counseling relationship so that there is no confusion about counseling work. There are times, however, when the student is in crisis and comes to the school counselor. When Sam was going through such crisis times, we ended our sessions with questions he thought would be useful to take to his next appointment with David.

In these ways, as a school counselor working in a narrative mode, I was bearing witness to a student's development of alternative stories during his time at school. A colleague describes this as "holding the past to the present and the present to the past." This witness role enables the school counselor to hold up a mirror of difference, so to speak, that facilitates the student's exploration of new experiences. We can ask questions that have the purpose of helping the student to see what he now knows about himself, how he was able to stand against "the problem," and what he is doing now that is making a difference.

School as a Resource for the Counselor

With Sam's lack of outside family support, school became his anchor. As he said six months later, "People in this place are really important to me. Like, when it was really tough, I could do things like drop in and say hi to Viv (our counseling receptionist), and just by smiling and talking with me, she'd remind me that I really was okay. It was a way of keeping hope alive, and there were other people I could do that with, too."

Despite the abuse and the isolating effects of the wall in Sam's life, he had managed to allow himself some opportunities for relationship. He had come to see a counselor. He had not allowed himself to be overtaken by unhappiness all the time. Gradually, piece by piece, a new story of himself was built, anchored in a set of events that did not fit with the influence of the wall in his life. This was a story of protest against oppression, of breaking the bonds of isolation.

In our particular school counseling setting, most of the students who come to see a counselor do so because of problems that are oppressing their families. Where possible, we involve the family, often meeting for one session and then referring on to an appropriate outside agency or therapist. But many students do not want their family to be invited to counseling. From a strict family therapy perspective, this could be seen as a limitation. However, we believe that working in a narrative way broadens the areas or stories with which a school counselor can work. Recognizing that the problem [rather than the person] is the problem gives me the freedom to explore and use the many relationships a student has in the school setting to not only understand the impact of the problem but also to search for alternative stories.

The narrative approach has, of course, grown out of a family therapy tradition. However, there are alternatives to looking for the problem solely in the family system. The narrative or text metaphor leads to a different emphasis. Narrative-informed counselors traffic in the meanings that are made by people out of the problems they face in life. These meanings are linked to more than the stories that circulate within a particular family. The family's stories are viewed as connected to social oppressions and language patterns that have currency in a community. For young people, the experiences that shape their lives are often powerfully defined within the school community as well as in the family. Therefore, the family does not need to be the therapeutic unit of choice (even for an approach to counseling that draws on family therapy ideas). We believe school counselors should be encouraged to think more of the opportunities the school community offers to work with problematic experiences. It is often the relational context that offers the most scope for useful work.

In Sam's case, finding relationships outside school that offered unique outcomes or ways of relating that challenged the wall was difficult. Sam saw no point in involving his mother, as he had little hope that his relationship with her could be any different. What he did hope was that by moving out of his family home into another environment, he would obtain opportunities for other relationship experiences and then perhaps develop a different experience of his mother. Because I was working from the assumption that Sam was not a "disturbed" young man or a member of a "dysfunctional" family but rather a person who had a problem that was oppressing him, I could use the school setting as a site for researching, identifying, or building on occasions when Sam escaped or challenged the isolation the wall had imposed on him.

So although a family meeting did not seem the appropriate way to work with Sam, he could find other relationships that offered unique outcomes within the school. The school was a community where a counterplot to the story of life dominated by the wall could evolve. Certainly, he had been labeled by many, but he had also encountered teachers who had appreciated him for his uniqueness rather than rejecting him for his difference. In counseling, we explored what it was they had experienced, and how he had been able to show them aspects of himself that they had valued. Although it took time for Sam to fully believe and feel some trust in these appreciating relationships, they often sustained him when the force of the wall spoke to him about his worthlessness.

The people he has related to in this way have continued to provide an important audience for the changes he has made in his life.

After the Demolition

A year later, Sam was in his final year of school. He was now living independently in a hostel, was in another relationship with a girl, and was planning to go to university. In preparation for using his story in this chapter, we met together with David Bullen to record and write up "Sam's story," which he says he might use one day—when he is a well-known poet—as part of his autobiography. What became clear as he recounted his story was that it had not been one of straightforward improvement.

Slipping Back

Eight months after our first meeting, Sam had come to see me, anxious that he was "slipping back." He spoke about what he called "the paranoids," who had made an attempt to get him behind that wall again. As we talked, it became clear that he had in fact made a stand against the paranoids when he had seen "how stupid they were" in an argument with his girlfriend. Talk about "the paranoids" came entirely from Sam. The habit of talking about the problem in an external way seemed to be catching.

I said to Sam, "So you saw through the paranoids . . ."

"Yeah," Sam said. "I just thought—ah, man, that's the end of it, they're not going to make a fool of me any more. And it just happened, see [holding up his arm], I stopped cutting myself ages ago."

"Sam," I responded, "it seems to me you've left a whole lot of 'stopped' things, a whole lot of old stuff, way behind."

His reply was a telling comment on the narrative practice of seeking audiences for the new story so that it can achieve enough salience for identity to be built around it. "Well, yeah . . . and I'm glad that someone else notices. You see, that's what I need—someone to acknowledge that, hey, I'm different now."

"That would help you to keep hold of the sense of yourself that you now have?"

"Yeah," he said thoughtfully. "I mean, look at how far I've come. I couldn't just *talk* to you like this."

"I remember you didn't talk to anyone. You used to walk the corridors with your hair all over your face—you couldn't even make eye contact with anyone."

"Whew!" said Sam, laughing.

We went on to talk about some of the other differences Sam was noticing. One of the most important for him was in the way he was thinking. As he said, "Even when I think now, even my thinking's been great, I've been thinking in terms of *me*, not someone else. You know how I used to have those voices sometimes, but now it's just, 'Should *I* eat that now? . . . What shall *I* say to that other person now? . . . What do *I* want now?' It's me."

We read these statements clearly as those of a person who has discovered his voice, who is no longer speaking in terms proposed by others, and who is actively engaged in becoming an agent, as Bronwyn Davies describes agency, in the conditions of his own life.

Sam then offered me a wonderful metaphor to describe this sense of himself: "I always think of it [his sense of himself] as an electrical wire that was broken but joined together again, but every so often the outside frays a bit."

When I asked what had helped mend it again, Sam went on to remember what he had done when he had thought for himself and acted for himself.

Documenting the New Story

Toward the end of the session, I asked Sam about using his story in this chapter. His response was that it would be "mind-boggling and awesome." "You mean other people would be interested in what I've done?" he asked incredulously.

I asked if he was interested in writing parts of the chapter, so that this really would be his story, not solely my account of his story. Following Sam's comment that his outside therapist might have some ideas, too, we arranged a meeting with David, in the spirit of Epston and White's notion of *consulting your consultant*. Sam decided that the account of this meeting was very important for him to keep, not just to help him write, but as a reminder of what we had talked about and how far he had come.

The meeting began with David asking questions about the problems Sam had faced a year ago and what had become of those problems since. It was clear from Sam's responses that he was now stronger than the problems. The conversation moved on to hope.

David asked Sam, "When things were really hopeless, what unique and powerful things in you enabled you to face fear?"

Sam's response was "There was always a bit of hope that things could change."

He had had what could be called "a hopeful way of thinking" that had led him to take hopeful steps against misery. In reply to a question about how he had learned about hope, Sam said that he thought it must have been there naturally, as there had been little hope in his family. David thought that perhaps Sam had been training himself, even as a very young child, to have hope, and although he had built the wall, hope had also enabled him to bring it down. David asked if it was hope that had first led Sam into my office.

"It sure was!" Sam replied. "It was hope that she would invite me to come and talk."

But an important part of bringing the wall down had been letting out the negativity. Sam said that, although he hadn't realized it at the time, he had discovered that "it was good to visualize things, as it took the misery out of me and pouring it onto paper in poetry changed the misery."

He had also shared his very powerful poetry with both of us, as well as with two of his teachers, and had gained a great deal of satisfaction in others' recognition not only of the content of his poetry but also of his ability to write.

"It was important," Sam said, "that I had someone I could express the negativity to, as my friends couldn't take it."

David then asked if we had a shower or some such thing at our counseling department so that, at the end of the day, we could walk out and wash the negativity off. We all laughed at this, but there was also among us the recognition that the pain often has to be heard before it can be looked at and some space gained around it.

In Sam's own account of the progress he made, he writes:

"Where do I begin? Before I came to see Aileen, I was alone. I had always been alone. To think about it now it's scary to acknowledge the power my problems had. The loneliness that I had become accustomed to had intensified the grip of the problems. The pain that I experienced led me to build what I now know was a special defense, my wall. The only people I had anything to do with were those who had similar defenses to myself. As the wall got more powerful, I cut myself off more and more from people and all there was, was a deep depression."

Sam went on to explore the events in his life that caused him to build the wall, a process that he says he found helpful, "as it showed me that I've come a long way from all that."

The wall had been a starting point for externalizing conversation with Sam, and although it was referred to from time to time in later sessions, other problems and other externalizations became more helpful. Sam had readily accepted the metaphor of the wall, and I noticed that a year later, he spoke about his problems as external beings. Maybe it could be said that he had internalized an externalizing way of thinking.

Short School Stories

Sam was not unusual in his willingness to label or name his problem. We have found that adolescents readily respond to conversations that identify the problem as something outside of "self." They seem to feel an enormous relief in seeing that they are not "mad" or "bad," which we find are the two most common self-descriptions. In counseling conversations, students are often quick to go along with the counselor's externalizing talk and frequently take delight in "naming" the problem, as the following story about Sally shows. For others like Mark and Alan, the problem was more clearly visible.

Sally and the Downs

Sally had made an appointment with me (Aileen) on the suggestion of the school nurse because she had been getting a number of migraine headaches. In our first session, she told me she was scared that she might end up like her mother, who had a history of depression. Sally herself was experiencing "really down times" and described herself as depressed.

We explored how long the "down times" had been around, when they came, and how long they lasted. The "down times" were having quite an effect on Sally's life at school, as her friends thought her moody and tended to avoid her if she seemed in a down mood. In response to my calling these times "the downs," Sally seized on the metaphor saying that "the downs" were like uninvited guests who gate-crashed her "place," took over, and then left, leaving her to clean up the mess. Not surprisingly, the headaches tended to accompany the downs. What she wanted was to have the downs over on an invitation-only basis so that she could be sad when she wanted to. She left our first meeting to watch for warning signs that the downs were going to gate-crash and to watch for any times when she was able to shut the door on them.

Sally reported a week later that the downs had gate-crashed only once because she had discovered some of their tricks and had been able to outwit them. She found that her main way of doing this was to talk to people. She had been spending more time around friends rather than walking off by herself (which is what she had previously done when the downs were around).

Like Sam, Sally had discovered some agency against the problem in the school setting. We then looked at how she might apply this knowledge in areas of her life outside of school. She went on to discover several things about herself that helped her control the downs' gate-crashing. Although there was more to our counseling work than this, as other family issues were impacting on Sally's life, her enjoyment in outwitting the downs allowed her a sense of agency against the problem and removed any tendency to see herself as a depressed person. This perspective gave her another way of looking at other issues in her life.

Escape from Stealing

A young man I (John) met in the company of his school counselor was working on a problem of "stealing." Although he was only thirteen years old, Alan had developed quite a career of stealing at school, at home, and in the neighborhood. He had been referred to the school counselor, "as a last resort," to see if she could find a way to overcome this problem. He was facing imminent suspension if things did not change.

The school counselor talked with Alan about "stealing" as an externalized influence on him rather than as an internalized moral defect. As she did this, he was able to separate himself from stealing and look at the influence it was having in his life. He could see that many of its effects were things he did not want. He did want to think of himself as an honest person, and he wanted others to trust him. He started to want to take back his life from stealing.

When I met Alan and his counselor, Alan was feeling proud of the steps he had taken toward responsibility and pleased with the developing prospect of a career other than one of crime. But he was also coming up against the fact that the story of stealing was not just a personal story under his control. There were other people who played roles in the story that featured him as thief.

Despite his attempts to break away from the influence of stealing in his life, the story of stealing invited the people in Alan's social world to continue to harbor negative expectations of him. Friends would still ask him to steal things for them. Family members would suspect him of theft when a sum of money could not be found in the house and would demand that he give it back. And at school, teachers were monitoring him all the time and waiting to pounce if he put a foot wrong.

His counselor, who was working with him to build an alternative story, was required to involve him in the active building of an audience for the new reputation he wanted to have. Alan himself underlined the importance of this exercise for his own sense of himself. It was very important to him to ask at two successive counseling sessions whether the school principal had noticed "that his name was not coming up" in relation to disciplinary issues. It was not enough just for it not to come up. In order for the new story to develop, he needed the steps he was taking to be noticed by a significant person with considerable power in his life. Such noticing would support the growth of an identity distinguishable from the one that stealing had built.

The school counselor took his question very seriously and was actively seeking the involvement of the principal and other significant teachers in the process of authoring a new reputation for Alan. She and Alan were realistic about the time it would take to achieve the reputation he desired, and there were many unique outcomes that needed to be woven together into the new fabric of this reputation.

In Trouble at School

Sometimes, of course, the problem issue is located squarely in the school domain. There are times when students seek help from counselors when they are "in trouble" at school. In this situation, they can often experience some separation from the problem through a conversation around "trouble" or some agreed-upon metaphor. Mark, in the sixth form (equivalent to twelfth grade), made an appointment with me (Aileen) for counseling after he got a strong message from his year-level dean that he was close to suspension for "being in trouble." There is an obvious externalization for the school counselor to make in such situations. Trouble can be separated from the person, and the student can be engaged in a conversation about the effects of trouble in his/her life.

In Mark's case, the very act of coming to counseling seemed to be an important and courageous move against the dominant problem story. It was his first attempt to take a stand against trouble and its potential to wreck his future and his image of himself. I expressed curiosity about how he had managed to make this step. We also spent time exploring the history of trouble and its effects on his relationship with his parents, his life at school, his hopes for the future, and his valuing of himself. Mark could see what trouble was doing to his life, but its invitation was still very compelling. His friends were united in a lifestyle of trouble, and his loyalty to them was strong.

However, he was now one of the last of his group of friends to be at school, and he was beginning to see himself as having a future that could be different from the "dead end" he saw his friends heading toward. I asked him what trouble had promised him. He replied that it had promised him fun, but it was now taking away his future hopes, and he was beginning to develop a stronger desire for a future free from trouble.

Further exploration identified not only some areas of his life that were trouble-free but also times when he had been able to turn down invitations from trouble. We used these to explore Mark's capabilities and resources for shaping his own life rather than having it shaped for him by trouble. We agreed that it would be helpful for certain teachers to know of his intentions, and he was able to enlist their aid. He asked that I assist by "paving the way" and talking with those teachers first.

Positions in the Counseling Relationship

In Mark's case, the initiative to come to counseling was a voluntary decision of his. The counselor can be placed in a very different relation to a client if a third party, such as a school administrator, refers a student to counseling. If the "trouble" is defined by someone else and ascribed to the person as a feature of her identity, the student may find herself in the position described by Edward Sampson: one of being only able to "speak in terms proposed by others." This is a position without the kind of voice or agency that Mark was able to find for himself.

Similarly, the counselor can be cast in the discursive position of "fixing" the problem. The modernist agenda invites professionals to think in such terms: problems are dealt with by isolating the variables and applying expert knowledge to their solution. From a narrative perspective, we would want to shine a deconstructive light on the assumptions underlying such thinking. One of these is the assumption of the individual moral agent responsible for her own actions. If those actions are causing "trouble," then there must be some "faulty wiring or programming" that can, potentially anyway, be identified and corrected.

If we start to think in more relational terms, these assumptions become much more problematic. We cannot escape an analysis of the ways in which power is constituted within the school. We have to think about how the stories that circulate in general educational discourse, and in school communities in particular, shape identities so that some people are labeled as "trouble." Our task from a narrative perspective is to find ways of talking that are deconstructive of these stories and position counselors and students in places that offer them agency and voice.

What the narrative perspective offers school counselors is not just a counseling method but a distinctive philosophical standpoint grounded in distinctive linguistic practices. These practices offer counselors tools for making sense of the influences that operate on their conversations with students. They also open up possibilities for disrupting the dominant thinking patterns implicated in the problems that young people consult their school counselors about. This holds true whether the problem issues are brought to school from students' homes and families or originate in the power relations of the school itself.

Notes

P. 216, *discursive position:* Davies, B. (1991). The concept of agency: a feminist poststructuralist analysis. *Postmodern Critical Theorising, 30,* 42–53.

P. 216, *set up relations:* Davies, B., & Harré, R. (1990). Positioning: The discursive production of selves. *Journal for the Theory of Social Behaviour, 20*(1), 43–63; Foucault, M. (1980). *Power/knowledge: Selected interviews and other writings.* New York: Pantheon Books.

P. 219, *the principle of externalizing conversation:* White, M., & Epston, D. (1990). *Narrative means to therapeutic ends.* New York: Norton; White, M. (1992). Deconstruction and therapy. In D. Epston & M. White, *Experience, contradiction, narrative and imagination.* Adelaide, Australia: Dulwich Centre Publications.

P. 219, *counterplot, or alternative story:* White, M., & Epston, D. (1990). *Narrative means to therapeutic ends.* New York: Norton; White, M. (1992). Deconstruction and therapy. In D. Epston & M. White, *Experience, contradiction, narrative and imagination.* Adelaide, Australia: Dulwich Centre Publications.

P. 225, *no longer speaking in terms proposed by others:* Sampson, E. (1993). Identity politics. *American Psychologist, 49*(5), 412–416.

P. 225, *as Bronwyn Davies describes agency:* Davies, B. (1991). The concept of agency: A feminist poststructuralist analysis. *Postmodern Critical Theorising, 30,* 42–53.

P. 225, *consulting your consultant:* Epston, D., & White, M. (1992). Consulting your consultants: The documentation of alternative knowledges. In D. Epston & M. White, *Experience, contradiction, narrative and imagination.* Adelaide, Australia: Dulwich Centre Publications.

P. 231, *only able to "speak in terms proposed by others":* Sampson, E. (1993). Identity politics. *American Psychologist, 49*(5), 412–416.

P. 231, *the discursive position:* Davies, B., & Harré, R. (1990). Positioning: The discursive production of selves. *Journal for the Theory of Social Behaviour, 20*(1), 43–63.

Chapter Nine

Appreciating Indigenous Knowledge in Groups

Glen Silvester

The differences between a traditional and a narrative approach to group work were highlighted for me after I had led a narrative-bascd group on assertiveness for people with disabilities. When I explained to a colleague that this group really knew a lot about assertiveness, she inquired, "Well why did someone suggest they needed assertiveness if they already knew a lot about it?"

Her reply was still on my mind when I heard a visiting African-American playwright and actress say in a radio interview that people of color in the United States were oppressed by mainstream culture but there were always stories of resistance. She went on to say that this made them innately political, and it was political stories that she was portraying on stage.

So it occurred to me that the stories of resistance that were told in the group of people with disabilities were not the stories that are usually given voice by group leaders. Group leaders usually elicit stories of unassertiveness and then provide skills training to overcome deficiencies. As a group leader in a narrative style, I seek to discover the history, context, and meaning people give to an issue—whether it be, for example, assertiveness, communication, or parenting—and to open space for them to story their own strengths and preferred ways of being. The difference is also highlighted by contrasting assumptions about what it means to be a group leader, what it means to be a group member, and what facilitative strategies will be helpful.

A traditional skills approach to groups assumes that the group leader has both good facilitative and good didactic skills. This positions her as the expert with knowledge, skills, and resources, and participants as being in deficit. If knowledge is power, participants are placed in the less powerful position. Further, the group leader is likely to support dominant cultural stories, thereby replicating the oppressive story the group participants bring in with them.

In taking a narrative approach, I assume that participants will have knowledge, skills, and expertise in their lived experience that can be shared in the group. These knowledges may be hidden by problem-dominated personal and cultural stories that describe the individuals as inadequate in some way. The dominant story of our traditional group work theories assumes that well-functioning people are rational, self-actualizing, and take responsibility for themselves. These individualistic ways of being are culture-specific. A narrative approach allows space for preferred alternative stories and searches out manifestations of expertise in those stories.

This chapter is about experimentation in and enthusiasm for a narrative approach to group work. I work with Relationship Services, an agency that has an education and a counseling function. It initiates courses in communication and assertiveness skills, self-esteem, and parenting, and also responds to requests from community groups for facilitation and training of groups in various relationship skills.

For a few years, I had been developing a narrative style in my counseling work, but my group work remained skills-based. At Relationship Services, I was inspired to experiment with a narrative approach in the groups I led. However, I could find very little written information about working with groups in this way and began to wonder how the theoretical concepts of narrative therapy could be applied in the group context.

A Group of People with Disabilities

"Do you think you are more nervous because we are disabled?" asked Mary.

I looked around the circle at the group. Many of its members were in wheelchairs; all were affected by disabilities that I had never experienced. However, I had been teaching assertiveness classes for years. *Was* I nervous? What had I said to invite this question?

The group had begun in the usual way with introductions. We placed ourselves on an imaginary map to show where we came from and shared in pairs and then with the whole group. Everyone spoke. Looking, in narrative fashion, for alternative behavior that supports assertiveness, I offered the following:

"My understanding from working with a lot of groups is that people find the most difficult thing to do is to speak up in a group. Would you agree with that?" There was agreement. "So what does it mean that everyone has spoken in the whole group? Does it mean that assertiveness is present?"

From people's expressions and nods, I could tell this was a welcome idea.

"For myself," I said, "when I was driving here today, I felt excited but also a little anxious about leading the group. I wondered who you were, where you came from, and how I could be useful to you."

That's when Mary asked me if I was more nervous because they were disabled. I knew I had thought a lot more about this group than was typical, wondering what voice our society gave people with disabilities. Did I know their stories? Did I think that teaching a few assertiveness skills would give them a powerful voice, or were these classes intended to soothe the frustrations of powerlessness?

In answer to Mary's question, I replied, "Yes, I have been thinking that from your experiences around disability you would know things that I wouldn't. You would have been assertive in ways that I have not had to be, and I would want to try to understand those stories. Would that be okay?"

This way of proceeding was okay with Mary, and I had an idea that there were already lots of stories in this group about assertiveness.

Establishing Rules

In establishing group rules, I wanted to begin from a narrative understanding that the participants would have life experiences that would tell them what rules were needed in a group. Consulting the participants was also a way of avoiding the power imbalance that is created when the leader asks the group to agree to an existing set of rules. So I said, "I'm wondering if there are any rules or ways of behaving you would like the group to observe that would help you to be able to share stories? Could you talk to the people sitting beside you about what, if any, rules you would like for this group?"

People talked in groups for a while, then I invited one person from each group to share ideas from that group with us all while I wrote them down. These were the things they said:

"If you want to cry, you don't want people telling you not to or trying to stop you," said Denise.

"How do they stop you?" I asked.

"They pat you on the back and say 'Never mind,'" replied Denise. "It's smothering."

"You can't say things if people talk behind your back," Stan offered from his group.

"And I don't want to be laughed at," added John.

"Has this happened to you in the past, John?" I inquired.

"Yes," he said. "And then I won't talk."

"Do you think 'being laughed at' would prevent most people from speaking up?" I asked.

"Definitely," he responded.

In this way, we produced a list of behavioral restraints that members wanted imposed on the group so that they could talk. Behind each statement was a story of personal experience that I elicited by showing curiosity. Further down on the list were statements like the following:

"You would need to have the right not to talk."

"You don't put people down."

"You would like what is said to stay here."

"You would like to be honest with each other."

"You would need to get to know each other."

I reflected to myself that if I had been using a more didactic model, I could have translated what each person said into "I" statements and asked people to speak for themselves, as in traditional "assertiveness speak." Similarly, I could have asked individuals in the group to agree to "the usual group norms." Had I done so, I might have stifled the group identity that was emerging and perhaps not heard the stories that were acting on people as restraints on being assertive. I might also have reinforced the dominant discourses on disability, in which the able-bodied and experts on disability commonly speak for people with disabilities. I would certainly have been supporting the dominant cultural portrayal of a healthy, functioning person as one who is autonomous and independent.

Establishing Group Norms

Warming the group up and establishing group norms are customary group leader functions. The process here was different in that the stories of people in the group were used to generate the group rules. Rather than just move on to the next exercise, as I might have done in my previous groups, I took time to consider whether people in the group appreciated their own authority in developing group norms. After all, here was an opportunity for assertive behavior.

"I wonder, what do *you* think about the wisdom in this group," I said, "that you could come up with a list like this? What would you say about a group of people who had just got together and who could produce this? Would it give you confidence that wisdom was present?"

I asked these questions not as positive feedback statements but as invitations to people in the group to affirm their own knowledge for themselves. Positive feedback or affirmation would have given my opinion on people's abilities, whereas these questions developed the group members' own knowledge of their abilities.

When I looked at the list of group rules and what people would need if they were to feel comfortable talking, one statement stood out for me: "You would need to get to know each other." Group wisdom was telling me that it would be difficult for people to speak in the group, and therefore that it would not be useful to address "assertiveness" until people knew each other better. Again using the narrative approach of taking my lead from the group, I asked Bob, the originator of that idea, if he had a way of getting to know others. He said "I just go up to a person and say, 'Hi, my name is Bob,' and I ask them something about themselves."

"Is it easier with one other person or with a group?" I asked.

"One person," he replied.

"Would it be helpful in getting to know each other if I asked you to find a partner and then gave you a question to ask them, and we did this several times so you would get to talk with a lot of people here?"

There was enthusiasm for this idea, so we proceeded with it until most people had met and talked in pairs. In this process, group activity and experience were coauthored rather than simply being directed by the leader.

The Language of Assertiveness

Thinking now about assertiveness courses I have taken in the past, I recall that people's behavior was described as passive, assertive, or aggressive. Role plays were often used to portray each category, with assertive behavior being the goal. People were told their "assertive rights" and how to make "I" statements asserting those rights. The process did not seem to provide any opportunity for the group members' own languages and voices to be heard, or the stories of oppression that prevented assertive behavior.

To counter this, I wanted to understand what assertiveness meant for this group of people affected by disability, and what stories they had around it.

"I have been asked to lead a session on assertiveness," I said, "but I would like to understand what assertiveness means to you. Could we brainstorm some of the words and meanings?"

"Saying what you think and feel," said Anne.

"Can you think of a time when you have had to fight to be able to say what you think and feel?" I asked.

"Yes, lots," Anne replied. "People come to our home and speak about me to my mother in front of me as if I don't exist. They think because you are in a wheelchair you are invisible or dumb."

"Are there ways you challenge these attempts to deny your presence?" I inquired.

"I just speak up and make them speak to me," said Anne firmly.

People started talking about 'being in control,' 'having a voice,' and being able to 'say no.' I asked about assertiveness in institutions, and Beth immediately said, "Don't talk to me about institutions. I've had forty years of fighting against institutions and people telling me what's good for me."

At this point, my group skills training might have suggested that I reflect the strong feeling evident in Beth's voice and role-play making assertive "I" statements. This would have signaled that I considered Beth to have an interpersonal communication problem and would have suppressed an opportunity to open space for the story of Beth's own ways of being assertive.

I thought it would be more useful to give voice to the story of how Beth managed to stand against the oppressive nature of some institutions. With this in mind, I asked, "How have you managed to keep your own voice?"

"I've got older and stronger," she said, "and I just won't put up with it now."

I asked if others related to Beth's story of standing against oppression. More stories about assertiveness emerged, which I wrote down. These were examples of unique outcomes and alternatives to the dominant story that had suggested that the group needed assertiveness training. I was understanding more clearly that in this group, there were many lived experiences of assertiveness. These people were teaching *me* about being assertive.

"Would you say that this group knows a lot about being assertive?" I asked. People in the group nodded assent. If there had not been assent, I would have further explored the oppressive forces that restrain people from being assertive. I continued: "Do you think it comes from times when you have fought for those things and stood up for yourselves not only in the face of personal experiences but with institutions and authorities?" The effect of these questions was to affirm people's assertiveness, not because the questions put positive thoughts into people's minds but because they were assisting the storying of assertiveness.

I gathered from people's stories that there had been times when they were restrained from being assertive. I think the traditional labels "passive" and "aggressive" for the opposite poles of assertiveness fail to provide an explanation of how a person comes to be at one pole or the other. They are part of a dominant story about assertiveness and do not account for inequalities of power in relationships. Assigning people positions seems to be another way of taking away their agency or ability to be assertive.

I wanted to find the words and meanings that people in this group gave to the effect of being restrained from assertiveness.

"Looking at this list of what it means to be assertive," I said, "what words describe the effect of not being those things?"

"Withdrawn," said Stan.

"Powerless," said Mary.

"Misunderstood," said John.

"Judged and bossed around," said Beth.

"It makes me angry," said Lisa.

"Yes," said Anne, "people should be respectful and not think they know better than you about your life."

In seeking to honor and acknowledge people's efforts in fighting the effects of restraint, I commented: "I have an idea there are quite a few rebels in this group. Would you agree?" There was much laughter. "There seem to be strong ideas of resisting others' power over you. Do you think people with disabilities know a lot about the idea of resisting others having power over them?" There was murmured agreement.

People had been sitting closely in a circle around the large sheet of paper I had spread on the floor to record their contributions. There seemed to be a lot of energy and satisfaction in the group from having shared these experiences.

To finish off the session, I asked the group if our discussion had been helpful and if so, how. People said that they felt more comfortable, had got to know each other better, had had fun, were looking forward to the rest of the week, felt energized, and just enjoyed it. There was an emerging story of a cohesive group with a strong voice.

Initially, my skills-based training had led me to doubt that a two-hour assertiveness session would be of much value. And in fact, I did not "teach" any of the skills that I would normally feature in a traditional group ("making requests," "saying no," "setting limits," "using 'I' statements"). What I did do was story the group members' definitions and knowledge of assertiveness and provide a context for understanding the restraints on being assertive. This context then opened space for the telling of alternative and preferred stories of group members as assertive people. Group building resulted from this process, and I appreciated being positioned as "coauthor" rather than "outside expert."

I decided that, for me, this was definitely a preferred way of leading a group, and that the two-hour session was worthwhile. I followed up our session with a letter to the people in the group that recorded the things they had said.

A Parenting Group

A further example of my making an assumption about the expertise of people in a group comes from the second session of a parenting course I led. In the first session, I had used my traditional skills to warm up group members to each other, to parenting themes, and to uncovering their "needs." The idea that people are motivated by "needs" and "expectations," and that these can be fulfilled by a course, is part of my traditional training in group work.

People in the group told me that the first session was useful and that they would like the next one to be on how to discipline children. In the first session, I had used good facilitative and didactic skills, but now I felt a certain amount of dread at being placed in the position of "expert parent." I understood that if they saw me as an expert with the answers, they would not be expecting to voice their own expertise.

I chose to open the session on discipline with a story from Maori mythology. The story is of Mahuika, the immortal guardian of fire on earth who keeps the flame in her flaring fingernails.

Maui, a young descendant, comes asking for flame, saying that fire has been lost to the world. Mahuika gives it to him, but when out of sight, Maui douses the flame in a stream and returns to ask for another. The cycle is then repeated. Maui wants to see what Mahuika will do when she has no more fire to give him. Because Maui is a relative, Mahuika repeatedly gives the flaring nails to Maui until she has only one nail left. At this point, she becomes angry and throws the last fire nail at his feet. The flames pursue Maui, and he has to call on his ancestor to send rain. Fire is almost lost to the world, but Mahuika asks certain trees to take over from her as the guardians of fire—a function that is visible in the red flowers of many native trees of New Zealand.

Group members were touched by this story, and I asked them how it spoke to them of parenting. They talked about how parenting was often a task of giving and giving until there was nothing left to give. I asked them what support our society gave to parents. They told me stories of social isolation and limited financial resources. I asked what messages the media transmitted about parenting. I heard about parent-blaming, and particularly mother-blaming. Stories emerged about parenting not being highly regarded, rewarded, resourced, or supported in our society and about its being undermined by media portrayals that blamed parents.

Discovering Skills

In asking the sorts of questions I did, I was giving a context to parenting in our culture that went beyond group members' personal stories about their behavior with their children. By talking about parenting in this way, we were externalizing "parenting." This offered space for the emergence of alternative stories that might be different from the dominant one of parental deficit. I thought that, with an understanding of the dominant stories relating to parenting and families, people in the group could better appreciate their own strengths as parents.

With this in mind, I asked, "How is it that parents manage to parent in spite of these stories?"

Stories of parenting wisdom and strength began to emerge as each person told of his or her particular coping strategies. I recalled to myself how different this was from the "Parenting Teens" course I had led years earlier, when parents had talked about their problems with their teens and looked expectantly to me for some magic formula to solve them. It was on my mind that this group of parents had asked for ideas on disciplining children, and I wanted to find a way of responding to their request that did not position me as "expert" and them as "deficient," thereby replicating the dominant story.

I told the group of my fears of being seen as an expert on discipline and said that my only position on discipline was that, in principle, it should be nonviolent and respectful. I asked what people had tried that seemed to work for them. One parent described a method that sounded like a time-out system. I asked if I could write it down. I spread out a large sheet of paper, and soon it was covered with ideas on discipline as people enthusiastically described their methods. I wondered to myself how parenting expertise had been taken out of the hands of parents by "experts" in our culture—a development that had undermined parents' confidence.

Had I taught this group some of the disciplinary methods found in books on parenting, I would not have heard participants' own stories of competence or storied with them their parenting expertise. Outside expert knowledge would have prevented their own expert knowledge from being voiced. I again appreciated this way of leading groups, which seemed to me to be about coauthoring preferred stories of parenting.

When sharing these experiences with a worker from a child protection agency, I was asked, "Considering that some of these parents are lacking in parenting skills and may be putting their children at risk, wouldn't a few skills be helpful?" The question put doubts in my mind, but then I reminded myself how taken-for-granted is our cultural practice of defining problems as deficits in people. I would like to say that I do have a position against abuse and I think that as a group leader it is okay for me to be transparent about this or any other position I have. It might be helpful to teach a few skills to parents, but I believe that unless a parent's story portrays her as being capable in spite of the difficulties of parenting in our culture, she is unlikely to be empowered. By empowerment, I mean people's discovery of their own agency, which gives them more influence and control in their lives. The process also involves challenging societal constructs that oppress people and limit their options.

Whenever a group leader is positioned as having expertise and group members as needing expertise, the leader exercises power *over* the members rather than empowering them. For myself, I have been well trained as a teacher, a trainer, and a group leader. Taking a nonexpert position in the lives of others and using a more collaborative style for the group process is new for me, but very exciting and energizing. It is something I want to develop further with all my group work.

An Organizational Group

An opportunity to experiment with the collaborative approach came when I was asked to facilitate part of a planning day for the staff of a parenting organization. This small local organization had five workers, who each fulfilled a number of functions: administration, counseling, foster care placement, parenting education, and family support.

I was told that people in the group would be spending the morning together in a planning meeting, and that they would produce an agenda for the afternoon session, which I would facilitate. I agreed to this, although not knowing in advance what the agenda would be or what the group would need was challenging. My skills-based training usually required me to have more information about group needs beforehand, and also to have at least a tentative plan.

On arrival, I was shown a mind map that outlined the concerns of people in the organization. This was the agenda. I was thrown into turmoil about what I was supposed to do with this map that I had no understanding of. I wondered what techniques I could use, and what the participants expected of me.

I asked myself what a narrative approach would suggest and realized that I could take a curious and nonexpert position. This freed me from anxieties about plans and techniques. The map that had been produced made no sense to me, but it obviously made sense to the people who made it. It seemed to me that if I were curious about the map and asked questions about the meaning it had for them, this would be a useful exercise.

Being Curious

I asked the group, "Would you mind if I asked questions about the meaning of this map, to try to understand it?" They agreed to this.

"Would you mind if I wrote down what you said?"

"No, go for it."

"Which issue is biggest?"

"Stress management."

"Can you tell me how stress affects the organization?"

They told me that a certain amount of stress was useful, but that too much affected energy levels. It was the sort of job where demand was greater than resources and time.

"Do you think you are doing a great social service job and saving the government money?" I inquired. They laughed, joking that they should enter the political arena. "I wonder how you as a group cope with the stress of this job," I said. The purpose of this question was to deconstruct the assumption that they might be responsible for the limited resources.

They responded by giving me a long list of the ways they as an organization coped with stress.

"I'm understanding from this list that you are a quite amazing and supportive group. Would you agree?" I inquired. "From this list of ways you cope with stress, are there any that would be helpful in addressing the stress management theme on the mind map?" I asked.

The group came up with strategies they wanted to put into place.

"What connections does stress have to the other items on the map?" I inquired.

The process involved my expressing curiosity about people's meanings and asking about the history of the issue, its effects, and people's ways of coping. In addition, I talked about issues in an externalizing way and gave a wider context to the participants' work. As a result of my curiosity and my nonexpert posture, people in the group came to a better understanding of each other's positions. At the end of our session, I asked them if our discussion had been helpful. People said it had given them direction, understanding, and clarification and had been specific and cohesive.

I reflected on how I could have looked at their map, taken an expert position, and given them stress management training. Doing so would have reinforced the dominant story of many social workers that if only they had better time management or worked longer hours, they could meet client demand. I then wondered about the assumptions of current training programs used by many organizations. For example, "The Quality Advantage" uses a problem-solving model that can be applied to any organization. Such programs focus on interpersonal problems and do not account for context or power issues. They also do not give voice to people's stories about what is going on or allow for alternative stories to emerge.

Women's Groups

One useful function of a group, from a narrative point of view, is that it becomes an audience for members' developing preferred descriptions of themselves. In one group I led on assertiveness, members chose their preferred description of themselves as assertive people from descriptions generated by the group. Some of the assertive descriptions were "an assertive action-taker," "a risk taker," "a conflict manager," "a banisher of useless guilt," "a self lover," "a creator of choices," and "an honest expresser of feelings."

Each woman in the group chose her own preferred assertive description and early in each of the subsequent weekly sessions, the women interviewed each other in pairs, asking

- What experiences have you had since last week that have contributed to the ongoing development of your preferred description?
- In what ways have you noticed others responding differently to you in your preferred description?
- How would you account for those developments in a way that makes sense of your own contribution?
- Do they have any connections with other occasions, or are they completely new?
- Are there ways that the group has been supporting these developments of yours?

In responding to these questions, the group members were developing an alternative story of themselves as assertive people. These stories are further strengthened by the group serving as audience and by the members responding to each other in new ways. When people develop their own assertiveness stories and self-descriptions that connect them to their existing knowledge and ability, they open up a greater sense of agency. Traditional forms of training assume a lack of assertiveness and teach the "correct" assertive skills to acquire it. In traditional assertiveness classes, definitions of assertive behavior and rights are put forward as essential truths rather than being developed within language communities.

This was illustrated for me at another women's assertiveness group, when I asked each woman to tell me what being assertive would mean for her.

One woman said, "I want to stand up for myself, but I want to still be caring and kind to others. That is an important part of me I don't want to lose." This woman was developing her own specifications for being assertive that were relational rather than just individual. The conventional specifications are about being responsible for oneself and ignoring many of the nurturing qualities common to women.

Cultural Messages

I also asked the women about the cultural messages we receive throughout our lives that prescribe how a woman is to behave. The intention here was first, to identify myself as someone subject to the same cultural influences that they experienced, and second, to remove personal blame for our style of communicating by offering a societal understanding of it. The women were then able to identify the cultural restraints on female assertiveness. This deconstructive process was empowering in itself, as the women described the effects of these restraints as "like tiptoeing around on broken glass, just waiting to get cut," "like being buried in a hole," "powerlessness," and "lacking choice." An understanding of the history and context of assertion had been developed, and this established a climate for reconstruction. By uncovering the cultural messages and practices that shape our lives as women, we become better able to exercise choice in relation to those practices.

I said it was a wonder that women could be assertive at all and asked if there were times when the group members had overcome the effects of these restraints. I knew that there are always stories of resistance to oppression; even coming to the group is a story of assertive behavior. Each woman told of ways she had been assertive. I then asked them all how they had been able to be assertive. They said things like "By being persistent in asking," "Taking a risk to try different styles of communicating," "Working out what's bothering me and saying it," and "Looking for solidarity and support."

Some of these ideas may be found in textbooks on assertiveness, and some are more idiosyncratic, but what is important is that they were all generated by the women present. Through voicing their own assertiveness, they established agency. As one of the women said in giving feedback about the course, "It was good to know that I had the basics inside me. It just needed to be nurtured."

This is a collaborative and respectful way of working with women that leaves them with an appreciation of their own self-knowledge and strengths.

A Community Group

From time to time, I am invited to do "group building" with a community group or to teach such a group "communication skills." The impetus might be particular communication problems or conflicts that the group is experiencing.

In the past, I might have used a combination of group-building exercises, communication skills, and problem-solving techniques.

Although these may still have their place, I chose to use a narrative approach with a staff group from a rest home. They had asked if I could come to their staff meeting to give them ideas on improving communication. I said I would be happy to come but I would prefer to find out about *their* ideas and ways of communicating and coping. The superintendent of the home agreed to my proposal, although she still wondered if some teaching would be useful. Again, I was reminded of our society's strong belief in the "expert." The superintendent clearly doubted that staff would have more knowledge about their styles of communication than I would.

I began by telling the staff about myself and the fact that I was experimenting with new ways of working that would give their understandings and knowledge of their situation precedence over mine. Before I asked any questions, I shared a story with them that I had just read myself in the introduction to *Solution Talk:*

A woman was complaining to a friend about the lack of courtesy of the local pharmacist. She said the pharmacist was the rudest person on earth, and someone should tell it straight to his face.

"I know the man," said the friend. "I'll see what I can do."

A few weeks later, the two women met each other again. "What did you do?" asked the woman who had complained about the pharmacist. "I went to the pharmacy again and the man was completely changed. He was nice and kind. Did you confront him about his behavior?"

"Well, not really," said the friend. "I told him that you thought he was a very charming man."

The staff laughed at the unexpected ending, and I asked if anyone could suggest a possible meaning. One popular suggestion was that "if we expect problems, we will find them." This may not have been the moral of the story that the original author intended, or that I had thought of, but the staff made sense of it for themselves in their own context.

It was further suggested that we talk about "challenges" rather than "problems." There was general agreement about this, so I asked them what their biggest "challenge" was.

"Changes," I was told.

In order to understand the extent of the changes they were alluding to, I asked if I could write them down. The staff members agreed and after a short while, they had told me of fifteen changes that had recently occurred. Focusing on "change" externalized the issue, and the participants were able to work together in understanding the extent of change and where it came from.

I asked them what effects they had noticed from "change." A list of "effects of change" was generated, but while these stories were being told, there were also alternative stories of coping that were emerging. I noted these "ways of coping" on a separate sheet as they came up so as not to lose them before we could focus more fully on them.

Given all the changes and their effects, I asked how staff managed to support each other, and if there were things they really appreciated about their work in spite of these changes. There were stories I recorded about support and appreciation. Someone commented, "We started looking at a problem and moved through to positive understandings."

My perception of what happened was that the problem or challenge was fully explored so that its effects on individual lives had meaning and context. In standing together against the problem, staff members were not seeking to assign blame, and this gave space for the emergence of alternative stories of coping and support that were there but had not been heard lately.

I asked if our short session had been helpful. The participants said it was good that they were socializing, sharing, and communicating, and also that everyone had contributed and there seemed to be general agreement. A month later, I contacted the superintendent again and asked if, on looking back, she still felt it had been helpful. She thought that it had been very worthwhile; staff had felt comfortable enough to share, and communication was continuing. I felt satisfied that the staff had developed agency in storying their own expertise in communication.

Group Leader Expertise in the Narrative Approach

In taking a narrative approach to group work, I have wondered what constitutes expertise as a narrative group leader, and how this is different from the expertise called for in a skills-based approach. Could anyone lead these groups?

As a skills-based group leader, I would assess the needs of the group and then develop a plan to meet those needs. I would provide an experience that would enable the group to develop a skill to satisfy the need or problem. In using a narrative approach, I assume that there is enough lived experience, expertise, or skill among people in the group to provide understanding and helpful alternatives.

The expertise I employ in narrative work is that of uncovering people's stories by means of a curious, *not-knowing* style of conversation. A not-knowing position means that I am asking questions without having preconceived ideas or theories about what the outcome or solution for the group will be. I am attempting to use their language and understand their meanings. I use externalizing language to separate group members from the issues or problems. I look at the meaning of the problem and its effects and listen for the alternative stories. The expertise lies in participating in this development of meaning and understanding. The process assists people in thinking about how they think.

At a recent daylong "communication" group where I had been using a narrative approach, I checked before the lunch break on whether people were getting what they wanted or whether they would prefer that I use a skills approach. One member spoke for others when she said, "No, this is much more personal." It was personal in that people were giving voice to their own helpful ways of communicating rather than learning a formula for "correct" styles of communication. For me, this is a productive way of collaborating with members of a group. In developing their own preferred ways of being, individuals come into a sense of their own power and form a new relationship with their contexts.

Notes

P. 234, *and good didactic skills:* Nelson-Jones, R. (1991). *Leading training groups.* Sydney, Australia: Holt, Rinehart & Winston.

P. 234, *If knowledge is power:* White, M. (1995). *Re-authoring lives: Interviews and essays.* Adelaide, Australia: Dulwich Centre Publications.

P. 234, *traditional group work theories:* Corey, G. (1990). *Theory and practice of group counselling.* (3rd ed). Pacific Grove, Calif.: Brooks/Cole.

P. 234, *culture-specific:* Gergen, K. (1991). *The saturated self: Dilemmas of identity in contemporary life.* New York: Basic Books.

P. 241, *her flaring fingernails:* P. Grace. (1984). *Wahine toa: Women of Maori myth.* Auckland, New Zealand: HarperCollins.

P. 245, *"The Quality Advantage"*: Labovitz, G. H. (1991). *The quality advantage.* Burlington, MA: Organizational Dynamics, Inc.

P. 247, *resistance to oppression:* Linnell, S., and Cora, D. (1993). *Discoveries.* Sydney, Australia: Dympna House.

P. 248, *Solution Talk:* Furman, B., and Ahola, T. (1992). *Solution talk: Hosting therapeutic conversations.* New York: Norton.

P. 250, *style of conversation:* Anderson, H., & Goolishian, H. (1992). The client is the expert: A not-knowing approach to therapy. In S. McNamee and K. Gergen (Eds.), *Therapy as social construction.* London: Sage.

Chapter Ten

Moving from Problem Solving to Narrative Approaches in Mediation

John Winslade
Alison Cotter

There is a growing recognition of the value of mediation as a process for resolving conflict. Whether the conflict is between landlords and tenants, employers and employees, separating marriage partners, neighbors, or people in other kinds of contractual relationship with each other, mediation is beginning to be recognized as worth trying—and in many countries, as worth including in legislation.

The practice of mediation has grown quickly, and the problem-solving approach outlined by such writers as Fisher and Ury has contributed much to the growth of mediation. In fact, we are so used to the ideas that form the basis of the problem-solving approach that we may not recognize them as part of a theory, as a set of ideas that have shaped our experience of conflict and its resolution. But there have been some criticisms of this approach.

In this chapter, we take notice of these criticisms and stretch the boundaries of problem solving by applying what we have learned from the development of narrative ideas in counseling. We have come to see the potential for a narrative perspective in mediation practice as well, and the chapter seeks to demonstrate some of this potential. We tell a story about a neighborhood mediation scenario and, as it unfolds, we explore the alternative views of conflict, mediation practice, and the role of the mediator that we think emerge when we take a narrative stance.

The Problem-Solving Model

The problem-solving orientation is woven through conflict literature in the fields of law, psychology, business, and communication. It is built on a set of assumptions that can be traced to certain background stories or discourses about conflict. One of these assumptions is that the world is made up of individuals who seek satisfaction of their needs and desires. This way of thinking emphasizes the pleasure-seeking principle as a driving force in human motivation and places individual needs ahead of cultural, collective, or relational aspects of personhood. Conflict is understood to occur because individual needs are not being met. The focal task of problem-solving mediation is therefore the search for solutions (often called win-win solutions) that will meet the needs of the parties concerned.

Central to this approach are the ideas that parties to mediation should be treated as equals and that the mediator should be objective and neutral. The mediator's stance should be disinterested with regard to the content of the conflict, and his primary concern should be to facilitate the process of generating solutions. Carefully applied, the mediation process should enable the mediator to work effectively with people regardless of differences of culture, gender, age, or other characteristics.

Over the last ten years, questions and dilemmas related to the problem-solving approach have begun to emerge. For example, there has been discussion about whether it is possible for mediators to stand outside time and space, and their own history and culture, and be objective and value-free. Might they not inadvertently legitimate certain stories at the expense of others? Will they not be more responsive to some people than to others? Likewise, questions have arisen about the ability of mediators to separate content and process. There is increasing awareness that disputes are influenced by mediators, and that mediators are influenced by the disputes with which they are involved.

Many observers believe that the content and process of mediation cannot be separated. Feminist and cultural critiques of mediation have pointed out that the outcome of a mediation process may simply reflect or reinforce the power relationship between the mediation participants. Mediation processes, they say, have not addressed power, gender, and cultural issues adequately.

The New Narrative Metaphor

The narrative metaphor has begun to be applied to the field of mediation in recent years. A narrative approach to mediation begins with a different set of assumptions about conflict. Rather than viewing conflict as resulting from a situation of dysfunction (such as unmet needs) that can be corrected, the narrative approach begins with a postmodern recognition of the existence of differences between people. People differ not only in the real conditions and opportunities of their lives but also in the stories they draw on to make sense of these differences. Thus conflict can be understood as the inevitable result of the articulation of difference.

If the stories we tell about ourselves and others and the stories in circulation around us are influential in the articulation of difference, then the role of language in conflict is important. The differences between us are constructed in the metaphors and ways of speaking that we hold in common as language communities. In this discourse, relations of power are often laid down according to whose experience is privileged and whose excluded in the dominant way of talking.

The attempt to understand conflict in narrative terms focuses on language as it shapes our sense of who we are and what our needs are. From this perspective, the differences between us that from time to time lead us into conflict are not necessarily to be resolved but understood. The valuing of difference is a principle highlighted by this approach.

Conflict is seen as emergent (changing as it emerges) and malleable, rather than fixed. There are different versions of meaning to be explored rather than sets of facts to be discovered. But let us examine these ideas in relation to a specific example of a conflict situation.

The Scenario

The following story has been adapted from one that has appeared in the mediation literature. Previously, it was discussed from a problem-solving standpoint. We have used the story as a case study for teaching purposes and, through role-play, have developed our own distinctive approach to it. The mediation reports in this chapter are a composite of several mediation exercises using this scenario for role-playing.

> Jim Brown is twenty-six. He works long hours as an auto mechanic and lives in a flat in Hamilton, New Zealand. Dr. Elizabeth Smith lives next door to Jim. In her early forties, she's in the last year of a medical residency at the local hospital.
>
> When Jim comes home from his day at work (which requires a substantial amount of physical labor), he likes to unwind by playing loud rock music on his new and very expensive stereo. When Elizabeth comes home from her noisy and tension-filled days at the hospital, she prefers quiet reading, restful music, and early bedtime as her relaxation. Elizabeth has asked Jim many times to turn down his stereo, to no avail, and the two have been engaged for many weeks in loud arguments that are upsetting the entire neighborhood.
>
> One evening, in desperation, Elizabeth calls the police to complain about the noise. The police arrive and threaten to arrest Jim for disturbing the peace. The next night, Jim again plays his loud music, and an argument develops with Elizabeth. In her frustration and anger, Elizabeth throws a flowerpot at Jim. It misses him, but breaks his window. Jim contemplates filing a criminal assault charge and a civil small claims action against Elizabeth, but a friend suggests that he try mediation instead. Elizabeth agrees to come to mediation.

Stories Behind the Story

From a narrative perspective, we might expect that Jim and Elizabeth's conflict has been shaped by the ways in which each of them has made sense of their interactions. We might read the scenario just recounted and begin to develop a curiosity, not so much about the facts of the matter as about the ways in which the two parties are organizing those facts into stories that fit with the background narratives they tell about themselves and their lives. Our assumption would be that people make meaning of the events of their lives by incorporating them into larger life narratives. Such narratives are not developed in a vacuum but through interaction with other people. These interactions might themselves be framed by dominant cultural and historical stories that influence which aspects of experience are selected out for expression.

So, for example, Jim's and Elizabeth's stories of conflict might contain descriptions of what has happened that make sense only by reference to each person's gender-specific and occupation-specific understandings of work and leisure. As the parties come to mediation, it is possible that their focus might narrow as other events in their lives fade in relation to the dominant conflict story. This narrowing restricts choices for possible action and makes available options seem unsatisfactory.

However, narrative theory would lead us to expect that there will still be a great deal of lived experience that falls outside of the dominant story. Jim and Elizabeth may be expected to have had many experiences of each other as neighbors that would not fit with the story of conflict now bringing them to mediation.

This field of unstoried experience provides "a rich and fertile source for the generation, or re-generation, of alternative stories." Stories that people live by are full of gaps and contradictions. Such is the richness and complexity of life. The contradictions are usually neglected and paid little attention because of the apparently overwhelming dominance of the conflict-saturated story. Giving these contradictions and gaps more attention can open up spaces for change if the mediator can provoke people to see things in different ways.

In the case of Jim and Elizabeth, the mediator's task, from a narrative perspective, would be to work collaboratively with them, both to explore the assumptions and beliefs behind their conflict story and to identify and develop alternative, preferred stories. In this way, mediation provides an interactive space in which nonadversarial narratives can be advanced. First of all, conflict narratives must be destabilized by means of carefully worded questions that encourage participants to see things in new ways. Then the stories of the conflict events can be opened up to alternative meanings and interpretations. This approach gives participants resources and skills to deal not only with their current conflict but with any conflicts that might develop in the future.

Our comments on this process have so far been on the level of generalities. In order to make them more concrete and to make the narrative method more transparent, let us follow the story of a mediation between Jim and Elizabeth step by step. The model of mediation used will be the one we have helped to develop at

Waikato Mediation Services, an organization in Hamilton, New Zealand.

The Mediation

One of our preferences is to always have two mediators in a situation such as the conflict between Jim and Elizabeth. Although this is sometimes labor-intensive and expensive, it offers several advantages. One is the possibility of the two mediators modeling cooperative relationship. Another is greater flexibility for handling power relations within the mediation process. Co-mediation enables us to attempt to match gender or cultural differences between the participants. With Jim and Elizabeth, it was appropriate to have one male and one female mediator.

Mediators' Premediation Discussion

Having agreed to co-mediate the situation between Jim and Elizabeth, we (John and Alison) met to plan how we were going to work together and what process we would follow. We also wanted to consider possible themes or issues within the conflict so that we would be alert to them when they arose in the mediation meetings. More fundamentally, we needed to consider the appropriateness of mediation in this situation. We reviewed the agreement to mediate that Jim and Elizabeth had already made. It was important that the agreement was not entered into under duress.

We were conscious of research showing that in marital mediation sessions, the meeting itself and the arrival and departure processes have been occasions when violence and abuse have been compounded. Safety is an important baseline for mediation, and when feelings are running high and conflict has taken place, responsible mediators are wise to be cautious about proceeding if there is any concern about safety. Mediation is only one method of conflict resolution, and it is not always the best one. Moreover, even when it may seem an appropriate path to follow, there is still the question of timing to examine.

Having reassured ourselves that mediation was appropriate and that both participants had agreed willingly to take part, we began to discuss the information we had already obtained about Jim and

Elizabeth from preliminary phone calls. In our discussion of this scenario, we were not trying to get ahead of the participants so that we could impress them with our understanding of the situation. Our aim was rather to reflect on how we might make sense of the preliminary information we had been given. Co-mediators need to have such discussions in order to establish a working relationship and an understanding of each other's views about the mediation process.

We speculated about how the prevailing discourses concerning age and gender might have been contributing to Jim's and Elizabeth's thinking about their conflict. For example, might Jim tend to take less seriously Elizabeth's concerns about his loud music because they were coming from a woman in her forties? There were also issues around work, economic position, and social status, and prevailing ideas about neighborliness, that we expected to be in the background of the conflict. All of these might have been interacting with the issue of their differing taste in music. Our purpose was to sensitize ourselves to matters about which we might want to be curious when we entered the mediation sessions.

In this meeting, we also talked about whom we would see first. We were aware of the research that shows that the first person to speak in a mediation session can often, by defining the agenda, exert influence over the direction that the mediation will take.

We find it necessary to plan how we will start mediation sessions: Which of us will explain the process? Who will start off the questioning? Who will take notes?

Separate Sessions

We planned to meet with Jim and Elizabeth separately to hear the story from each person's perspective. Sometimes, this can be done with both participants present, and some approaches to mediation seem to suggest that mediation does not actually begin until both parties are in the same room together. But we have found that we have much more opportunity to develop rapport with each participant, to build trust in the process, and to hear the full story in a relaxed fashion when the other person is not present. So, unless circumstances preclude it, we opt for a separate session with each participant before a joint meeting. Sometimes, in long-standing and complicated conflicts, these separate sessions may extend over several meetings before it becomes appropriate to move to a joint meeting. We do not favor the use of the word *caucus* to describe such meetings because of the connotation that they are somehow outside the process of the "real" mediation.

Sara Cobb has shown how the person who is able to achieve greater closure in the articulation of his or her story has a much greater chance of being influential in the mediation process. The word *closure* refers to the process through which narratives seal off alternative interpretations. The more "complete" the narrative, the less vulnerable it is to alternative interpretations and transformation. This is another reason for having separate meetings before the mediation proper. As mediators, we have an opportunity to assist the person who is in the position of disadvantage in a given power relation to articulate her story before she gets into dialogue with the other party. We can also try to open up windows to new understandings with the person who is in the position of advantage, in order to ease the pressure towards premature closure that he might exert in later joint meetings.

We held a meeting with Jim on his own, inviting him to tell his story of the events that had led up to the current conflict. Later, we did the same with Elizabeth. During these initial conversations, we had several deconstructive aims in mind.

Inviting Story

The first aim was to give each person a chance to have his or her story heard by a respectful and empathic audience. We believe this in itself can often be transformative. From a narrative perspective, each telling of a story is a new version, and each new version is likely to have a shaping effect on the consciousness of the person telling it. A story is a construction of events into a sequence. The form a story takes creates the meaning that gives impetus to current or future actions. Kathy Weingarten and Sara Cobb have demonstrated how significant the retelling of a story can be in making meaning around experiences of sexual abuse. We were therefore seeking to give Jim and Elizabeth a chance to tell their stories fully by listening respectfully to each of them.

Often in this kind of situation, people tell their story in a fuller way than they have done in the past; previously, the story may have been told only in fragmentary form. What is also important is that they *hear* themselves tell the story more fully than they have told it before. The fact that someone else is listening and taking their story seriously provides an opportunity for them to become audience as well as author. As mediators, we might express interest in what it feels like for Jim and Elizabeth to hear themselves speak about the events. We might be curious about the effect on them of shifting the story from the more private world of thought to the more public world of conversation. In this shift, perspectives can start to change. Moreover, the telling of the story has in itself become an event in the story line that will have to be accounted for in any future renderings of the story. The story has become, from this point on, one that has been listened to attentively.

Developing an Externalizing Conversation

Our second aim was to let each person know that we were not going to blame him or her for being in conflict. We wanted to convey that we do not regard conflict as a bad thing, to be done away with as quickly and as often as possible, but as an inevitable outcome of difference. We would not want Jim and Elizabeth to assume that we thought they were in some way bad people because they were in conflict. So, as much as possible, we would avoid using internalizing language—for example, any references to personal inadequacy. The issues on which the conflict has centered are therefore identified and spoken about in ways that separate the person from the problem.

We spent an hour each with Jim and Elizabeth, inviting them to talk about the circumstances that had led up to the mediation. The following were among the questions we used to generate this conversation:

- What is it we need to know about what has brought you here?
- What's the history of your relationship with Jim/Elizabeth?
- When did it come under siege? What started undermining it?

These questions do more than trace the history of the conflict. They also place the conflict and its history into a larger historical context. In their answers, we listened for the issues emerging through Jim's and Elizabeth's stories, translating what they said into externalizing conversation when it seemed appropriate. We thus began to talk about "invasive music," "work stress," "home as a haven," "neighborliness," and "arguments." We wanted Jim and Elizabeth to begin to see and speak of the problem as *external* to themselves rather than *internalizing* it as personal failure or blaming the other person. We wanted to encourage them to see the situation as a problem against which they could eventually take a joint stand. However, until they met together, we would be careful not to push for too solid an externalization of the problem issue.

Mapping the Effect of the Problem on the Persons

The third aim was to find out about the effect of the conflict itself on each of the participants. In addition, the externalized issues we had identified could be developed into fuller metaphors by our asking questions that would explore the effects of these issues on Jim and Elizabeth. For example, we took some time in the separate meetings to discuss ways in which "arguments" were affecting each person. We asked

- Can you help us understand how "arguments" have been affecting

   your enjoyment of life,
   your enjoyment of work,
   your physical and mental health,
   the quality of your rest and relaxation, and
   your relationship with each other?

- What part has "work stress" played in shaping your relationships or your ideas about how you want to spend leisure time?

Both Jim and Elizabeth were happy to talk about these issues. They seemed to feel relieved to be asked, relieved that someone was taking an interest in their personal experience of the situation—and in a way that was not producing in them a sense of deficit, shame, or failure. The conflict had been taking its toll on Elizabeth, who at work was feeling exhausted from lost sleep. Both she and Jim reported feeling tense about coming home; they were watchful of each other. "Aggro" (aggressive behavior) had led Jim to stop listening to music as much as he would have liked, and he was resentful about this.

These themes were pursued with curious questioning for some time. Jim was asked about the effect of the conflict on his way of playing music, on his stress levels, on his sleep, on his relationships. Elizabeth was asked about the effects of the conflict on her work, her relations with neighbors, her thoughts about herself. The chance to talk about these things without the other person present can be very important. Feelings of vulnerability can be expressed that might be more difficult to share in front of someone with whom one is in conflict. The recounting of these effects to an appreciative audience, the mediators, can help significantly to develop the motivation needed to move the story past the point of impasse.

Mapping the Influence of the Persons on the Problem Story

Another concern we had as mediators in this early meeting was to recognize the participants as agents (without suggesting that they were sole agents) in the production of the social conditions of their own lives. We raised tentatively with each the possibility of an alternative story:

- Was there a time when your relationship as neighbors felt stronger or more positive? What was happening? Who would have observed that?
- Are there any aspects of "being neighbors" that you have managed to prevent arguments from undermining?

We also wanted each to begin thinking about the personal coping strategies and resources they had been able to draw on to help them cope during this time of "arguments":

- You've been in this conflict for a number of weeks now. How have you coped? For example, what strategies have you used to keep on doing a good job at work while having this issue on your mind?

Our aim with such questions was to focus attention (our own as well as Jim's and Elizabeth's) on the ways in which they had resisted being overwhelmed by the conflict. This kind of attention would highlight their agency against the problematic conflict, removing them from a position of victimhood or subjection. We planned to return to these stories (the exceptions to the dominant conflict story) and develop them more in the ensuing joint session.

Joint Session

We were now ready for a meeting with both parties. Some preliminaries would be necessary, though, before the stories were revisited. We welcomed the participants and took time to affirm our respect for their commitment to seeking better understanding as neighbors through mediation.

Notice the emphasis on "understanding" rather than "solutions." This is not to imply a complete rejection of the traditional mediation emphasis on securing agreements. But we do think that agreements work best in the context of increased mutual understanding. We also believe that pressure to settle is removed if understanding is presented as a significant goal at the start of the mediation. In many situations, agreements are not possible, and sometimes the pressure to settle can produce premature "solutions" that are not in the best interests of at least one of the participants.

At the start of this meeting, we outlined to Jim and Elizabeth the process we had planned. This included a set of guidelines to ensure safety and comfort:

Time out	Anyone can stop the mediation on request.
Confidentiality	What is said in the session stays in the session unless personal safety issues arise.
Respect for differences	Parties maintain a respectful style of communicating—for example, by not interrupting or using abusive language.

Mediators' Role

We explained that we wanted to be open in the way we worked, and that we would be checking with the participants about the direction in which the mediation was heading and whether they were comfortable with it. We also said that we would be asking questions with the intention of opening up space for new possibilities. If they felt uncomfortable with any question, we invited them to say so.

We then began to address the content of the dispute. We summarized the issues and themes as we had heard them in the separate sessions, then invited each of the participants to fill in any gaps in content or emphasis that we may have left. In this way, we were able to reintroduce the externalizing conversations we had developed in the separate sessions. On the whole, we prefer this type of opening to asking the participants to tell the story again in front of each other. In our experience, the latter approach can lead to reactivation of the conflicted stances from which the participants have already begun to move away in the separate sessions. Instead, we give them each a chance to overhear the other person discussing briefly with the mediator their additions or corrections to the conflict story.

In this exploration, each of them might experience a further elaboration of the issues and their impact. In addition, another layer of meaning is added to the matters discussed in the separate sessions as a result of their being aired again in front of a significant audience—the other participant in the conflict.

Narrative Questioning Style

In using a narrative questioning style, we were trying to do more than find specific answers or gather information. Like explorers, we were looking for things that might have been missed, elements that might shift perspectives or help the participants see things differently. Narrative approaches use a particular questioning style to explore assumptions and challenge dominant meanings. The questions focus attention on the subtext of the conflict, including its history, exceptions to the conflict story, and future possibilities of freedom from conflict. They also invite participants to redescribe themselves, others, and relationships.

The conflict between Jim and Elizabeth was similar to most, in that a raft of issues had constructed the dominant problem. We now attempted to unravel or deconstruct the issues surrounding the conflict, and the assumptions and beliefs behind them:

- How might your daily work experience affect how you see this conflict? (Work issue)
- How would you describe the place of work and of leisure in your life? (Work issue)
- What are your expectations of your leisure time? (Home-as-a-haven issue)
- What's the relationship between the stress you feel as a result of work and the kind of music you play? (Stress issue)
- How has stress been affecting your relationship with each other? (Stress issue)

It became apparent that Jim and Elizabeth both found their work stressful and chose music that helped them relax. However, the nature of the music was an emotional issue for Elizabeth because of her intense dislike of Jim's loud rock music and its effects on her. Jim also had strong feelings about the fact that his pleasure in his new stereo and in his rock music was being disturbed. As mediators working from a narrative approach, we wanted to acknowledge these strong feelings but to treat them as only one part of the conflict story. If we brushed over the feelings, Jim and Elizabeth would quickly slip back into the dominant conflict story.

We would not, however, place a strong emphasis on the cathartic expression of feeling as a key to changes in a relationship. Rather than seeing feelings as the essential origins of people's actions, we understand them as exchanges within social relations, which are scripted by the stories in which people are situated. We therefore tried to externalize the participants' differing tastes in music and respond to the emotions expressed while still relating these emotions to the broader issues of the conflict:

- So "differing tastes in music" is an important issue for you, Elizabeth? And you need both Jim and us to appreciate that . . .
- Jim, what would you hope Elizabeth might understand about "differing tastes in music"?
- *(To Jim:)* How might such an understanding affect neighborliness? Would it make more space for neighborliness to emerge? (Neighborliness issue)
- *(To each:)* How important are neighborly relationships to you? Would you, overall, prefer neighborly relationships that feature respect and trust to relationships of conflict?

- How did the police being brought in affect each of you? And the flowerpot throwing? (Arguments issue)

Our aim at this stage of the mediation was to work toward an externalized description of the conflict issue that included the experiences of both Jim and Elizabeth. There is a temptation in conflict situations for the parties to externalize issues by attributing their origin to the other person. It is obviously unhelpful for the mediators to collude with this kind of response. The temptation needs to be understood as one of the tricks that conflict can play to distract people from positive dialogue about their differences.

Our hope was that, with our joint resources, we could agree on a mutual definition of the problem issue that pointed to the aspects of an external discourse that were subjugating both participants. For example, "work stress" might, in combination with other discourses, have been exacting such a high price from Jim and Elizabeth that they were thrown into conflict with each other. This use of language positions them on the same side in opposition to the problem and clears the way for the building of solidarity to overcome the oppressive effects of "work stress" in their lives.

To make such solidarity possible, it is sometimes useful to look at the patterns of communication that have established themselves around the problem issue. Often, blame has been exchanged in a repetitive pattern of complementary transactions. Each move in the chain of interactions feeds on the previous one. A vicious circle of conflict develops in which every attempt made by either party to extract himself or herself from the situation ends in discouragement and a deepening of the quagmire. Mediators can work with the participants to identify this pattern by first of all establishing the sequence of communications that has occurred in relation to the problem:

- So when Jim did that, what did you do next? And so when Elizabeth said that, what did you say?

After the sequence of responses has been teased out, the mediator can summarize the circular effects of the communication in a way that highlights the complementary aspects of each person's attempts to deal with the conflict issues. For example:

- Would it be fair to say that there's been something of a vicious circle here—the louder the music played, the more angry you, Elizabeth, became with Jim, which led to you, Jim, playing the music just as loud next time and Elizabeth getting even angrier?
- Is this cycle something you want to continue? What would you like to be different?

In this way, the repeating cycle of conflict is mapped out and then externalized so that the participants are given a chance to disengage from their contributions to it.

Before going further, we checked out Jim's and Elizabeth's desire for change. Without this step, a mediation can be time-consuming and unproductive. But there is another reason to ask this kind of question: after hearing each other speak about the personal effects of the conflict, they are then given the opportunity to hear each other express a desire for change.

- Is this conflict something that you want to continue, or is it something you'd like to change?
- What's in favor of it? What's against it?

Each confirmed that the tension was highly stressful and not the way he or she wanted to live (although Elizabeth again repeated that could she not live and work with such loud music either). This gave the mediators a chance to point out Jim and Elizabeth's level of agreement on the desire to resolve the tension. Because any agreements stand in contradiction to the story of conflict, this can be construed as a *unique outcome* in itself.

Developing an Alternative Story

We began to look for such unique outcomes—times in which the participants' behavior was in contradiction to their current difficulties. What we were seeking at this stage was to identify moments in Jim and Elizabeth's relationship when "arguments'" grip on their interactions was loosened a little. And the more recently these moments could be found, the better.

- Have there been any occasions when you, Jim, have taken Elizabeth's concerns into account, or when you, Elizabeth, have made room in your thinking for Jim's wishes?

- Can you think of a time or an incident when your relationship as neighbors felt better than it does now? Have there been any other times?
- What did you do at those times?
- What enabled you to do that?
- What difference did that make?

Though acknowledging that they had never been particularly close as neighbors, Jim and Elizabeth, with encouragement, recalled incidents such as being happy to bring in each other's mail and garbage containers when one was on vacation, and being in the habit of greeting each other when their paths crossed. As mediators, we made efforts to anchor these small unique outcomes by asking each:

- What does looking after each other's mail and rubbish containers suggest about the possibilities for cooperation?
- How would you feel if cooperation were a bigger part of your relationship?
- How was it that you managed to keep up "neighborliness" for ten of the twelve months in which you've been neighbors?
- In what ways did you find "neighborliness" preferable to "arguments"?

We also wanted the parties to think about and identify personal resources they would bring to the task of establishing and sustaining an alternative or preferred story to the problem story of "arguments." We asked each:

- What attributes have you used in handling difficult situations in the past that might help you move forward from this point? Which could be applied now?
- How does having listened to Elizabeth/Jim affect your understanding of the situation? Can you think of ways in which you could build on these possibilities?

At this point, Elizabeth spoke of how embarrassed she felt about her out-of-character behavior in throwing the flowerpot, and how it was important to her to make amends for this. She offered to pay the costs of fixing the window. Jim was willing to accept this but was asked by the mediator:

- If your relationship were to become characterized more by cooperation, what concessions might you consider?

Jim said he had been thinking about using earphones when Elizabeth was home. In reply, she offered to give him a schedule of her work shifts with the idea that he might like to play his music loudly when she was not home.

These are possible new developments in the relationship between Jim and Elizabeth. They are the kind of plot developments that suggest a different story line from that in which "arguments" are a dominant theme. But they are still fragile developments, and there is a strong possibility that the old plot will retain its powerful influence in the minds of the participants. As narrative mediators, our task now is to invite increased attention to the new story so that it becomes cemented into consciousness as a viable alternative to the story written by "arguments." We ask questions that seek to focus Jim and Elizabeth's attention on what they might do to develop the new story of cooperation:

- Given your present understandings, what do you think are some of the possibilities now? What would you like to have happen?
- What difference could these new understandings of each other make to your ongoing relationship? How might these ideas affect the future?
- How would you know that you had developed a positive working relationship? What sorts of things would be happening? Who would be seeing them? How might they react?

The concept of dual landscapes of action and consciousness, which Michael White borrowed from the anthropologist Edward Bruner is a useful touchstone at this time. We can ask questions that serve the purpose of developing the new story on either of these landscapes. On the landscape of action, we became interested in the details of the steps that each participant proposed to take and engaged in discussion about the expected consequences of these steps. On the landscape of consciousness, we asked about the meaning each person was making or might possibly make of these developments. We asked questions like

- What difference might it make to your relationship if Jim were to take the steps he is thinking about, and if Elizabeth was to do the things she is suggesting?
- What is it like for both of you here now to be talking about cooperation?
- Could this kind of discussion we are having now indicate anything about the kind of relationship you would prefer to have as neighbors?
- How does cooperation fit with your history of getting on with neighbors?
- What other steps could you put in place to ensure that next week is more trouble-free for you both?

Developing Agreements

Traditional understandings of negotiation that are well established in the mediation literature can be employed at this point. As the new story of cooperation starts to germinate and grow, a spirit of give-and-take and mutual respect can replace suspicion and "arguments." This is a useful climate for negotiation. The brainstorming of ideas in a cooperative spirit can be introduced and tied to the newly emerging alternative narrative about the relationship. This process can be a unique outcome in itself, and the participants can be invited to reflect on the difference between the new way of speaking and those associated with "arguments."

Moreover, the development of a written agreement can enhance the new story and extend the ripples of its influence. Jim and Elizabeth were encouraged to help the mediators write down the steps they had agreed to take in the interests of cooperation and to sign a statement of commitment to take these steps. This is another act in the evolution of the counterplot to "arguments." The signed document would be, for each of them, a reference point for the performance of meaning in the future.

Sustaining the New Story

At this point in the process, it is usual for the participants to be infused with more hope than they have felt in the past. The mediators may take on this feeling and be tempted to engage in too much celebration about the shifts that have taken place. It is easy for the mediators to be swept away by expectations that the new story will be easily woven into the relationship between the participants. They may forget that the old story has been around for some time, and that the new one still needs plenty of time to develop strongly.

Rather than becoming overly positive at this time, we think that it is more useful for mediators to show respect for the power of the old story and to be cautious about its chances of reexerting its influence. This, we believe, is a useful stance to take, for two reasons: first, it is realistic and usually makes sense to the participants; second, it reduces the probability that the participants will attempt to demonstrate the old story's power to undermine the new. If they do not have to correct us for our undue optimism about the future, then they are freer to be more optimistic themselves. Similarly, if they are correcting our more conservative expectations of the new story's chances of success, they are more likely to take credit for the success when it occurs, rather than attributing it to our influence. And this in turn is likely to increase their commitment to the new story.

We therefore believe it is important that when the participants have reached a point of agreement, mediators question the chances of success. We need to ask the "what if" questions. We need to point out the possibility that the "arguments" story will be more tricky than expected and will not give up easily in the face of efforts to defeat its influence. By taking this stance, we are also inviting the participants to prepare themselves against the possibilities of failure or relapse. We are inviting the performance of meaning around these possibilities so that they do not sneak up and take Jim and Elizabeth by surprise, thereby threatening the fragile new story's chances of survival. We ask how they might deal with failures and relapses and how they might prevent themselves from becoming downhearted if they do not achieve success overnight.

We warned that all may not be plain sailing for Jim and Elizabeth's new agreement. We voiced concern about the obstacles that none of us could currently foresee. We spoke about other people who might be able to interfere with the intentions that the two participants had stated. We talked about honeymoon periods and about what can happen when the novelty of the spirit of cooperation wears off. We wondered about how hard it would be to keep the documented agreements (without overdoing this and scaring the participants). We asked how long the participants thought it would take before the old story of "arguments" lost its influence over their relationship, and we offered more cautious estimates than they did. We discussed this issue between ourselves in front of the participants and familiarized each other with our cautions in a way that increased the cautious spirit in each of us. At the same time, we stated that we would be happy to be surprised by Jim and Elizabeth if they managed to prove us wrong.

Reviewing the Agreements

The next step in the mediation process would be a review of the developments that took place after the joint meeting(s). Sufficient time needs to elapse before this review meeting to allow the agreed steps to be taken and any unplanned developments to occur.

From a narrative perspective, we consider this review meeting far more important than a perfunctory chat about whether the agreements have been kept. We see it as an opportunity to build on what has already been achieved in the development of the new story. With Jim and Elizabeth, we were not only interested in whether the agreements about wearing headphones and exchanging information on work schedules and the like had been kept. We were also concerned with the meaning constructed out of these events and the contexts in which new understandings had been developing.

We expected that events had happened in the relationship between Jim and Elizabeth that had not yet been storied but that had the potential to contribute to the emerging story of respect and cooperation. So we directed our curiosity toward the discovery of these unique outcomes and their integration into a story of some coherence. We knew that this kind of curiosity might require persistence because such events, simply because they are still unstoried, often lie outside the participants' immediate awareness. Examples might be a passing smile at the gate or a new idea about music-playing that one participant thought of and raised with the other. It might be a new initiative for handling personal stress. It might be a neighborhood crisis like a car accident that draws both people into the street and into conversation about what they have seen. Once these kinds of events have been identified, we might ask Jim and Elizabeth questions to ascertain how they have made meaning of the events in relation to the new story. For example:

- Has anything happened in the last two weeks that could be considered to have contributed to the development of cooperation and respect between you?
- What difference did this event make to each of you? What bearing do you think it might have on the struggle against "arguments"?
- How did you manage to prevent "arguments" from reentering your relationship on this occasion?

The field of mediation has developed over the last few decades on the basis of a number of untested assumptions about conflict, human needs and motivation, the nature of "community," and the nature of resolution. A narrative approach to mediation is more than a stylistic variation on previous approaches. Rather, it marks a theoretical shift from the individualist and objectivist assumptions of the problem-solving model to a postmodern perspective that acknowledges the social construction of reality. Conflict develops in a social context; meanings are created and negotiated by individuals in conversation with one another.

In a narrative approach to mediation, the conflict story is unraveled or deconstructed to reveal the themes or discourses within it. The fact that different discourses exist alongside each other creates a source of tension and conflict. But it is this lack of discursive unity that also creates spaces and the potential for change. In these spaces, alternative preferred stories can be developed. A narrative approach to mediation thus entails an intricate weaving together of positions and the meanings that go with them.

Notes

P. 252, *Fisher and Ury:* Fisher, R., & Ury, W. (1981). *Getting to yes.* Boston: Houghton Mifflin.

P. 253, *the parties concerned:* Menkel-Meadow, C. (1984). Toward another view of legal negotiation: The structure of problem-solving. *UCLA Law Review, 31,* 754–842.

P. 254, *the field of mediation in recent years:* Folger, J. P., & Jones, T. S. (Eds.). (1994). *New directions in mediation: Communication research and perspectives.* Thousand Oaks, Calif.: Sage.

P. 254, *the mediation literature:* Menkel-Meadow, C. (1984). Toward another view of legal negotiation: The structure of problem-solving. *UCLA Law Review, 31,* 754–842.

P. 256, *generation, or re-generation, of alternative stories:* White, M., & Epston, D. (1990). *Narrative means to therapeutic ends.* New York: Norton.

P. 257, *violence and abuse have been compounded:* Lapsley, H., Robertson, N., & Busch, R. (1992). *The domestic protection study: Family court counselling.* Hamilton, New Zealand: University of Waikato; Newark, L., Harrell, A., & Salem, P. (1994). *Domestic violence and empowerment in custody and visitation cases.* Madison, Wis.: Association of Family and Conciliation Courts.

P. 258, *the direction that the mediation will take:* S. (1994). A narrative perspective on mediation. In J. P. Folger & T. S. Jones (Eds.), *New directions in mediation: Communication research and perspectives.* Thousand Oaks, Calif.: Sage.

P. 259, *influential in the mediation process:* Cobb, S. (1994). A narrative perspective on mediation. In J. P. Folger & T. S. Jones (Eds.), *New directions in mediation: Communication research and perspectives.* Thousand Oaks, Calif.: Sage.

P. 259, *making meaning around experiences of sexual abuse:* Weingarten, K., & Cobb, S. (1995). Timing and disclosure sessions: Adding a narrative perspective to clinical work with adult survivors of childhood sexual abuse. *Family Process, 34,* 257–259.

P. 269, *a useful touchstone at this time:* White, M. (1991). Deconstruction and therapy. In D. Epston & M. White (Eds.), *Experience, contradiction, narrative and imagination.* Adelaide, Australia: Dulwich Centre Publications.

Chapter Eleven

Health-Promoting Conversations

Bev McKenzie

It was now 2 A.M., and this was the fourth place we had been to this night. Mere led me into a crowded room thick with smoke. A party was in progress. Maori women and men (indigenous people of New Zealand) were standing in groups clutching beer bottles or glasses. Some were singing to the sounds of a guitar. I was aware that I was the only Pakeha (white person) present.

"Sit down." Mere indicated with her head that there was a chair available for me. "But if you want to be with us, stand up," she said out of the corner of her mouth. I mentally thanked Mere for making the local culture explicit and smiled. People were looking at me with that question in their minds: "I wonder what she is doing here."

In the Returned Services Association (RSA) Club, men had called out, "Hey, *taringa* woman," wanting to share their experiences of going deaf during the war with the gun blasts. (*Taringa* is the Maori word for ear). In the karaoke bar, we had met some of Mere's relations. One, a gang member, stared at me for some time, then said, "I want to know more about the glue ear thing." I was excited by who had asked the question, and now I was intrigued to find out just how far into the community information on our program had reached.

A Serious Health Problem

Glue ear is a condition that, if undetected or untreated in early childhood, can cause hearing loss. This can seriously affect a child's ability to learn. Many public health reports have been written on the extent and impact of glue ear in the Maori population. These reports have repeatedly called for the involvement of Maori people in any programmatic responses. One such report identified isolated parts of the Waikato region as in particular need of resource support. Within these isolated communities, Maori children up to five years of age were the group given priority.

Taumarunui was one of the rural communities identified. It has a center that is a focus for shopping and rural supplies and services. Some of the people targeted lived close to the town, but many lived in small villages or near *marae* (tribal ceremonial meeting places) in isolated pockets at some distance from the town center. On each of the *marae,* there was a *kohanga reo* (where Maori language and culture are taught to preschool children). The *kohanga reo* community consisted of *kaiako* (teachers) and *kaiawhina* (assistant teachers) from nine *kohanga* and their *whanau* (extended families), and they were already well aware of the problem of glue ear within the community. With the help of a local doctor, they had surveyed the children's ears and found that 50 percent of the children were affected. They had written to the Area Health Board (the local health authority) for support in developing a program to address the problem. However, the board did not have a good track record in helping the Maori community.

The health promotion unit of which I was a part was originally set up to address such issues with communities, in collaborative ways. In planning programs, the unit drew on the Ottawa Charter. This charter acknowledges that health and illness are constructions, the effects of inequities in social relations. A basic tenet of the charter is that within the resources of the community most affected by the problem lies the solution. Building on this perspective, narrative theory suggests that people are not overcome by the problem all the time and will have found some short-term solutions for themselves.

In this case, our manager challenged us to "find innovative answers to old problems"—the old answers having been to provide screening tests and medical support through a specialist ear nurse. I relished the chance to try a different kind of intervention.

Listening, Speaking, and *Tino Rangatiratanga*

Maori often feel blamed by health professionals, even when this is clearly not the professionals' intention. Constructionist theory helps me understand how this happens. The health professional is usually positioned as the expert. Because of unquestioning Western belief in the power of modern medicine, such "experts" often take up advice-giving roles and project an expectation that "patients" must do what they are told. The very term, *patient,* indicates passivity—surrender of one's active power over one's life. This power is called *tino rangatiratanga,* or sovereignty, by Maori. It is something that Maori have become very sensitive about because, as they explain, some of our Western ways can take this power away. The loss of *tino rangatiratanga* and recruitment into ways of being that deny productive power over one's own life are part of the process of colonization. Health professionals in the Western medical system have developed particular ideas of doctoring, nursing, diagnosis, and treatment. This in itself is not necessarily wrong, but in order to make a diagnosis, medical professionals are often drawn into a style of questioning that seems to demand a "colonized" demeanor on the patient's part. As one Maori explained: "It is the interrogation that they feel when they get in there.... 'Oh God, they are going to ask me all these questions!' and 'Oh God, I'm not going to understand what they are talking about!'— and I think it scares a lot of our Maori people off."

It is not hard to see why this is a reasonable fear. For example, medical "experts" say things like "Your child failed the ear test" or, if community members have not responded to a letter asking them to attend the ear clinic, "The people are lazy." Maori people know that these things are said about them. They also appreciate, perhaps more than those who use such words, the connotations of cultural inadequacy that these ways of speaking imply. What is often not made clear to the recipients of the letter is that the medical language in which such letters are written and the authoritative judgments about "failure" presume certain knowledge about ear problems.

I am told by Maori women that Maori are not used to asking questions of health professionals. The health professional is seen as the person who knows. Often, the Maori may sit and look as if they understand what the health professional is saying, refraining from asking questions out of respect for the professional's expert status. But at the same time, Maori do not give up their self-determination. This cultural mix can result in some important misunderstandings going unrecognized. Health professionals often mistakenly think that they are communicating well with Maori because interviews are conducted in a very polite, respectful manner on both sides. But Maori tell it differently: "We look at the health professionals with their confidence and their big words, and we sit back and say nothing."

For Maori, this sitting back and saying nothing is a mark of respect. For Pakeha experts, it could be taken as ignorance or acquiescence.

Fighting the Effects of Colonization: Within Myself

You may be asking what a white, middle-class woman is doing in a program dealing with Maori health. When I ask myself that question, I find there are several answers. The same systems that oppress Maori oppress me as a Pakeha woman, though differently. Having experienced oppression in my own life in painful and far-reaching ways, I want and need to be working with others, personally and politically, to push for change in systems that oppress. Therefore, at the core of my health promotion practice, I want to use methods that empower people and communities.

In calling myself a Pakeha, I acknowledge that my ancestors came to New Zealand several generations ago and contributed to the colonial heritage that even today is still largely monocultural. As a Pakeha, I have no wish to perpetuate colonizing practices. Instead, I wish to take seriously in my work a partnership with Maori that is based on power sharing. Paulo Freire's statement is a significant beacon for me: "Washing one's hands of the conflict between the powerful and the powerless is to side with the powerful, not to be neutral." But this is not simply a matter of fighting for justice for others. It is a deliberate positioning of myself in relation to the practices of health professionals. In locating myself as a community educator working with Maori, I have had echoing through my mind the words of an Aboriginal woman at a health conference: "If you have come to help me, you are wasting your time, but if your liberation is tied up with mine, then we can work together."

I heard her words as an invitation to partnership with indigenous people: if we have a common purpose in striving against oppression, then there are ways to work together. But these ways required me to take up a different position in my practice as a health educator. I see health information as a resource for healthy living rather than an authority. I see health as defined by the people whose well-being is in question rather than by health experts.

Community Work in Narrative Mode

I came across social constructionist thinking through living with a partner who used narrative ideas in his work as a therapist. The ideas appealed to my sense of justice and fairness and helped me theorize the process of empowerment. I have worked to translate these ideas into a health promotion setting—an adaptation that has taken place over a number of years. I have also been exploring the use of narrative in community settings as a qualitative evaluation tool, as a model for facilitating group work, and as a model for community intervention.

To approach the community around Taumarunui in a narrative way I needed to develop a relationship with the people affected by glue ear. I needed to listen to their experiences around this condition and to their stories of its effect on their lives and relationships. Understanding health and illness as social constructions, I became interested in the discursive practices that make up people's experiences of glue ear as they live in the community, and in the glue ear experiences of health professionals. Believing that health is not something we give to people but a process created in the dynamic moments of our relationships, and believing that it is my work as a health educator to foster such health-promoting conversations, I set about listening to the stories of community people, unearthing new insights and new learnings (sometimes for them, sometimes for me). Together, we discovered their current knowledges and thought about how they were producing their worlds in light of these knowledges.

Working with the Community

Becoming engaged with a community is probably the single most important process that determines what eventually becomes possible in a project, especially with groups thought of as "minority" and "disadvantaged." It requires cultural sensitivity and awareness of different interests and understandings. Recognizing this, the health promotion unit employed a Maori "interface" worker, Koro, whose task was to find the most appropriate Maori group to drive our project. Koro was to negotiate with the community group—in this case, the local health committee—to bring key community people together for a training program. Following the training, these key networkers would take the educative process back to their own *whanau*.

My involvement began when Koro judged that the community was ready for the six-week training program, which was designed to take place one day a week. Before it began, I went to meet with one of the "key" women, Arohina, and the *kuia* (an older woman of high standing in the community). We talked together about the idea of health-promoting conversations and what they would mean in practice. It was important for me to take up a different stance from that of the more usual expert coming to tell these people what to do. I suggested that I had some skills that could be used alongside the skills of the community, and that together we could learn from each other. As the next step, Arohina agreed to distribute among her networks a flyer that we prepared together.

Features of the Training Program: Deconstructing the Problem

When facilitating a program with Maori, the day begins with a *karakia* (prayer) and welcome from a *kaumatua* (an elder of status). This program belonged to the Maori from the start. The *karakia* set the scene and brought people together spiritually. The prayer and welcome were acknowledged and replied to. A relaxed time followed as we shared who we were, creating a warmth and interconnectedness in the group. This stage in the process is called *whakawhanaungatanga*.

Only after these (in)formalities was I given the role of establishing the *kaupapa* (agenda) for the day. We had come to share and learn more about our experiences of glue ear. I adopted the words used by the group for glue ear rather than the one used by the medical profession: *taringa pirau* (rotten ears), *taringa pikako* (smelly ears), and *taringa maemae* (sore ears). I asked them for stories of themselves in relation to health. What were their experiences of coping with ear problems? As we began to share stories, many issues emerged: difficulties in talking to the doctors; the privacy of health for Maori; how people felt about going to the doctor and specialists; how they coped with children or grandchildren with glue ear. Many remembered what it was like for them as children when they had a sore ear but did not say anything about it; they kept quiet so that they did not annoy their parents in the middle of the night—or because they somehow knew that there was already enough pressure on the family. There were stories of going to the doctor and trying to make sense of the doctor's medical way of talking.

As the facilitator, it was my role to develop a discourse out of which solutions could be drawn. I understood participants to have a wisdom that Michel Foucault calls indigenous. This is knowledge that is very well known—in fact, it is so embedded in cultural discourse and taken-for-granted that it previously may have been unrecognized by the users of that knowledge. Or it may have been disqualified or accorded lower status than the knowledge promoted within dominant communities. I carefully listened for the context, language, and belief structure of the group while continuing to develop an externalizing conversation.

As the process continued and the participants became more relaxed with each other and with me, we reflected on how each person acted in relation to the problem of glue ear. What did participants notice about glue ear? How did it come to their attention? What did the children do? What led them to do that and not something else? What did the parents do? These questions invited the group to reflect on and reexamine the meanings of their experiences. The process drew out many of the commonly held ways of thinking and speaking that pathologize Maori and offered the opportunity to look at them differently. This is the process of externalizing; the objective is to move the blame from the people being the problem to the problem being the problem.

Participants talked of how the children's behavior was often described as frustrated, distracted, dreamy. Young children were described as grizzly, off their food, rubbing their ear. The parents observed the symptoms but did not necessarily connect these to glue ear unless they had some prior experience of the problem. There were also stories of how parents had responded to their children's pain. They described how they had warmed the ear using remedies learned from their own parents: a warm potato in a sock or warm olive oil, for example. Some of the group noted that parents who were not aware of the classic symptoms said, "He hears when he wants to hear." (Part of the problem is that glue ear comes and goes, and some days the children can hear well.) Some parents related that they felt "dumb" because they had not recognized the symptoms (which are invisible until you know what you are looking at). Because glue ear has been such a common problem for a number of years, most members of the group have heard people say, "All of my children had runny ears. So did we as kids, so it must be hereditary."

I then asked some other reflexive questions so that we would continue to reexamine the meanings of participants' experiences and to draw on the alternative knowledges in the room. For example, I asked, "In your opinion, what did the parents believe the health professionals thought about it?" The participants said that parents often felt blamed by the health professionals—and dumb because they had not recognized the symptoms. The participants reported that some health professionals thought the parents were lazy and unintelligent and did not care for their children. Others thought that parents should be more responsible for their own health needs. Health professionals in general often think that parents lack knowledge and parenting skills.

I went on and asked, "If it was the teachers who noticed runny ears, what did the parents believe the teachers thought about them as parents and about the child with glue ear?"

"That it was our fault as parents that nothing had been done about it," someone replied. "I think the teachers think that Maori don't care about their children."

One woman said, "I can remember a teacher saying to me as a child, 'Doesn't your mother look after you? Doesn't she give you a hankie?'"

Some people would recognize my questions as circular, but the importance of the questions is that they enable the deconstruction of the judgments of health professionals and others and seek to reestablish the authority of the knowledge of parents and children. In this room was a wealth of experience and knowledge waiting to be drawn out; all that was needed was space for the experiences to be heard. Once the knowledge was validated, it could be put to good use.

As the day proceeded, a doctor known to the group talked about the medical aspects of glue ear. This information, given to the group in a straightforward manner, dealt with the structure of the ear, the mechanisms of hearing, ear infections, and the consequences of leaving ear infections untreated. We wanted to emphasize that medical knowledge is not mystical or beyond the participants' understanding; rather, it is knowledge to be shared and made use of.

I remembered Koro saying that in order to preserve *mana* (authority, dignity), Maori often closed themselves off from the Pakeha support system. I wondered how much this closing off was an effect of Pakeha ways of speaking. If one has a health problem and knows that teachers and health professionals think about Maori in "Why don't they?" or "Why haven't they?" terms, one might close off as a way of maintaining some pride, *mana*, control over one's circumstances. An accusatory attitude does not invite collaboration.

Cindy, Cindy, Why Don't You Ever Pay Attention?

Later, we examined the child's experiences of glue ear and how the child was positioned by peers, teachers, and parents. To do this, we used video clips that showed a child in a classroom who was suffering from the effects of glue ear. The child could not hear the teacher's commands and, as a result, was in a world of her own, unaware of her deafness or of its effects on her and on those around her. She was described as a dreamy little girl. The teacher called out to her in a frustrated tone, "Cindy, Cindy, why don't you ever pay attention?" I asked the group about the effect of such experiences on the child. They mentioned, among other effects, isolation, anger, frustration, and low self-esteem.

We examined possible explanations of parents' and teachers' observed behavior in this scenario and what support was needed if change was to take place. The group was clear that parents and teachers needed help in comprehending why the child was not paying attention. The child, meanwhile, needed responses built on love, acceptance, and understanding. Some people recognized themselves in the video scene and "confessed" to the group that they had interacted with their own children or grandchildren in a similar way: "I never realized that my child may have had glue ear and couldn't hear and I have talked to him like that."

After this exercise, we looked at what needed to change. The group felt that doctors needed more education on ear problems. They said parents and health workers needed to get together to understand each other. Consistent messages needed to be given by health professionals; there needed to be more communication between schools and health services. Schools needed to understand and be made more aware of hearing problems. Hearing problems needed to be detected at infancy. A wealth of knowledge was present, drawn from personal experience of the problem.

In the final round of the day, some participants expressed relief that they no longer felt so alone with the problem. They clearly had enjoyed listening to others' stories and sharing common experiences. One woman expressed it this way: "It's great to have a common goal. I learnt a lot today. I can hardly wait to get out there and tell others." She was going home to tell her *whanau* about what she had learned, but like several others in the group, she wondered whether this would be possible.

The Next Step: Spreading the News

On the way home, I reflected on the day and on how I could facilitate a discussion about the difficulty of talking with certain *whanau* members about health problems. I wondered who was able to speak within that *whanau,* and what could be spoken about. What cultural forces were operating here? Foucault takes the position that what can be spoken about and who can speak are issues of power. Were such issues operating in this case? Were some people in the *whanau* actively preventing "key" health workers from speaking about glue ear? As a Pakeha and therefore of a different culture, I would need to work with sensitivity to determine the answers to these questions. I also could not be sure what action the community members needed to take; however, I did have a responsibility as a facilitator to set up a process for finding out.

As a result of my reflection, I initiated a process the following week. We had externalized the problem as "ear problems." I asked the group, "How do you think it has come about that it is difficult to talk to some people about ear problems?" Many of the responses were about the sacredness of the head to Maori—for example, "I remember, growing up, we never walked across another person's head."

The idea of sacredness or *tapu* associated with the body explained to these women why health and ears were private. The discussion touched on the spiritual dimension of health. It was important to acknowledge and to use *karakia* (prayer) and to have faith in traditional healing methods, which are used interchangeably with Western medical knowledge. As these matters were sacred, I allowed space for the discussion and did not intrude.

The participants then talked about some parents they knew who were really shy about discussing problems and kept to themselves. Shyness, I thought—here it is again. The women spoke about how Maori have a "hidden pride," and how some *whanau* like to keep to themselves and not let outsiders in. I thought of the times when Maori had regarded me as an outsider, a Pakeha health professional, and responded to my questions at a superficial level or gave me an answer they thought I wanted. Did this have anything to do with the effect of colonization? Had Maori been driven to build a protective shell around themselves? The difference in culture left me no way of asking this, so I went on to the next question.

Reconstruction: Getting to Action

"Understanding this problem now and how it comes about, are there ways that Maori culture can be used or developed by Maori to overcome it?" The purpose of this question was to start the process of reconstruction. It helped the group to uncover and give voice to the cultural resources they already had to overcome the problem. The women said the topic could be brought up in *whanau* meetings. They also suggested that a person could ask her mother or the elders for cures or advice.

The discussion moved on to ways they had found to talk within the *whanau*. One approach was to call on the skills and spontaneity of a young *kaiawhina* (assistant teacher). Mere was one such woman; she was called on often to be a translator between cultures. Other people suggested that within the *whanau* there might be someone who could take the health message to others. "Someone close to that *whanau* might be able to observe who that could be and send the information in to them." Another woman later reported that she had not been sure whether the new information would be received by her sister, so she had talked about it in terms of her own discoveries on the course: "You know, on this course that I was on today, I learnt that when Sonny turns the TV up and is yelling a lot this could mean that he has a hearing problem, and I need to take him to that van thing and get it checked out." This conversation opened up the way for her sister to talk about ear problems.

Alternative Stories

At the beginning of each weekly session, I asked the women to catch me up on what had happened during that week. There was always a multitude of stories about their going back to their own *whanau* to give the information to others. Some had talked at *whanau* meetings, or *hui;* others to friends or family. I was always excited by the stories that unfolded. It seemed that within some *whanau* settings—such as in a *kohanga* meeting or with friends—it was permissible to talk about the health of the children.

"We had a *whanau* meeting, and I had a talk about what I had done, and the parents were coming forward and asking more questions. It was amazing."

In response, I was very curious about how the situation had arisen and developed. "What did you say and do, and what was the reaction of the people there?" I asked. "How did you manage to capture people's attention?" The answers to such questions turned each incident into a full story. The tellers were the actors in the scene, which had a specific setting, time, and cast of characters. Through the telling of the stories, preferred self-descriptions began to emerge. The importance of this storying was that meaning was being *made*—a new history claimed.

The women from various *kohanga* told how they had realized the importance of nose blowing and had begun to teach the procedure to children. One woman began to recruit children who knew how to blow their noses to teach others to do so. It was through the storying of their experiences that they gave recognition to and received recognition for the discoveries they had made. They were taking control of the problem.

At the end of the training program, I asked the participants what they would tell others about it. Some said simply that they would share the information; others said they would talk about how enjoyable it had been to share common problems. Many spoke about how much confidence they had gained. One woman commented that hearing about participants' experiences with their own children or with others had given her new insights into herself.

I asked some reflexive questions about their learnings. "If someone important to you had observed you over the period of time that you attended the education days, what different things might they have noticed about you during this time?"

One woman replied, "People may have noticed that I am a more understanding and *aroha* (loving) person towards my children, instead of the yelling person that I was. My approach with children has changed. When I see that a child has an ear problem, I also look at what might be going on for that child—my attitude has changed."

Becoming Health Educators

Following the training program, I took every opportunity to story the experiences of the women, either directly—if I met them during a follow-up visit—or through Arohina. It seemed that the women had become so enthusiastic about their knowledge, they wished to share it wherever they went, whether to the home of friends, to the club, or to a party. As someone said at the end of the program, "I can't wait to get out there and tell others." I was interested in listening to the success stories of the educators who took the information back to their own *whanau*. It was in these stories that the unique outcomes lay. Telling the stories offered the possibility of changing them from mere anecdotes to a new history of glue ear in the community. These women's perceptions of themselves began to change, and their confidence in themselves as educators grew.

I asked Rehua, "What sort of things have you discovered about yourself during and since the training program?"

She replied, "I was not very interested in health, to be very honest, but this has prompted me. Breast-feeding babies—I used to think, Oh gosh! But then I suddenly realized through this course how valuable breast milk was to preventing children from getting glue ear—natural antibodies and that. Now, when I see mothers breast-feeding their babies, I say that's really good. Little health things like that. Now I carry a hanky around with me to help blow my little mates' [the children's] noses. Just little things like that. They are little things but *important* things."

Often, when I met the educators, they had a story to tell me. Hoki was the Maori Plunket worker and had been very shy on the course. When I met her, I asked her how things were going. She looked pleased with herself and told me the following story:

"I saw Lilly the other day, and she looked like she hadn't had any sleep, and she looked worried. When I asked her what was wrong, she told me the baby had been crying a lot. We went over to her house. We both looked at the baby. The baby's cheek was red, and it looked like it had been crying for some time. I asked Lilly how long this had been going on, and when I heard it had been going on for two days, it seemed like we needed to get medical help. We took the baby to the doctor, and sure enough, it had an ear infection and needed antibiotics."

"What was it about the situation that you responded to?" I asked.

Hoki replied, "The way the baby was crying, the redness around the cheek and ear, and that it had gone on for so long."

Rehua's and Hoki's confidence had grown. They were becoming educators of others and primary health care providers.

Changing the Position of Maori Women in the Discourse

Through the new knowledge gained at the training course, Rehua's position in the discourse about health began to change.

Hekia and Rehua discussed with me their plans to hold a *hui* where they would share the information with their own *whanau*. Hekia was unsure whether they could do it without the health professionals helping them to talk to the parents. She said to Rehua:

"If it was to come from the professional side, maybe they [the parents] will start taking it all in, and they will take it on board. Do you think that is appropriate or not?"

Rehua paused for a moment. "No. I feel confident enough. . . . I don't know about going out there [to the wider community,] but for starters, presenting our package here, to our *whanau*, we have got to say that we went on this course, this really intense course that showed us everything about the ear, and we feel confident enough to stand here to tell you exactly all about it. We were taught it in simple terms, how to talk one on one to mothers. Especially if we are concerned enough. Polish up on our first performance, of course. Get it down to a fine art. I feel very confident."

Rehua thinks she will get a better response than the professionals who visit the *kohanga*, because she knows the families. She is confident about and capable of holding a meeting with the *whanau* to talk about ear problems and does not need to rely on the health professionals. She has changed her position in the medical discourse. In the *hui* that followed, the women capably demonstrated that they were taking responsibility for their own health. One of their stated objectives for the day was "to be our own educators."

Through the training course, Maori women had gained confidence, including the confidence to ask questions of health professionals. Hera described her interaction with a medical professional after the training program:

"I had a good experience yesterday. I went to Rotorua hospital. My baby got burnt a couple of years back and they sent me this card. I get to the hospital and I thought, Oh yeah, we are going to see about his burns . . . and get in there, and I say his burns are quite nice, and he says, 'No, dear, you are not here for the burns, you are here for his ear.' I had been referred to him in 1991 for my baby's ears . . . and there I am sitting there talking to the wrong doctor . . . but he came out, and he started showing me all these diagrams, and before he started saying anything, I said, 'Oh yeah, that's the Eustachian tube, and he said to me 'Where did you learn all of this?' and I said we had a course, and I said it is a pity I had to wait two years to get to see him, . . . but he definitely needs a grommet [a small tube inserted into the ear drum to allow healing to take place].

". . . Usually, with people like that, I feel *whakamaa* [shy], and I don't say very much, I just sit there. But because I knew about it, I felt like I was up there, too, on the same level."

Rewina said, "It is just giving you that confidence, eh, to be able to speak."

"Oh," replied Hera, "my friends have me on, and they say, 'You think you are an ear specialist now!' and I say, 'Well, I am. I have got my certificate to prove it, too.' Yes, it has given me a lot of confidence."

I was excited to hear Hera repositioning herself within the discourse of what it was to be a Maori woman and visit a doctor. Her old position is described by her as *whakamaa*. Her new position of confidence enables her to explain to the doctor what she knows about the workings of the ear and the formation of glue ear.

The Alternative Story Emerges

The educators formed a team to take the information to three outlying *marae* that had not sent representatives to the course. We had several practice meetings, where it became clear that each woman had a specific preference for the part of the program she wanted to present. Each would start her presentation with an account of how she had become involved in the program and would then relate a story from her own life that was relevant to the part of the program she was leading. I went along as a resource person but did not take a very visible role.

On the way home after one of these *hui*, I asked Arohina how she felt when she saw the Maori women up front. She said she felt very proud. "The more they see us up front, the more Maori people will see us as a role model. They will get to see us as educators of our own people."

These Maori women were speaking themselves and each other into existence in new and preferred ways that held significant cultural meaning. They call themselves Maori educators.

Performance of the New Story

At the end of the first phase of the program, the organizations involved held an evaluation *hui*, where the educators took key roles in front of their community. The mayor, local doctors, the ear, nose, and throat specialist, *kaumatua* and *kuia* (elders) were present. There was also a group of Aboriginal health workers from Australia who had come to find out what was happening in New Zealand programs for the prevention of glue ear. Thus an audience had been recruited for the performance of the educators' new skills.

The educators were by now well practiced in their presentation style, each leading a segment of the event. This impressed the audience. The local doctor, who had been involved with the program ever since the problem was identified among the *kohanga* children, was delighted both by the presentation and by the fact that Maori women were in the forefront. The ear specialist commented on the level of knowledge he had found in patients when he was working at the ear caravan. He was also very pleasantly surprised by the quality of the educators' questions. Not only were these women confident about their own knowledge in their own communities, but they were now claiming legitimacy for their roles before an audience of health professionals. The professionals, for their part, could now see how Maori could respond to their own health needs.

Despite my optimism, I recognized that not everyone was able to understand these new positions. The newspaper report of the event gave evidence that, for some, dominant discourses still prevailed. The headline read, "Ear specialist nurses win the battle over glue ear." The reporter had talked to all of us—the Maori workers, *kuia*, myself, and the ear specialists—but the newspaper space had been given solely to the ear specialists: "Thanks to the good work of the specialist ear nurses, the battle against glue ear in the . . . district seems to be working. That was the conclusion drawn by the ear and nose specialist . . ."

Arohina sent me the newspaper cutting. In the margin of the report, she gave expression to what was now a widely held alternative knowledge: "Credit must go to the grass roots, participating voluntarily to meet their needs. There are battles at both ends of the system. The biggest battle is where people do not get paid and still strive to help themselves."

Reflections

I was interested to hear how Arohina felt the changes had taken place. What were the steps that had led to this?

She said: "Well, I think in all that you did and I did, we downplayed that 'we are dumb mothers' idea. We said, 'No, you are not. You have the knowledge, just like everyone else. You are not a dumb Maori.'

"So the story was fostered in some way?" I asked.

"Well, we followed that up by involving them. We played down the professional story and built on their story. That's what we did."

"We gave them a place for their story?"

"We gave them a place for their stories. We listened to their stories and praised their stories. They were beautiful stories that were told. We created that environment, and they did it, and you did it by encouraging them. The fact that we were in among them, it was team work, we didn't move without having our community on board. We discussed things—the starting steps. They knew what was happening. They were prepared. The educators are not brought out into unsafe waters. They are working in a way that is culturally appropriate, as in working among their own *whanau*. It is not disrupting the concept of *whanau* [extended family], *hapu* [subtribe], *iwi* [tribe]. Within that *whanau, hapu, iwi,* their knowledge and experience they can relate to each other. . . . You [Bev] were breaking the status quo. You may as well say you were being colonized, too, like us. You were reacting against the system with us, so you couldn't be seen as a colonizer to us. It was the people who were behind you that were the colonizers, and we were together trying to stop them."

Postscript

As politically inspired nationwide "reforms" of the health system took hold, restructuring occurred within the organization in which I worked. The health promotion unit was disbanded, and with it went the mandate for partnership with the community. The new health authority management had different and definite ideas about how relationships between communities and the health system were to be managed. The new contract set up with the community health committee was written in terms of statistical targets, which left the community feeling blamed when the targets, which were arbitrarily set, were not reached. Outcomes of empowerment proposed by health promotion practice were not seen as valid in the new managerial framework; they could not be counted. New methods of consultation have not proven satisfactory to the community, and if anything, have served only to enhance colonizing Pakeha practices. The success of our efforts has been rendered invisible to management.

Our accomplishments may have been partially erased in the health system, with restructuring and the redesigning of contracts. The dominant discourse has reasserted itself. But in this particular community, what we achieved has become unstoppable because the people have begun to hear their own voices and to see their own stories in action. Although this has been on a relatively small scale and over a short period of time, it has given to the community real hope that cannot be denied.

There were effects on myself as well as on the community. Narrative thinking invited me into a way of working with people in which they become my senior partners. This produces a respectful and collaborative approach to naming problems and initiating action. It also captures in practice the principle set forth by Ron Labonte that "the experience of health belongs to those experiencing it." As a health professional, I am very aware that I do not have the privilege of naming anyone else's reality. Narrative certainly offers me a clearer way to support the development of agency among Maori so that they act on their own behalf and name their own needs.

The story of this chapter demonstrates the effect of narrative practices in a community. It shows how a group of women who at one time described themselves as "dumb mothers" now describe themselves as "educators of our own people." Along with this redescription is visible evidence of empowerment: improved confidence, self-esteem, and cultural identity; enhanced ability to reflect critically and solve problems; expanded capacity to make choices; increased collective bargaining power; and greater legitimation of the women's own perceived needs.

I believe that through our project these Maori women have gained a voice for themselves that they can hear and that they are beginning to insist that others hear also. This was evident when the group went to see the area manager of the new health authority to ask for funding to continue the program. Though this was a Pakeha arena, they were not intimidated and held their ground. One of the group, Arohina, described the scene:

"They were Maori women in a Pakeha environment, and they moved into it. Maori are usually reluctant to go into a Pakeha environment. 'We are here because we know what we want and what is good for us. The days are gone where you are going to tell us what is good for us,' and we voiced it."

She reflected: "I think it is quite a shock for Pakeha to come up against Maori women like this. These women come from the Ponsonbies (a low socioeconomic sector of Taumarunui). They are seen as having no brains. They are 'nobodies' in the eyes of a lot of people. Here they are speaking out for themselves."

These women are insistent that Maori will provide services to Maori, and that any Pakeha health workers in the community will be asked to work in ways that are culturally appropriate. This is social change at a profound level.

Traditional Pakeha methods still have colonizing effects on Maori, and alternative community methods need to be found. The best hope, I believe, lies in the domain of postmodern thinking, where approaches such as narrative give at least as much weight to the experiences, knowledges, and preferences of Maori as to practices of Pakeha health professionals. Maori ideas and preferences need to be more than just acknowledged as "being there." They need to be worked with in a respectful way.

Traditionally, collaborative methods are merely paraded on appropriate special occasions. Narrative provides a way of thinking that is always with us, encouraging a shift from shallow performance to constructive approaches to people and problems.

Notes

P. 276, *in any programmatic responses:* The Review Team to Consider Hearing Impairment Among Maori People (1989). *Whakaronga mai: Maori hearing impairment. Report to the Minister of Maori Affairs.* Wellington, New Zealand: Government Printers.

P. 276, *the Ottawa Charter:* A charter for health promotion developed at the First International Conference for Health Promotion in Ottawa, Canada, 1986. *Canadian Journal of Public Health, 77,* 426–427.

P. 276, *inequities in social relations:* Labonte, R. (1991). Empowerment: Notes on community and professional dimensions. *Canadian Research on Social Policy, 26,* 64–75.

P. 276, *short-term solutions for themselves:* Bruner, E. (1986). Ethnography as narrative. In V. Turner & E. Bruner (Eds.), *The anthropology of experience.* Chicago: University of Illinois Press.

P. 278, *still largely monocultural:* Spoonley, P. (1992). Pakeha ethnicity: A response to Maori sovereignty. In P. Spoonley, D. Pearson, & C. McPherson (Eds.), *Nga take: Ethnic relations and racism in Aotearoa/New Zealand.* Dunmore, New Zealand: Palmerston North.

P. 278, *not to be neutral:* Freire, P. (1978). *Pedagogy in process: The letters from Guinea Bissau.* New York: Seabury Press.

P. 279, *dynamic moments of our relationships:* Labonte, R. (1989). Community and professional empowerment. *Canadian Nurse, 85*(3), 23–28.

P. 279, *their current knowledges:* White, M. (1992). Deconstruction and therapy. In D. Epston & M. White (Eds.), *Experience, contradiction, narrative and imagination.* Adelaide, Australia: Dulwich Centre Publications.

P. 280, *"minority" and "disadvantaged":* Wallarck, L. & Wallerstein, N. (1986). Health education and prevention: Designing community initiatives. *International Quarterly of Community Health Education, 7*(4), 319–342.

P. 281, *Michel Foucault calls indigenous:* Foucault, M. (1980). *Power/knowledge: Selected interviews and other writings.* New York: Pantheon Books.

P. 284, *issues of power:* Parker, I. (1989). Discourse and power. In K. Gergen & J. Shotter (Eds.), *Texts of identity.* London: Sage.

P. 291, *battle over glue ear:* "Ear specialist nurses win the battle over glue ear." (1993, November 17). *Ruapehu Press,* p. 10.

P. 293, *my senior partners:* Epston, D., & White, M. (1992). Consulting your consultants: The documentation of alternative knowledges. In D. Epston & M. White (Eds.), *Experience, contradiction, narrative and imagination.* Adelaide, Australia: Dulwich Centre Publications.

P. 293, *and initiating action:* Gray, B. (1989). *Collaborating: Finding common ground for multiparty problems.* San Francisco: Jossey-Bass.

P. 293, *belongs to those experiencing it:* Labonte, R. (1989). Community and professional empowerment. *Canadian Nurse, 85*(3), 23–28.

P. 293, *own perceived needs:* Kindervatter, S. (1979). Nonformal education as an empowering process. Centre for International Education.

Epilogue

Wendy Drewery

Well, now, if you have stayed with us through this book, you will, we hope, have gathered something of the flavor of what we try to do in our practice. As we come to the end of what has been a wonderful experience in community achievement, we are mostly feeling amazed—and even a little chastened. We knew that narrative ideas were powerful and would drive the writing of the book along, but for several of us the experience of participating in this project and our pride in what we have done is marvelous beyond anything we could have imagined. It is not so much that we think the product is wonderful (although we do feel pleased with it). Our exhilaration is more about what can be achieved when a group of people try to interact according to the ideas we have enunciated here.

We began this project because we believed in these ideas and in the creative work being done by the various people who have contributed to the book. What we also believed in was the power of collaboration on the basis of shared understanding. At the beginning, we talked a lot about what the project meant to us and what each of us had to give to it. We met sometimes every two weeks, sometimes once a month, depending on the stage the project had reached and the needs of the authors. We talked about our insecurities, our different strengths and weaknesses. We sat around a large coffee table and carefully thought through such things as the reasons why some ways of writing felt better than others. Some doubts had been voiced in the early stages by various individuals about their capacity to complete the task. We decided

296

that we would not ask people to write in a vacuum. So even in the embryonic stages we all read each other's writing.

Sometimes it was hard to hand one's writing over, knowing how rough and ill-formed it was. But doing so was always an uplifting experience. Feedback often came later in the week, in the mail, always with some good suggestions and a lot of encouragement. In spite of the misgivings of those who did not think of themselves as strong writers, we have not compromised on quality at all.

We watched our group dynamics change as power shifted among the members. Occasionally there were tears as people struggled with issues, but we focused on the strength that was laboring to find expression, and this resulted in the emergence of some very lovely stories as long-standing insecurities gradually faded away. In short, we believe we practiced what we have been talking about in these pages.

We have learned a great deal. One of our startling discoveries was that authorship is not necessarily a matter of individuals scribbling away in their separate rooms. Many of the ideas—indeed, much of the writing—in this book were generated from group interactions rather than from the labor of single individuals. Instead of reaching into our personal stock of experience for inspiration, each of us often reached into the rich pool of knowledge collectively possessed by our evolving community of writers. This is not to deny the contribution of every individual author; it is to suggest, though, that each of our contributions was enhanced through our interactions with others. Indeed, in some of the chapters, we have had difficulty deciding where the lines of authorship are to be drawn. We hope no injustice has been done in the final decisions, but we can at least note here the contributions of each to all.

Our theory suggests that everybody has tales to tell, everybody has a legitimate claim to his or her place in the world. We tried to practice this in the group. Each meeting began with an agenda to which we all contributed. By the time we came to our last meetings, we could point to many signs of mutual learning, sharing, support, and challenge, not only in our writing but also in the dynamics of the group.

Aileen Cheshire observed: "We have students working and writing alongside lecturers here. That seems really special." This comment prompted Lorraine Smith—like Aileen, a student in our program—to ask, "How did that happen? I joined you all late, and at first I was really unconfident. We've somehow allowed students to have some knowledge. We've developed a two-way process of learning. I feel really validated professionally."

And so she should. I don't see any reason why lecturers ought to know everything. As a lecturer myself, I find such an idea very constraining, not to mention frightening.

As these pages demonstrate, every contributor has something interesting and innovative to offer. Some of us surprised ourselves. We have simply tried to create the space for such surprises. We mounted an explicit challenge to the discourses that dominate our usual working relationships: unfavorable comparison, hierarchy, lack of knowledge—the very same discourses that so many of our clients struggle against. The group process was interesting, approximating what I would like to think of as a new form of democracy— one that makes space for minority voices. We sometimes went around in circles, or so it seemed, as we revisited decisions we had thought were final, argued about the nuances of different terms, wondered how to make decisions when no one actually knew "the answer." We pondered the ethics of professional practice, writing, and life in general a lot—and sometimes "got it wrong." But we learned that even this was not disastrous. We could revisit. We could change our minds in the light of new experience, new understanding. Such a process is called "recursive." To us, it represents a strong commitment to a project—one that involves an ongoing attempt to define what one is doing. The naming is very much a part of the doing.

We talked of how we wanted this book to have a New Zealand feel to it. Being a little sensitive to the marginality of life in the Antipodes, we feel we know something about the effects of colonization, and this knowledge has contributed to our understanding of the hegemonic nature of Western rationality. We wanted to speak directly about this to colleagues from the "North" who might read this book. We wanted to show how our thoughts and our work have been informed by Maori challenges to colonial discourses and feminist challenges to patriarchal ones—and by our responses to each. We are still a little worried about coming on too strong when we make these points. As Wally McKenzie put it, "We don't want to poke you in the eye with a sharp stick, but these things are important." I am sure they are important to many, if not most, of our readers. We would like to have more dialogue with you on these topics.

Even though we have tried to temper our tendency to evangelize, I am sure some of it comes through. But we would not want you to think we are setting ourselves up as authorities on narrative ideas. We have dared to speak our enthusiasm, dared to sound authoritative, dared to speak about the work of others without consultation, dared to leap into some uncharted waters. Leaping off like this would be much more frightening if we did not have first-hand knowledge of the power of collaboration in a warm, loving community.

From where I sit, the postmodern world is a frightening place: too many nuclear weapons, too much technology, too little skill in peacemaking. One would think that counselors have a lot to offer such a world. However, having lived much of my life with the fear of being wrong, I am learning that the world is also a very forgiving place—a place where many possibilities lie untapped, where there is increasing room for differences, where more and more people understand how little they know. These are the real advances in human development, in my view—not that we are closer to the answers, but we are closer to living with uncertainty and can find this prospect exciting.

Please write to us. We are eager to continue the conversations begun in these pages, eager to include you as readers in the authoring of what you have been reading. We are interested to know how our writing brings to mind aspects of your experience, personal or professional, and allows them to be seen differently. We would like to hear about any experiments you try on the basis of your reading. We are also interested to know whether things that are taught to you by your clients relate to the ideas we have been discussing.

Our intention is to share in the ongoing production of discourses that enrich people's lives.

You can contact us through the editors at the University of Waikato, Private Bag 3105, Hamilton, New Zealand.

A Narrative Glossary

agency   The extent to which individuals can act for themselves and speak on their own behalf. Such agency is more of an achievement than a right. It is established in the face of dominant discourses, and it often involves a deliberate break from the influence of such discourses.

agentive self gap   The gap between an actual description of a life change in passive terms and a potential description in which the narrator portrays himself as an agent in the production of the change.

alternative story   The story that develops in therapy in contradiction to the dominant story in which the problem holds sway.

anti-anorexia/anti-bulimia leagues   Communities of people who have taken a stand against the oppressive regimes of anorexia and bulimia in their own lives and are prepared to share their stories with others who are struggling with these problems.

archives   Collections of documents produced as outcomes of narrative therapy and dealing with the conquest of a specific problem issue. With the permission of their originators, they can be used in therapeutic meetings with other clients as sources of local knowledge about the problem and how to defeat it.

audiences for the new story   Significant others in the life of the person struggling with a problem who might appreciate the development of the new story.

coauthoring   The ideal therapeutic relation, in which counselor and client share responsibility for the development of alternative stories.

consulting your consultants   Seeking information from a client about the special knowledge he or she has developed as a result of struggling with and defeating a problem. The counselor does this for the benefit of future clients after progress has been made in performing a new story.

counterplot   The significant events in the development of the alternative story.

curiosity   The "naive" inquiring spirit that is essential in narrative therapy. It differs from the kind of curiosity that seeks to confirm existing knowledge or assumptions; it is marked by a genuine desire to learn from the client, especially about the alternative story.

deconstruction   The process of unpacking the taken-for-granted assumptions and ideas underlying social practices that masquerade as truth or reality. It is achieved by bringing to light the gaps or inconsistencies in a text or discourse or dominant story so that acceptance of the story's message or logic no longer appears inevitable. Deconstruction is less adversarial and more playful than critique or confrontation.

deliberate ignorance   Lynn Hoffman's term for the stance of naïveté and curiosity from which questions are asked in narrative therapy. It signifies both the narrative therapist's eschewing of the right to impose her own expert knowledge and a respectful attitude towards the client's knowledge about his own life.

discourse   A set of ideas embodied as structuring statements that underlie and give meaning to social practices, personal experience, and organizations or institutions. Discourses often include the taken-for-granted assumptions that allow us to know how to "go on" in social situations of all kinds. They are linguistic in nature (provided that language is taken to include nonverbal as well as verbal practices).

discursive   Pertaining to or originating in a discourse or in the background from which a discourse is formed.

discursive practice   A poststructuralist term for the way in which a discourse is acted on and circulated within a culture. For example, it is a discursive practice within some cultures for a man to shake hands when he greets another man but to refrain from doing so when greeting a woman.

discursively present   Maintaining a full awareness of the discourses at work in a social situation and endeavoring to sustain a subjective position in relation to these.

dominant story   The "normal" way of construing a situation, or the set of assumptions about an issue that has become so ingrained or widely accepted within a culture that it appears to represent "reality."

experience-near description   A description of events that relies on a personal or local understanding rather than on an understanding borrowed from established knowledge or expert opinion.

externalizing conversation   A way of speaking in which space is introduced between the person and the problem issue. The problem may be spoken of as if it were a distinct entity or even a personality in its own right rather than part of the person. This creates an opportunity for the relationship between the person and the problem to be articulated.

gaze   A social process of evaluation and isolation of individuals or groups. This process serves to subjugate people to authorities and leads them to monitor or discipline themselves according to external regimes, as if they were constantly being watched.

historicizing question   A question that serves a deconstructive purpose by examining how things have come to be the way they are, thereby opening up the possibility that they could be otherwise.

indigenous knowledge   Local knowledge (personal, familial, or cultural) of how to live that lies dormant or hidden in the shadow of colonizing practices or dominant stories that lay claim to universal truth.

internalizing conversation   A way of speaking that locates problem issues firmly in the personality of the person suffering under them.

landscape of action   The realm of human experience in which events occur and out of which we fashion the stories with which we make sense of our lives.

landscape of consciousness   The realm of human experience in which we make meaning of the events that happen to us and develop understandings of the connections between events by reference to culturally learned discourse.

mapping-the-influence question   A question asked about an externalized problem to detail the relationship between the person and the problem. The map may be about the influence of the problem on the person or vice versa.

modernist Pertaining to the ways of speaking promoted in the modern era, which can loosely be said to have begun in the eighteenth century with the age of reason, in which the search for universal scientific truth takes precedence over other forms of knowledge.

not-knowing position Anderson and Goolishian's term for the narrative stance of naive curiosity (as opposed to expert certainty) concerning the ways in which clients might effectively address the problem issues in their lives.

performance of meaning The process by which, as we situate our experience in stories, the stories come to provide us with systems of meaning, from which we then draw to make decisions about our actions and to make sense of the actions of those around us.

position call A use of language by one party in a relationship that invites the other party to take up a particular relational position. Position calls structure people's responses and the meanings that are made of them.

positioning The process by which discourses place people in relation to each other—usually in power relations of some kind.

postmodernism A philosophical movement across a variety of disciplines that has sought to dismantle many of the assumptions that underlie the established truths of the modern era. It is marked by acceptance of plurality and the challenging of norms. In particular, postmodernism tends to reject the view that science and technology necessarily provide hope for human progress.

poststructuralism A set of ideas that can be called postmodern but that, following Michel Foucault, critically examine structuralist concepts of truth, reality, self, and culture. This way of thinking rejects the idea that power is centralized in the major structures of society. It also rejects the idea of social structures as natural or given. Instead, power is understood as diffused throughout society as a result of the function of discourse.

power/knowledge According to Foucault, the form of power developed in the modern world that, rather than being repressive, is productive of relations and subjectivities. It tends to be decentralized and language-based. This idea stresses the role of professional and academic disciplines in the production of the systems of thought by which society is governed. Power/ knowledge operates everywhere to produce truth, reality, and normality. Power is not considered a commodity held by one group at the expense of another but a feature of all human interactions in everyday contexts.

problem-saturated story   The story that a client presents to a therapist in which the problem is so dominant that there at first appears little sign of any alternative story.

reauthoring   The process of developing an alternative story in therapy. When a narrative approach is used, this project is jointly undertaken by the counselor and the client.

reflexive loop   A process of reflecting on previous actions and in doing so, changing future actions. For example, in narrative therapy, the counselor deliberately asks the client questions that invite comments on the power relations in the counseling relationship itself.

reflexivity   The activity of reflecting on a power relation in order to understand it better and to break from its taken-for-granted influences.

romantic   Pertaining to a movement in Western art and culture, originating in the nineteenth century, that laid stress on individual subjective experience as a source of truth in the face of a hostile society.

self-description   The identity that a human being adopts. The term points to the provisional nature of all identities and to the possibilities of other descriptions, thus contradicting the notion of a fixed, essential personality.

smalling question   A question asked in therapy that is designed to focus curiosity on the tiny details of experience rather than on the larger elements of consciousness. Such questions are used in the search for unique outcomes or in an attempt to flesh out a fragment of experience so that a new story can be built around it.

social constructionism   The movement in the social sciences that stresses the role played by language in the production of meaning. A central tenet is that people produce through discourse the social conditions by which their thoughts, feelings, and actions are determined. In this way, meaning is made in social contexts rather than given.

sparkling moment   A moment in any problem-saturated story when the client demonstrates a surprising achievement in defeating or limiting the influence of the problem in her life. Such moments, which are often isolated and neglected, are the shining stars in a sky darkened by the dominance of the problem. Same as *unique outcome.*

story of protest or resistance   A subversive story of the rejection—however feeble and spasmodic—of dominant truths. One of the important aims of the narrative therapist is to build a coherent series of connections between moments of protest or resistance.

subjectivity   Our own sense of ourselves and our location in relation to others. Subjective experience is shaped by discourse (or subject to power/knowledge), but it is also the basis for our attempts to break out of the given descriptions of ourselves. Another word for identity.

totalizing story   A culturally accepted story, particularly one drawn from professional discourses, that subsumes individual subjectivity under an all-embracing description of personhood.

unique account   A story developed in narrative therapy through the connection of several unique outcomes. The coherence of a unique account makes possible the performance of alternative meanings.

unique outcome   An aspect of lived experience that lies outside of or in contradiction to the problem story. Michael White's term, borrowed from Erving Goffman.

unstoried experience   Aspects of lived experience that lie outside the realms in which dominant stories have sway or demand attention.

voice   The capacity to speak on one's own behalf, in terms that are not given by others.

About the Authors

Aileen Cheshire is in her sixth year as a school counselor at Selwyn College in Auckland, New Zealand. After a number of years teaching English, she took an eclectic training in counseling but was led into narrative work by participating in workshops given by Johnella Bird and David Epston. She then embarked on the master's program in counseling at the University of Waikato. While still studying part-time, Aileen applies the narrative approach to her work at Selwyn College.

Alison Cotter is an educator and mediator. After teaching at schools in England, Scotland, Canada, and Indonesia, she became involved in adult education at the Waikato Polytechnic in Hamilton, New Zealand, and taught communication, counseling, and women's studies for fourteen years. Having recently completed a master's degree at the University of Waikato, she works with Waikato Mediation Services, a community-oriented group of professionals who offer mediation, training, and consultation.

Kathie Crocket is a counselor in the student counseling service of the University of Waikato and also contributes, as part of a teaching team in the Department of Education Studies, to undergraduate and graduate courses in counseling. She has a particular interest in the interface between the study and the practice of counseling.

Wendy Drewery is a senior lecturer in education studies at the University of Waikato, where she contributes to the counseling, health development, and human development programs. She has a master's degree in philosophy. Her doctoral thesis was on women's decision making at midlife.

David Epston is one of the codevelopers of narrative therapy. He is codirector of the Family Therapy Centre in Auckland and is a writer and teacher in the field of narrative ideas. His numerous publications include *Collected Papers* (1989) and *Narrative Means to Therapeutic Ends* (1991). He is a constant international traveler, presenting lectures and workshops mainly in Australasia, Europe, and North America.

Tim Harker is a counselor and family therapist working in private practice at the Hamilton Therapy Centre, Hamilton, New Zealand. Before entering his specialty he was a counselor/coordinator with the Men's Action Network, a Hamilton organization working with issues of violence.

Bev McKenzie has been a passionate agent for change in a number of settings. She has been a teacher, has worked in rehabilitation and in a girls' remand home, and for ten years worked in public health. She has a longtime interest in working with people who are not adequately catered for within established systems. Bev has now stepped out of those system constraints to explore new possibilities for working with people and communities.

Wally McKenzie is a family therapist at the Hamilton Therapy Centre and teaches in counselor education at the University of Waikato. He began his university training in his late thirties after working for a number of years in electronics. He comes from a family with a rich storytelling tradition.

Gerald Monk is director of the counselor education program at the University of Waikato. He has worked with narrative ideas in his part-time private practice over many years, and he introduced narrative therapy as the primary approach to training in the University of Waikato's Master of Counseling program in 1993. He has conducted workshops on narrative approaches in both New Zealand and the United States.

Glen Silvester is a licensed "Relationship Services" group leader and counselor practicing in Thames, a small town in rural New Zealand. She has focused her practice and her thesis for the Master of Counseling on a narrative approach to group work.

Glen J. Simblett, a native of England, is a psychiatrist working in private practice and in a publicly funded psychiatric day hospital in Hamilton, New Zealand. His psychiatric training included biological treatments, individual and group dynamic psychotherapy, and strategic family therapies. David Epston introduced him to narrative ideas at a seminar, and he subsequently spent four years trying to understand and integrate them into his everyday psychiatric practice.

Lorraine Smith is a mother and a part-time drug and alcohol counselor. She is interested in counseling practice that has a strong focus on the political and cultural contexts of the problems that bring people to therapy. Lorraine has focused her Master of Counseling research on applying a narrative approach to alcohol counseling.

John Winslade is a counselor educator at the University of Waikato. He has a background in school and marriage counseling. As a member of Waikato Mediation Services, he is involved in the development of narrative ideas in mediation. He also has a strong interest in alcohol and drug education and counseling.

Index

The Seattle School
2510 Elliott Ave.
Seattle, WA 98121
theseattleschool.edu